D0952895

Presidential Passions

The Love Affairs of
America's Presidents—
From Washington and Jefferson
to Kennedy and Johnson

Presidential Passions

The Love Affairs of
America's Presidents—
From Washington and Jefferson
to Kennedy and Johnson

Michael John Sullivan

Foreword by John H. Davis

SHAPOLSKY PUBLISHERS, INC.
NEW YORK

A Shapolsky Book

For any additional information, contact:
Shapolsky Publishers, Inc.
136 West 22nd Street, New York, NY 10011
(212) 633-2022

10 9 8 7 6 5 4 3 2 1

Library of Congress Cataloging-in-Publication Data

Sullivan, Michael John, 19–
    Presidential passions: the love affairs of America's presidents—from
Washington and Jefferson to Kennedy and Johnson / Michael John
Sullivan; foreword by John H. Davis.
        p.   cm.
    ISBN 1-56171-004-0
    1. Presidents—United States—Mistresses. 2. Presidents—United
States—Wives. I. Title.
E176.4.S86   1991
973'. 0992—dc20   90-47321

Book Design and Typography by Printworks Limited, Madison, CT

Printed and bound by Graficromo s.a., Cordoba, Spain

for my mother and father

AKNOWLEDGMENTS

*Thunder and lightning, wars, fires, plagues, have not
done that mischief to mankind as this burning lust,
this brutal passion.*

—Robert Burton

To my parents, Clifton and Mary Ann Sullivan, I would like to
say thank you for making this book possible. Their unfailing
love and support, as well as that of my two beautiful sisters,
Kathleen Sullivan Ciraulo and Karen Sullivan Gaffney, have always
been life's greatest blessing.

I would also like to thank my publisher, Ian Shapolsky, for his
enthusiastic guidance and his many creative contributions to this book,
and my editor, G. Donn Teal, of whose expertise and great patience I
have been the fortunate recipient. Another important source of encour-
agement and support was author/photographer Tom Zimmerman, who
generously provided his sage advice and invaluable sense of humor
when they were most needed.

In the creation of my book I am greatly indebted to *People* and
Playboy magazines for their authoritative personal interviews of
Madeleine Brown, Judith Exner, and Jimmy Carter, and to ex-President
Ronald Reagan for his autobiographical study *Where's the Rest of Me?*
Much appreciation must also be extended to author Fawn Brodie, whose
perceptive and sensitive insights into the psychologies of
several of our Presidents was a constant source of guidance and
inspiration to me.

It takes a great many people to bring a book from the typewriter to
the bookstore shelf. The author is just one of them. The others are far too
numerous to mention name by name, but each one—whether anonymous
worker or valued friend—must know how greatly I appreciate their
contributions.

Michael John Sullivan
Westchester, California
1991

CONTENTS

FOREWORD

For men han ever a likerous appetite
On lower things to perform their delight
Than on their wyves, be they never so faire ...
                                        —Chaucer

According to an unwritten code that probably had its origin in the strictures of seventeenth-century puritanical New England, Presidents of the United States are not supposed to have girlfriends, God forbid mistresses. But, as Michael John Sullivan ably demonstrates in his book, some of our greatest and most popular Presidents have indeed had girlfriends and mistresses—although the general public, until very recently, has chosen not to believe it.

What? George Washington, the Father of His Country, held the torch all his life for a secret love? Thomas Jefferson, drafter of the Declaration of Independence, kept a black slave mistress who bore him three illegitimate children during his Presidency? Sacrilege! Rather than countenance these outrageous infractions of the country's ancient puritanical code, the American people have historically refused to believe their presidential heroes were ever unfaithful to their wives.

The Kings of England and France may have had their Royal Favorites and their Royal Bastards, but American Presidents did not. This has been the traditional American attitude toward the notion of presidential extramarital affairs.

Such a position of collective self-deception stands in marked contrast to the unspoken codes of presidential sexual behavior in other parts of the world.

I recall that once I went to a reception in Mexico City given by a former President of Mexico that, to my initial surprise, was being held in the villa the ex-President had bought for his mistress, rather than in the home he maintained for himself and his wife and family. Upon registering a degree of amazement over this, my Mexican friend laughed and exclaimed: "Here in Mexico if a

1

President *didn't* have a beautiful young mistress, people would think something was wrong with him."

Mr. Sullivan's treatment of presidential love affairs is so frank and unabashed, I fear his book runs the risk of being put down by critics as a mere exercise in backstairs gossip. Such a dismissal, however, would be unfair. For Sullivan's book goes far beyond gossip. *Presidential Passions* is a valid contribution to the history of the American Presidency, and a much-needed one at that.

Granted, if the illicit sexual escapades of a given President were only harmless dalliances that offered a harried Chief Executive temporary respite from the crushing burdens of his office, the telling of these escapades in a book would amount to little more than idle gossip. But, as the author demonstrates, in his four chapters on the rampant sexual promiscuity of President John F. Kennedy, there are times when a President's sexual escapades go far beyond being harmless dalliances. In the case of President Kennedy, his extramarital affairs were so reckless they could have indirectly destroyed a government and compromised the security of an entire nation. When presidential infidelity threatens consequences such as these, it is automatically elevated from the petty spectacle of servants gossiping about their masters as they eavesdrop on them from the backstairs to the higher realm of history with a capital H.

Consider the implications of Kennedy's reckless affairs with Judith Campbell (later Mrs. Exner) and Marilyn Monroe. In the entire 200-year panorama of the U.S. Presidency these two dalliances were surely the most reckless *liaisons dangereuses* of all.

In the spring of 1961, the President's brother, Attorney General Robert F. Kennedy, was launching a massive attack on organized crime—what was to become the most intensive and widespread assault on the Mob in U.S. history up to that time. One of the Attorney General's primary targets in this campaign was Chicago Mafia boss Sam Giancana.

Concurrently, the CIA and various groups of Cuban exiles were conspiring, with President Kennedy's approval, to invade Cuba in April 1961 and to overthrow the Communist government of Fidel Castro. Furthermore, as part of the effort to topple Castro, the CIA had entered into an alliance with several notorious organized-crime bosses to plot the assassination of Castro. The first attempt on the Cuban dictator's life was to be made on the day of the planned invasion of Cuba by CIA-backed Cuban exiles. Foremost among the Mafia bosses recruited by the CIA to plot and carry out the murder of Fidel Castro was Chicago mobster Sam Giancana. Others involved were Mob front man in Las Vegas and Los Angeles, Johnny Roselli, and Florida boss Santos Trafficante, Jr.

It was while Attorney General Kennedy was mounting his campaign to get Sam Giancana, and while the CIA was at the same time plotting with Giancana to get Castro, that President Kennedy was carrying on the most dangerous sexual affair of his life. He was meeting regularly with none other than one of Giancana's girlfriends, Judith Campbell, a Hollywood starlet Kennedy had been introduced to by Frank Sinatra in 1960 at the height of his campaign for the Democratic presidential nomination.

When, in 1975, a United States Senate committee headed by Senator Frank Church discovered Kennedy's relationship with Miss Campbell and Miss Campbell's relationship with Sam Giancana, it immediately sought to cover all of it up. However, word soon leaked out of the Senate committee chambers, and Campbell was compelled to hold a press conference on the matter. At the conference, and later in a book, Campbell—then married to a golf pro by the name of Dan Exner—admitted that she had had a year-and-a-half-long affair with President Kennedy while she was also seeing Giancana, but she insisted that Kennedy knew nothing of her relationship with Giancana and that there was no communication between the President and the mobster.

Time passed. Then, in early 1988, as she struggled with terminal cancer, Judith Campbell Exner reversed her story and

3

told author Kitty Kelley in an interview published by *People* magazine that President Kennedy did indeed know of her relationship with Sam Giancana (and also with Johnny Roselli) and that she, in fact, did carry messages back and forth between Kennedy, Giancana, and Roselli, acting as a personal courier between the President of the United States and the head of the Chicago Mob.

What did Judith Campbell Exner believe her courier activity between Kennedy and Giancana was all about? She believes today that initially it had to do with Giancana's role in helping to finance Kennedy's campaign to win the West Virginia primary in 1960, a contention for which there is ample corroboration in the form of FBI reports.* Later, however, after Kennedy was inaugurated President, Judith believed that the messages she was carrying from Kennedy to Giancana had to do with the CIA's ongoing conspiracy with organized crime to assassinate the President of Cuba.

What credence can we give to Judith Campbell Exner's latest revelations? Do we have any basis for believing them? Might Judith have dropped these bombshells in *People* magazine simply for the money? (She reportedly received $50,000 for the new information.)

Not long after Mrs. Exner came forth with her new revelations, the British writer Anthony Summers and I decided to test a few of Judith's contentions to see if her facts held up to close scrutiny.

Judith had alleged in the *People* interview that she had once made love to Kennedy in the Georgetown townhouse he and his wife, Jacqueline, were living in prior to moving into the White House. She remarked that while she was there with Kennedy, a well-known "railroad lobbyist" was present. Summers, a brilliant investigative journalist, went to work to find out if this could be

---

*Details are available in my book *The Kennedys: Dynasty and Disaster* (New York: McGraw-Hill, 1987).

true, and discovered that the then-Senator Kennedy had been meeting with a railroad lobbyist at the time, both at home and in his office. His name was Bill Thompson, now deceased.

Judith had also alleged in *People* that she even arranged to have President Kennedy meet Sam Giancana in Chicago's Ambassador East Hotel. Was it possible that the Secret Service could have allowed such a notorious criminal as Giancana to meet with the President of the United States? I decided to investigate this incredible aspect of her story.

I located a member of Kennedy's 1961 Secret Service detail, one Tony Sherman, asking him if it would have been possible for someone like Sam Giancana to get past the tough Secret Service security at the Ambassador East Hotel.

Sherman replied: "Sure, if Kenney O'Donnell gave the O.K." (Kenneth O'Donnell was one of Kennedy's most trusted aides, a member of Kennedy's so-called "Irish Mafia.")

"You mean if O'Donnell passed on someone, he could see the President in his hotel suite?" I inquired.

"Yeah, that was all we needed and we'd let him by."

"But would you check his ID, his credentials?"

"If Kenney said it was O.K. to let the guy in, we let him in, we didn't have to check nothing."

"But wouldn't you have recognized Giancana, if he showed up at the President's suite, or at least sensed he looked somewhat shady and—"

"The President told us that if Mr. O'Donnell said the man could pass, he passed."

"With no ID?"

"With no ID."

"Sam Giancana at the time carried an ID," I added, "made up for him by the CIA, in which his name was given as Sam Gold. Do you recall coming across such a name?"

"Nope, but it doesn't matter. You have to understand that if O'Donnell came out and saw someone and okayed him, we let him

5

in without even asking for his ID."

Thus it appears that it was indeed possible for the Chicago Mafia boss to have met with Kennedy in Chicago's Ambassador East Hotel.

Let us pause a moment to consider the implications of Judith Exner's 1988 revelation that she carried messages from President Kennedy to mobster Sam Giancana throughout the first year of Kennedy's Presidency.

We have observed that the President's brother had ordered the Justice Department to go after Giancana and that the CIA had hired Giancana to murder Fidel Castro.

Thus, precisely when the U.S. government was both pursuing Giancana and using him in a covert assassination operation, the head of our government was using one of his illicit sexual partners to carry secret messages back and forth to Giancana.

The implications are obvious. By carrying on an affair with one of Giancana's girlfriends and using her to carry messages to Giancana, President Kennedy was compromising his brother's efforts to prosecute the mobster and at the same time placing himself—and, by extension, the American government—open to blackmail on the part of organized crime. But that was only a minor problem, if indeed President Kennedy was directly plotting with Giancana the murder of the President of a neighboring state—as Judith Exner has come to believe was the purpose of her courier activity between Kennedy and Giancana throughout 1961. Such actions on the part of an American President, if discovered by Cuba, could have resulted in war, and if they had been discovered by the President's enemies in the U.S. Congress, they could have resulted in Kennedy's impeachment.

But perhaps all Kennedy was doing was monitoring Giancana's CIA-backed efforts to assassinate Castro and was not actively engaged in the plotting. Kennedy did not trust the CIA, and this may have been his way of keeping track of the CIA's conspiracy to kill Castro, among other things. It is quite possible. But still, if he was only monitoring the CIA–Mafia plot to murder Castro, Kennedy would still be, from a legal standpoint, an accessory to the crime.

If Kennedy was using the girlfriend he shared with mobster Giancana to communicate with Giancana about the Castro assassination plots, then he was indeed playing with fire. He was running the risk of utter catastrophe, as well as his own personal ruin.

In 1979, a committee of the House of Representatives reinvestigated the assassination of President John F. Kennedy. During the course of its investigation it discovered that one ally of Sam Giancana, Jimmy Hoffa, had threatened to assassinate both John and Robert Kennedy, that Carlos Marcello, a fellow Mob boss friendly with Giancana, had also threatened to kill President Kennedy, and that another Mafia boss close to Giancana, Santos Trafficante, Jr., a fellow CIA–Mafia conspirator against Castro, had expressed foreknowledge of the assassination of John F. Kennedy as early as the fall of 1962.(Trafficante told Cuban exile leader José Alemán: "Kennedy is going to be hit." Alemán later reported this remark to the FBI.*) The House Assassinations Committee further discovered that both the President's suspected assassin, Lee Harvey Oswald, and Oswald's killer, Jack Ruby, had strong ties to organized crime. It is not difficult to hypothesize from these discoveries that Kennedy literally courted catastrophe as a result of his dealings with Judith Campbell and Sam Giancana, and not only had he made himself vulnerable to blackmail but also to assassination because of them.

Then there was the affair with Marilyn Monroe, also ably dealt with by Michael Sullivan, and also a matter far transcending mere tabloid gossip. As Sullivan emphasizes in *Presidential Passions*, it eventually came to light that the President's lovemaking sessions

---

*The details are available in my book *Mafia Kingfish: Carlos Marcello and the Assassination of John F. Kennedy* (McGraw-Hill and New American Library, 1989) and in David E. Scheim's *Contract on America: The Mafia Murder of President John F. Kennedy* (Shapolsky Publishers, 1988).

with the sex goddess of the sixties were being secretly taped by agents of Mob-controlled Jimmy Hoffa, with all that implies in terms of President Kennedy's vulnerability to blackmail and the compromising of Attorney General Kennedy's prosecution of Hoffa and his crusade against the Mob.

Toward the end of her tragic life, Marilyn Monroe, feeling dejected over what she felt was Kennedy's jilting of her, threatened to call a press conference and reveal all about her relationships with the President and the Attorney General. If she had done this, the Mob's Hoffa tapes could have backed up her claims and caused the utter ruin of the Kennedy Presidency and Administration.

Yes, Jack Kennedy enjoyed playing with fire. But, in light of what we now know about the dangers of that fire, was his conduct fair to the people who elected him? What the reckless personal life of John F. Kennedy has taught us is that the extramarital affairs of a President are much more than the stuff of tabloid journalism, they are a legitimate concern of the people of the United States.

John H. Davis
New York
1991

INTRODUCTION

*Love is a great force in private life; it is indeed the greatest
of all things; but love in public affairs does not work.*
—E.M. Forster

The subject of the love affairs and private lives of America's Presidents will always be of immediate interest to a large segment of the reading public. Those who are fascinated by the unique and complex workings of the human mind and heart will certainly read this book with enthusiasm and pleasure, as will those who are interested in discovering the true and honest facts behind the elaborate fantasies and deceptions of the carefully crafted "official" images.

However, many other readers are uncomfortable—and even resentful—of any intimate biographical investigation that presents information conflicting with the sanctity of their idealized heroes. These people often defend their dream men and women with an aggressive hostility aimed at crushing all factual opposition to their cherished fictions. For them, examining the most vital and personal attributes of an American President's life is either offensively improper or an unjust invasion of privacy. These prejudiced critics always attempt to conveniently censor and disavow biographical studies of any facts that may prove distasteful or disturbingly inconsistent.

If it were only a question of benign celebrities, such as movie stars and social figures, the fantasy-loving reader could afford the luxury of condemning or ignoring the truthful revelation of these figures' private lives. When the object of consideration is the leader of the nation, it becomes an absolute *necessity* to put self-indulgent make-believe aside and acquire a firm and accurate knowledge of their most human traits.

The nature of a man's deepest passions is the most vital part of his being. The basic morality and love impulses of an individual determine the particulars of every other factor and action of his or her existence. There is an undeniable consistency in the mechanics of the psyche and soul. Intimate feelings and private acts display a definite moral structure that, although oftentimes successfully hidden, is solidly present behind every public performance. Attitudes of love and moral responsibility permeate a man's life and find a constant and predictable expression through the labyrinthine progression of his existence. Although surface appearances may greatly differ, what a man does in private will be faithfully translated into his public actions.

Therefore, the intimate lives of our national leaders is not only a legitimate subject for examination, it is almost an imperative duty for every citizen to conduct such a full and thorough investigation. For several decades the American Chief Executive has been the most powerful person on earth. The wielding of such gigantic power involves an incredible amount of trust, and it is only logical that this trust must be based on the fullest and most accurate knowledge possible.

What type of man seeks to capture this exalted place in history? What is at the core of this type of personality that drives him forward in his seemingly impossible quest for the ultimate heights of power and authority? What crucial role do his love impulses and romantic relationships play in enabling him to reach higher and grasp stronger than all others.

About the American Presidents, numerous volumes have been written, detailing personality and character analyses, family history; an of course there have been multitudinous biographies. Nevertheless, the enigma remains: Each of the forty-one illustrious gentlemen has eluded a true and complete understanding. Each has escaped—in one way, at least—back into the shadows of history as a superhuman specimen gifted with abilities and talents rarely visited upon mankind, but with little truly personal/sexual history.

Except for those few victims of capricious fortune who were unlucky enough to have been vividly caught in public scandal, almost all of America's Presidents have been deified, given a somewhat godlike status. Whatever their ultimate ranking and/or academic evaluation, almost all of the Chief Executives have retained some degree of glorified mythology. This has helped obscure many of their singular human traits and conveniently camouflaged their strongest passions and desires.

Passion—whether focused sexually, politically, or militarily— has been a key ingredient in the personalities of the forty-one Presidents of the United States. Most of them had an exceptionally passionate nature, and the manner in which they dealt with their feeling made them different from their fellow patriots. Some of them, usually very precariously, were exceptionally successful in mastering and controlling their temperaments, while others were unable or unwilling to do so—much to their misfortune and regret.

History would have us easily believe that all of our Presidents were happily married, domestically satisfied men, as devoted to their wives and families as they were to the service of their country. We have always lived with the mistaken but much-cherished belief that to admit that an American President was anything less than a perfect paragon of middle-class respectability and saintly sexual morality would also force the nation, collectively and individually, to confess its own failings and moral shortcomings and arrive at an undesired confrontation between the idealized myth of our nation and the true reality.

Although a few of the presidential marriages were as happy as any could be, and some were as practical and compatible as the average marital union, many others were nothing more than cynically constructed, well-publicized fronts or elaborate shams. These marriages of advantage and convenience naturally were not the true focus of the gentlemen's romantic passions. Thus, because this book is interested in firmly establishing the truth, its purpose is not to report on the genuinely happy and successful marriages featured prominently in so many other histories, but rather to cover new territory in revealing some of the illicit relationships hidden behind the fable of presidential wedded bliss.

Proven facts and documented evidence are the essence of the book. Gossip, rumor, and speculation have been identified as such and kept to a minimum. There has sometimes been a need for the interpretation of facts and the establishing of logical and obvious conclusions.

Sexual passion is a man's most intimate and complete expression of himself. With the recent surge of maturity and honesty of our present age, it is finally time for America to fully examine and accept the most secret and misrepresented aspects—yes, their most precious resources—of the men who have created and guided our nation and shaped our modern world: their hearts and souls.

Michael John Sullivan
Westchester, California
1991

The body searches for that
which has injured the mind with love.
—Lucretius

1

THE DARKER SIDE
OF CAMELOT

reparing to take office as President, the newly elected John Fitzgerald Kennedy had lunch with his old friend Charles Bartlett and sincerely informed him that he was planning on stopping his womanizing ways. He intended to keep "the White House white." Only a few hours later, Kennedy was arranging for his beautiful, accommodating private stewardess, Janet Des Rosiers, to be put on the payroll of the White House secretarial staff.

John Kennedy was such an extraordinarily compulsive womanizer that it seems he was almost totally helpless in controlling this aspect of his behavior. This part of his life, although successfully obscured from public view during his term of office and for several years after, has become so well known during the last decade and a half that it has assumed legendary status. However, what most people do not realize is the incredible extent of his sexual activities and the dark implications of its psychological tones.

Without a doubt, Kennedy was the most promiscuous and

13

sexually active man ever to occupy the Oval Office.

The song "Camelot" from the popular Lerner and Loewe musical of the same name was one of President Kennedy's favorite melodies. The magic, mystical quality of the romantic Arthurian legend appears to have suited the glamorous Kennedy Administration and the word "Camelot" came to be the commonly accepted metaphor for the Kennedy years. But, ironically, the key ingredient of the mythical Camelot—the purity and chastity of the high-minded knights remaining true to their one and only lady love—was completely opposite from the reality of Kennedy's personal nature and beliefs. What's more, the Camelot of King Arthur was, in fact, much less fanciful and fictional than the Camelot of President Kennedy.

An intriguing enigma, John Kennedy is best understood by looking closely at the unique and emotionally unhealthy family that produced him. The famous Kennedy clan of Boston was, itself, a fascinating riddle of opposites and extremes. With a wealth measured in hundreds of millions of dollars, the Kennedys were unlike other dynasties of the super-rich in that they continued to pitilessly fight and climb their way high beyond the top with the overachieving, single-minded tenacity of the poor and hungry. Greed seemed to be the only family motto, and somehow every member was thoroughly indoctrinated at a very early age. Greed for ever greater wealth—greed for power—greed for prominence and recognition—greed for winning at any cost. Life was nothing more than a series of contests for the Kennedys, and they existed only to win. This and other conflicts and emotional problems raging beneath the glamour and glittering accomplishments would permanently scar most of the sons and daughters.

The bulk of the family's psychic ills came directly from its head, Joseph Kennedy, a crudely ruthless, supremely egocentric self-made plutocrat. As a father, he was something of a benign dictator, obsessed with his many offspring and centering his entire world upon their growth and material success. Usually absent from the home, he perhaps overcompensated, when there, by mercilessly focusing his concentration on making demands on his children. The foremost of these edicts was that each child must compete and *win*! Unfortunately, the competition that was most encouraged was between the children themselves, and it was so intense that to a great extent, it became the theme of each life.

Next to his large flock of hyperachieving children, Joseph Kennedy's greatest preoccupation in life was womanizing. And it was a full-time endeavor of prodigious proportions. With an almost perverse pleasure, he not only refused to be discreet about his incessant philandering, but went out of his way to flaunt his vulgar infidelities with boastful pride in his own home in front of his wife and children. He seemed to take special delight in displaying his sexual conquests before his young sons.

The most famous of Joseph Kennedy's mistresses was silent film star Gloria Swanson. While his wife sat placidly in another room, he forcefully seduced Swanson at his Palm Beach mansion. Taking the beautiful cinema queen along on luxurious trips to Europe with his wife, the senior Kennedy wanted to father a child by Gloria and tried to prove his devoted faithfulness to her by noting that his wife had gone an entire year without becoming pregnant!

For her part, Joe Kennedy's wife, Rose, was a somewhat simple woman whose entire mental powers appeared to center on her religion. A devout if not fanatical Catholic, Rose Kennedy told friends that she didn't mind how many women her husband was involved with as long as she had her family and they didn't interfere with her personal life. When someone once boldly inquired of Rose whether or not she dealt with her husband's unfaithfulness by assuming an icy demeanor, she thought for a long moment, then replied: "Yes, I have. And I make him pay for that iciness—I made him give me everything I wanted. Clothes. Jewels. Everything! You have to know how to use that iciness."

In addition, a devoted slave to strict manners and rigid

discipline, Rose Kennedy apparently was deficient when it came to the maternal attributes of love and affection. John F. Kennedy would later confess to his good friend Bill Walton: " My mother was either at some Paris fashion house or else on her knees in some church. She was never there when we really needed her. My mother never held me and hugged me. Never! Never!" Kennedy admitted to another friend that living at home when he was a boy had been like "living in an institution." Indeed, as parents, Joe and Rose Kennedy must have been a formidable pair. The man whom Franklin D. Roosevelt, Jr., called one of the most evil, disgusting men he had ever known, and the cold, shallow woman of almost unbalanced religious devotion, must have provided a very bleak emotional environment for their swarm of children.

Encouraged by his own licentious father, John Kennedy began his Olympian sexual career at the age of seventeen in a Harlem whorehouse. At college he quickly established the reputation of a playboy by being caught with girls in his dorm room. His fellow classmates remember him as always being extremely successful with girls—literally only needing to snap his fingers to have them surround him. However, he never seemed to have only one special girlfriend at a time. Instead, he had several girls he would constantly be seeing.

Langdon Marvin, a longtime aide and consultant to Kennedy, remembers the strong habit of the men of the family sexually sharing their women as being almost "incestuous." Marvin closely observed the intimate lives of the Kennedys for years, and he always noticed that the men of the family considered all women to be objects to be mutually shared among themselves, swapping sex partners and trading girls back and forth "like baseball cards."

The most vivid inheritance from father to son in this nouveau riche Boston family was a weirdly complex mixture of insatiable lust and cruel disdain for women. In his bluntly arrogant manner, Jack Kennedy was exactly like his father: He went after women with only one thing on his mind—sexual conquest. And he never

16

made the slightest attempt to disguise his crude and selfish motives. There was no long, skillful courtship when JFK went after a girl, no soft, moonlit conversations in which emotions could forge stronger bonds of understanding and affection. Kennedy neither had the time nor the interest to pursue a relationship that would demand even the smallest investment of his inner self. He was in too much of a hurry to make as many sexual scores as he possibly could.

Carnal opportunities seemed endless for the Kennedy men. Their incredible wealth, alone, was an irresistible magnet for the great majority of women who crossed their path. Attractive looks added extra bait to the trap, and an amazingly cynical and cold-blooded cooperative networking of their available feminine stock greatly facilitated the effectiveness of their amorous logistics. By pooling their female conquests in this manner, passing their girlfriends back and forth from son to father, from brother to brother, from father to son, they succeeded in multiplying their myriad liaisons.

Just merely warming up at Harvard for his fantastic future career of womanizing, Jack Kennedy graduated and went off to discover the world and its women. During the summer of 1940 he lived in the "bohemian" Hollywood Hills of Southern California and shared a swank bachelor apartment with a handsome and energetic young actor named Robert Stack. Stack was just beginning to make a name for himself in films and would win stardom the following year when he would present child superstar Deanna Durbin with her first screen kiss in the film *Nice Girl?* After decades of being one of Hollywood's most popular and reliable stars, Stack enthusiastically remembered John Kennedy in his autobiography as being more irresistible to women than any of the top matinee idols of the screen. There must have been both admiration, and some frustration, on Stack's part while watching the young JFK effortlessly capturing the interest of every beautiful girl they encountered. With almost palpable envy, the distinguished actor wrote that "he'd just look at them and they'd tumble."

17

Kennedy didn't have too much time to enjoy the glittering delights of the film capital. In September he had to head north to Palo Alto to enroll in graduate school at Stanford University. Although the air was cooler and the scenery not as exotic as Hollywood, Jack did not stop his playboy lifestyle. He proceeded to get involved with as many beautiful women as possible.

One night at a posh Nob Hill party in San Francisco, he made the acquaintance of a pretty former airline stewardess named Susan Imhoff. They began dating and became intimate. Although their affair was relatively brief, Susan, almost a half-century later, still had vivid memories of the future President, recalling him as a tall, handsome young man with a slender physique and an irresistibly boyish smile. She also remembered that he liked having sex with the girl on top, finding it more stimulating and satisfying for her to do all the work. (This was several years before his famous wartime back injury, which he would afterward always use as an excuse for this favorite, passive sexual position.) Significantly, she was also impressed by the fact that he didn't like to cuddle or be lovingly affectionate after the physical act of making love.

When war was declared in late 1941, Kennedy enlisted in the Navy. Stationed in Washington, he met and immediately became romantically involved with a Danish journalist, Inga Arvad. Inga was tall, blond, and statuesque. She was also married. And she was also secretly suspected by the FBI of being a Nazi spy. Federal agents were maintaining a full-time surveillance on Inga's activities, and, thus, the twenty-four-year-old Kennedy inadvertently became a constant subject of top-secret FBI reports.

One such report, filed on February 9, 1942, documented one of Inga Arvad's recent trips to Charleston, South Carolina, and officially stated that Kennedy had spent every night with her in her hotel room and had engaged in sexual intercourse with her on "numerous occasions."

The Director of the Office of Naval Intelligence wanted to promptly cashier Jack flat out of the Navy, but Joseph Kennedy had powerful connections in Washington and he arranged for his hedonistic and impulsive young son to be transferred to active duty. It was only then that the dangerous relationship with Inga finally came to an end. Jack went to the South Pacific and Inga went on to have a fling with elderly financier Bernard Baruch, eventually drifting to Hollywood, where she married aging cowboy star Tim McCoy.

Because of his involvement with a suspected Nazi spy, Jack Kennedy remained the subject of continuing FBI investigations. His personal life and casual romantic encounters were followed very closely, becoming the focus of several years of detailed reports. These, just recently released to the public, confirm the incredibly active nature of Kennedy's love life.

In Paris, in 1945, Jack spent a pleasant evening with the gorgeous movie star Hedy Lamarr. Back in New York, he steadily dated actress Angela Greene. The beautiful members of the acting profession seemed to have consumed much of Kennedy's interest during the years after the war and he spent time in Hollywood dating as many of them as he could. According to FBI reports, he was frequently seen with Susan Hayward as well as with Joan Crawford. Lana Turner, Sonja Henie, and newly imported English actress Peggy Cummins were likewise seen in his company.

Jack's only romantic failures were his pursuits of Olivia de Havilland and her equally famous sister, Joan Fontaine. They successfully resisted his prodigious charm, and when Fontaine deflected his advances by telling him of how his father had previously propositioned her, Jack proudly listened, and then responded with: "I only hope I'm the same way he is when I reach his age."

However, it was the brightest star of the 20th Century–Fox lot, Gene Tierney, who became Jack's most serious romance during

19

this time. The exquisite and elegant Miss Tierney, who had recently reached super-stardom with her highly praised portrayals in the films *Laura, Leave Her to Heaven,* and *The Razor's Edge,* was preparing to divorce her husband, Oleg Cassini. She noticed Kennedy visiting the set of her current film, *Dragonwyck,* and suddenly became conscious of "the most perfect blue eyes I had ever seen on a man." For the emotional young actress, it was love at first sight.

The long-lasting affair was taken very seriously by the sensitive actress. She visited Kennedy often in the East and even went to Cape Cod to meet his family. She was hoping for, if not counting on, marriage. But for Jack Kennedy, marriage with a divorced, non-Catholic film star was not even a remote possibility. He was already looking far enough into the future to foresee trying for the Presidency. When Jack finally told Gene that marriage was definitely out of the question, the relationship instantly ended with her abrupt departure.

Kennedy had so many affairs with so many girls at the same time that it is almost impossible to give a name-by-name account. Of these myriad lovers, one of the most interesting was Durie Malcolm, a Palm Beach socialite who would later serve prominently in a popular and absurdly erroneous rumor. The false story, which gained national attention in 1962, claimed that Jack and Durie were secretly married in 1939 and divorced in Reno in 1948. There was not a bit of truth to the story, but by using a recorded clerical error Kennedy's political enemies did the best they could to attack him.

The other possible political embarrassment coming from his frequent affairs involved a stunningly statuesque model named Pamela Farrington. Pamela had often traveled with Jack, and was in the habit of sunbathing in the nude. A few years later, when Kennedy was running for the Senate in 1952, a photograph of him lying next to a very naked Pamela on a Florida beach began privately changing hands. Jack's staff and advisors panicked and prepared for the worst, but when the future young senator was shown the scandalous photo he laughed and casually commented, "Yeah, I remember her. She was great!"

After winning his Senate seat, Kennedy continued to perfect his affectionate reputation of "Washington's Gay Young Bachelor" that he had established as a congressman (1947–53). The public viewed him in a rather innocent and uncritical light as someone extremely charming and attractive who loved the company of beautiful women. But the amorous activities of the boyishly smiling Jack Kennedy had a much darker implication than the naively casual observer could see. Beneath the laughing and happy exterior lurked the sadness and loneliness of a callous and hardened womanizer.

Kennedy's compulsive sexual pursuit of women bore the very negative and self-destructive characteristics of the classic "Don Juan" complex. There was very little *quality* in his sexual affairs and even less *love*. Word around town among the many women he had taken to bed was that Kennedy was a severe disappointment as a lover. One of Kennedy's girlfriends of his Senate years described his lovemaking as disastrous. The young senator had been so terrible in bed that the poor woman was convinced for years after that she was frigid. It was not until she finally entered a loving relationship with someone else that she realized it wasn't her fault. Many of Kennedy's other sex partners unhappily came to the conclusion that if he was a great lover, he was only a great lover of himself.

Rushed and mechanical in his lovemaking, Kennedy was only interested in the conquest of his opponent and the quantity of his partners. The pursuit of his victim and the establishment of a new "score" were apparently his chief and only interests in romance. And as if to safely ensure against the threat of any meaningful intimacy or emotional involvement occurring, Kennedy's favorite arrangement for having sex was with two girls at the same time.

"I'm never through with a girl until I've had her three ways," he once, with remarkable tactlessness, proudly told a group of reporters.

While in the Senate, Kennedy shared an apartment with fellow Senator George Smathers. "No one was off limits to Jack—not even your wife, your mother, your sister," Smathers once recalled. On one occasion, Smathers was suddenly called away to the Senate and had to leave his own date with Kennedy and his date. When Smathers later returned, he found Kennedy attempting to have sex with both girls.

The very definite pattern of Jack's womanizing had an either conscious or unconscious purpose. His targets were Hollywood actresses, divorcees, and models. Each of them was beautiful, bright, and amusing. And each was also a "safe" woman: one whom he *would not* and *could not* marry.

Certainly sex was nothing special for Jack Kennedy. He once told British Prime Minister Harold Macmillan, as he frequently told many others, that if he didn't have sex at least once a day, he got a headache. To famed authoress Clare Boothe Luce he charmingly boasted: "Dad told all the boys to get laid as often as possible. I can't get to sleep unless I've had a lay."

Psychiatrically speaking, the "Don Juan" complex from which John Kennedy so obviously suffered can be attributed to a blocked personality, from which threatening problems of either a sexual or emotional nature were kept securely hidden in the unconscious by the relentless pursuit and conquest of every woman whom the subject encountered. Of course, any kind of psychic intimacy or emotional involvement was avoided at all cost, this being not only unattractive and undesirable for the Don Juan, but also a complete impossibility because of the problems lurking in the subconscious.

Many victims of the Don Juan complex are latent homosexuals, who keep their true desires hidden behind the constant lovemaking performances to display and "prove" their heterosexuality. There is no evidence that Kennedy was latently homosexual. Other Don Juans are emotionally crippled early in life and demonstrate hostility and aggression toward women and an inability to form intimate relationships with them. This would appear to be an accurate portrait of John F. Kennedy. Considering the crushingly pernicious influence of his immoral father and the acute lack of affection and cold indifference of his mother, it is no surprise that the young Kennedy should have developed exactly such a complex.

Television news commentator Nancy Dickerson dated Jack when he was a senator, and her memories of him echo perfectly what all of his other intimates had to say. She was convinced that the chase and eventual conquest meant much more to Kennedy than the quick act of making love. For Kennedy, sex was nothing more than "a cup of coffee," Dickerson firmly believed.

Kennedy was more than satisfied with his shallow, carefree, bachelor existence. He didn't want to get married. Nevertheless, his tyrannical father, still avidly stage-managing his son's promising future, began pressuring him to make a choice and start a family.

Instead of selecting one of his favorite voluptuous types, Jack chose a nervously introverted, elegantly attractive socialite named Jacqueline Bouvier. The product of a broken home, "Jackie" Bouvier was working, as a lark, as a journalistic photographer for *Look* magazine when she met Kennedy. Her colleagues remember her as being shy and likeable and somewhat like "a boy, not much interested in sex." Her stepbrother, author Gore Vidal, once commented: "Jackie, you know, is ultra-fastidious. Therefore, she never particularly concerned herself with sex. She finds it untidy."

It seems strange that Jack Kennedy would appeal to such a woman as Jackie Bouvier. However, the ethereal, cultured young beauty had a father who was cut from the same cloth as Kennedy. The two men were very much alike, especially in the way they related to women. And if Jack suffered from a Don Juan complex, than in an equally Freudian way Jackie was the victim of a Father complex. She had always been attracted primarily to dangerous,

23

compulsive womanizers like her father. Whatever needs there were to play out with her future husband this troubled and disturbed relationship with her father, Jackie could not have made a better psychological choice than John F. Kennedy.

With each so perfectly fulfilling the other's uniquely distorted emotional requirements, there were also other reasons why Jack Kennedy and Jackie Bouvier appeared to be a perfect match.

Behind the shy, childlike facade, Jackie was extremely ambitious, and eager for a brilliant position in life. One of her closest friends, John White, observed the romance develop from the very beginning and sadly watched it disintegrate during the disastrous marriage. In his excellent biography, *A Woman Named Jackie*, author C. David Heymann quoted White as saying:

> I think, for Jackie, the desire to conquer JFK was first of all the money, then the challenge and finally the fact, as far as I could see, that she had very little experience dealing with love and didn't know what to expect. . . . She maybe just thought that JFK wasn't the worst bargain in the world. And certainly the idea that he was on the way up appealed to her.
>
> I'd known other girls who had dealt with him. I used to hear their stories. Some of them would say to deal with such raw power and such open contempt—being checked off in a little black book—was a hell of a challenge. They thought they might break through to him. And the fact that he was also such a cold fish also played a role. He had warm blood but a cold heart. Most of these women had dealt with other men and regarded JFK as a oddity to be treasured. He was different—totally cold and ruthless toward women, which I suppose many of them found charming. It was almost the idea of being able to say the next morning you were drunk and didn't know what you were doing.

Later on, when John White talked to Jackie about the amorous Kennedy, he got the impression that she wasn't especially concerned about his severely deficient morals, and that she had knowledge of the situation and was willing to take the risk. White felt that, for Jackie, her future husband's great potential success was far more important than his private morality, particularly if he provided her with "a decent role in the drama." After Kennedy had become President and Jackie turned herself into one of the most dazzling First Ladies in American history, White simply concluded, "It's fair to say that they both lived up to their ends of the bargain."

For his part, Jack Kennedy was both pleasing his father and gaining a vital career asset. One of his best friends, Lem Billings, knew the family extremely well, and asserted: "Joe Kennedy not only condoned the marriage, he ordained it. 'A politician has to have a wife,' he said, 'and a Catholic politician has to have a Catholic wife. She should have class. Jackie probably has more class than any girl we've ever seen around here.' "

Also of critical importance to John F. Kennedy was the selection of a particular type of woman who would not place demands on him for the deeper feelings of love and emotional intimacy that he was unable or unwilling to give. Jackie, unusually bright and intuitive, knew the isolated and reserved nature of her own personality and saw how it would be comfortably compatible with her future mate's "pool of privacy," as she optimistically phrased it. Indeed, she characterized herself and Jack Kennedy as "icebergs"—the major part of themselves existing unseen beneath the surface. She felt that they both "sensed this in each other, and that this was a bond between us."

"In their strangulated way, Jack and Jackie loved each other," one of Jackie's oldest friends, Betty Spalding, observed, "but neither was able to relate to the other, and there was never any affection between them at any time. He was always quite diffident towards her. He had a total lack of ability to relate emotionally to anyone. I think that was one of the things that was so difficult for Jack when he finally married Jackie." Spalding watched the Kennedy marriage at close range for several years. "Both of them were blocked emotionally," she recalled. "[Jackie] had the same emotional block and panics that Jack had. And their relationship was extremely stormy at the beginning."

was extremely stormy at the beginning."

Just before the wedding, Jack went off on a two-week Mediterranean pleasure cruise with his former college roommate, telling his bride-to-be it was "a last fling." This gave Jackie pause for thought. Was Jack really sincere in his promises to change his promiscuous lifestyle?

Beautiful Jacqueline Bouvier appears to be having some serious doubts as she arrives, unsmiling, at the altar with a "prize catch" husband, Senator John F. Kennedy. It's the warm summer of 1953 in exclusive Newport, Rhode Island.

All the same, they were married. The year was 1953. They went to Acapulco on their honeymoon and stayed at the sumptuous villa of the Mexican President. Within a day or two, Jack's promises were totally forgotten and his attention slowly drifted to every young woman who happened by. He soon began flirting outrageously. When they returned from their trip, their friends noticed a growing tension between the newlyweds.

Marriage brought almost no change to John Kennedy's womanizing ways. Jackie certainly must have been aware of what was going on, from the very earliest days of their marriage. She was extremely hurt, and her hurt eventually turned to anger. As the marriage progressed and they failed to grow closer together, divorce seemed the only answer. Jack was still carrying on with every available woman in exactly the same manner as when he was a bachelor, and Jackie was becoming so moody and severely depressed that there were rumors she was being treated at a famous psychiatric clinic specializing in electro-shock therapy.

Finally, as Jack approached his drive for the Presidency of the United States, his father stepped in and, reportedly, offered Jackie a million dollars not to divorce Jack. The couple stayed married, and made an effort to launch a harmonious display of their marriage for the upcoming campaign.

During the 1960 presidential race, John Fitzgerald Kennedy not only fully exploited his magnetic masculine charm on potential women voters, he also indulged his insatiable lust in private. After his cliff-hanger victory, he entered the White House, continuing his lifestyle of numerous and indiscriminate sexual affairs, setting something of an infamous record that has remained unsurpassed.

As time passed, his wife would seem to have almost philosophically accepted the President's gross infidelities as something that could not be changed. Eventually, Jackie Kennedy would be compromising enough to calmly accept her husband's mistress as her own press secretary.

One positive change in JFK's extracurricular love life after he entered the White House was the forced need to use at least some decorum and caution in the conduct of his affairs. According to the files of the FBI, from 1955 until 1959 he had maintained a suite on the eighth floor of the Mayflower Hotel in Washington. The reports refer to the suite as "Kennedy's personal playpen." A witness who attended a party there was quoted in one report as saying that Kennedy and Senator Estes Kefauver and their female companions engaged in sex right in front of the other couples at the party and then, swapped partners and began making love again.

Giving up his suite at the Mayflower, Kennedy as President was forced to restrict the public visibility of his philandering and, given the great power, prestige, and means of his exalted office, he was able to carry on surreptitiously with far more famous and interesting partners. One such long-term relationship had begun just before he won the Presidency. It involved one of the most beautiful, glamorous, and well-known women of the century.

Love alone is the true seed of every merit in you,
and for all acts for which you must atone.
                                                        —Dante

----

2

JACK AND THE
SEX GODDESS

arilyn Monroe was at the pinnacle of her great beauty, glamour, and fame when she met John F. Kennedy at the home of Peter Lawford in 1957. Kennedy had long been fascinated by the gorgeous blond actress. Lawford was his brother-in-law, the husband of his sister Pat, and lived at a luxurious beach house on the exclusive Santa Monica shoreline of Los Angeles. His home served as a headquarters for Jack's romantic operations on the West Coast. Having met many top Hollywood celebrities there, Jack asked his brother-in-law to arrange an introduction to Marilyn.

Jeanne Martin, the former wife of singer Dean Martin, remembers the years when she and her husband were very frequent guests at the Lawford home and both Jack Kennedy and his younger brother Robert were there:

> I saw Peter in the role of pimp for Jack Kennedy. It was a nasty business—they were just too gleeful about it, not discreet at all. Of course there was nothing discreet about either of the Kennedys,

Bob or Jack. It was like high-school time, very sophomoric. The things that went on in that beach house were just mind-boggling. Ethel could be in one room and Bobby could be in the other with this or that woman. Yes, Bobby was a grabber, but not in the terms that Jack was. Jack was really instinctive, you know, straight for the jugular—'Come upstairs, come in the bathroom, anything.' Bobby didn't have eyes for me, but I do know this. I have a friend who was in the library with him, and before she knew it the door was locked and he threw her on the couch—amazing! It was so blatant. Here were the President of the United States and the Attorney General.

Martin witnessed Marilyn Monroe with the Kennedy brothers at Lawford's beach house several times and she was "quite sure" that the glamorous star was sexually involved with both of them.

Toward the end of his life, Peter Lawford told his last two wives that both Jack and Bobby Kennedy had been romantically involved with Marilyn, although he continued publicly to deny it. Numerous friends and associates of Marilyn's support the existence of a prolonged and highly secret affair with Jack Kennedy, especially after he became President. Marilyn herself confided to her most intimate and trusted friends at the time that she was having an affair with "the President."

By the time the affair with Jack Kennedy began in 1959, Marilyn Monroe had experienced an incredibly successful professional life and a tempestuously unhappy personal life of her own. Love had seemed to mysteriously elude her from her earliest days, and although she and her ultra-privileged lover were of different worlds and radically opposite backgrounds, they were close to being emotional twins. Each was the product of a psychologically unhealthful childhood and each was the victim of deficient paternal love. Each, too, tragically lacked the ability to commit exclusively to another person in a meaningful relationship. Therefore, ironically, Marilyn and Jack's inability to deeply love was the greatest thing they had in common and the link to the intensity and duration of their sexual affair.

Marilyn and Kennedy's elegant young wife, Jackie, also had something important in common. The insecure screen goddess also suffered from a Father complex. However, instead of idolizing a dangerous, womanizing absent father, as Kennedy's wife did, Marilyn never knew her father, but had desperately searched for a suitable replacement all her life. Her emotional quest for the perfect father took her from bed to bed through three failed marriages and dozens of casual affairs, right to the doorstep of the man who would likely be the nation's next President. Marilyn could have hardly asked for anything more. What greater, more perfect father-figure could there possibly be than the President of the United States?

Until the advent of her glittering stardom, life had treated Marilyn Monroe very unkindly. Born into poverty, she was first deserted by her father when she was a baby, then abandoned by her mother a few years later, when the unstable woman was declared insane and committed to an asylum. Marilyn was left alone. Without family or relatives, she was placed in an orphanage, then raised in institutions and foster homes until she married her first husband in 1942, when she was sixteen. He was only a boy of twenty, but she called him "Daddy" and he called her "Baby."

Marilyn never really grew up emotionally. The fact that both of her parents lost their sanity and ended up in asylums must have eroded what little confidence in the future she had left. With this sinister knowledge of her flawed mental heritage, Marilyn was overwhelmed by fears and self-doubts. It is no wonder that she chose a lifelong course of self-indulgence and irresponsibility and remained, primarily, a child—an insatiable child starved for love and recognition.

It was this childlike quality that was most vital to her unique stardom. Marilyn combined her powerful sexual appeal with an equally powerful innocence. One of her directors, Joshua Logan, once described her as: "Luminous and completely desirable. Yet naive about herself and touching, rather like a frightened animal, a fawn or a baby chick." The critic Molly Haskell always noticed in Marilyn a "painful, naked, and embarrassing need for love." It was all of these conflicting and contrasting elements that magically transformed her inner anguish into an irresistibly seductive image on the warmly glowing movie screen.

After seven years of struggling and slowly climbing through the acting ranks in Hollywood, Marilyn landed her first starring role in 1953 in an undistinguished melodrama entitled *Niagara*. Her all-stops-out sexy performance as an evil and adulterous wife instantly made her a superstar of the cinema. It also made her a national sex symbol.

The following year, she entered into a brief and disastrous marriage with baseball hero Joe DiMaggio. In 1956, she tried matrimony again with celebrated playwright Arthur Miller. This union was more successful than its predecessor and lasted five years, until another divorce in 1961. While engaged in these misalliances with polarized opposites, Marilyn starred in *Gentlemen Prefer Blondes, How to Marry a Millionaire, The Seven-Year Itch*, and *Some Like It Hot*—all of them popular and critical smash hits that made her one of the most famous and sought-after actresses in the world.

Meeting Jack Kennedy at his brother-in-law's beach house in 1957, Marilyn did not become intimate with him, however, until two years later. Mainly geography and the intense demands of their separate careers had kept them from becoming lovers more quickly. But finally, in 1959, Kennedy managed to spend several secluded days in Palm Springs with the celebrated sex goddess. It was during this secret rendezvous that the President-to-be and Marilyn consummated their relationship and their love affair began.

Immediately, for Marilyn, it was a serious and hopeful involvement, which she desperately hoped would eventually lead to marriage. She would only strengthen this naive ambition and belief in the next few years as Kennedy became President and dangerously continued the illicit affair. It is truly the supreme testament to Marilyn Monroe's total detachment from reality that she still believed that marriage was even a remote possibility with President John F. Kennedy.

Naturally, Kennedy found Marilyn an exciting and interesting romantic diversion, and he obviously enjoyed the constant danger and the challenge that such a famous liaison brought with it. However, even if he had never become President, without a doubt he never would have seriously considered becoming permanently involved with Marilyn—let alone divorcing his wife and marrying her.

As Jack and Marilyn initiated their lovemaking under the torrid desert sun and continued their passionate union all through the several long, sizzling days and nights to follow, neither could have suspected that they were doomed figures of history, both destined swift and tragic ends. Within four years, both of these glamorous icons of the mid-twentieth century would be dead.

From the very beginning, logistics was the major problem of the affair. Privacy and secrecy were vital elements of their rendezvous, and it would become necessary for the distinctive sex goddess to wear elaborate disguises when traveling with Kennedy or meeting him in public places. The Lawford beach house in Santa Monica became their principal love nest, as did the President's sumptuous penthouse suite at the Carlyle Hotel in New York City.

An ideal bachelor pad with a spectacular view of the city's skyline, the penthouse at the Carlyle guaranteed total privacy for Kennedy's secret romantic activities. Protected from any outside access whatsoever, the top-secret interior of the suite was even immune from important communications from Washington. Instead, any messages for the President were held for him at the desk down in the hotel lobby. No one could disturb the President at the Carlyle. Even Kennedy's closest advisors and aides never knew the steady stream of sex partners constantly filling the hedonistic hideout, Marilyn was the most famous.

The President's association with the actress was not kept totally secret from the public. With a remarkable degree of calculated cynicism and caution, Kennedy arrogantly attempted to have it both ways by establishing a highly visible public "friendship" with Marilyn. Perhaps it was his idea to use this as a protective cover. Carefully playing out an emphatically open and innocent relationship for all the world to see might possibly provide a very valuable and effective decoy against any future accidental discovery or speculative gossip. The simplistic moral logic of the time would have provided this blatantly hypocritical charade with a foolproof interpretation: John F. Kennedy would never associate with Marilyn Monroe in public if they were really lovers in private!

Thus, the seemingly casual friendship they displayed helped discourage the dangerous discovery of their passionate affair. Kennedy was even shrewd enough to recognize that there was a great benefit to be had in using the enormously popular star's presence in his presidential campaign. The endorsement of Marilyn Monroe could not only bring more votes, but it could also add a radiance and exotic glamour to the Kennedy candidacy. As it happened, this is exactly what occurred. Much of the glitter and sparkle of the nationally emerging Kennedy image was due to Marilyn's magical presence at the 1960 Democratic Convention in Los Angeles.

During that fateful July, when the whole Kennedy clan gathered in Los Angeles to scratch and slave for Jack's nomination, Jackie stayed home in Hyannisport while Marilyn occupied a prominent position front-stage in the exciting and historic drama. Most of Kennedy's spare time away from his duties at the convention was spent with the sexy star. She was in a highly emotional state at this time; she was not only involved with a man who might soon occupy the White House, but her marriage (to Arthur Miller) was deteriorating and coming to an end.

Marilyn had also just gotten over a serious love affair with French film star Yves Montand, who had recently appeared with her in *Let's Make Love*, a weak, uneven comedy that had been a commercial disappointment and a critical failure. The Monroe–Montand romance had been a recklessly indiscreet one, fully covered by the press. In typical fashion, Marilyn had naively hoped that it was going to turn magically into a permanent relationship and bring some degree of much-needed stability and meaning to her empty and precarious life. But this didn't happen. Montand had never intended to leave his adored wife, Academy Award–winning French actress Simone Signoret; and when *Let's Make Love* finished production, so did his fling with his promiscuous co-star. Marilyn took it very badly, for she found herself publicly humiliated by his casual rejection.

Now, more than ever, Marilyn was in need of the all-powerful and totally secure father-figure she had spent her life so desperately searching for. And John F. Kennedy was fitting the bill more and more perfectly.

With the prospect of a new and exciting romantic involvement that promised everything she sought, the glamorous sex-symbol joyfully joined Kennedy and his brother-in-law Peter Lawford and another male friend for dinner at Puccini's, a fashionable Italian restaurant, on the second night of the 1960 Democratic Convention. That evening, Lawford observed how serious the affair was becoming. Marilyn announced during dinner that she found Jack's performance "very democratic"—even "very penetrating"—and she later giggled that she thought she had made his back feel better. In return, Kennedy continually patted and squeezed her voluptuous body, moving his hands under the table to feel as much of her as he could. While doing this, a sudden intrigued expression appeared on his smiling face: The actress later told Lawford that this was because Kennedy had slid his hand way up her dress and had happily discovered that she wore no underwear.

Lawford, the most intimate link between John F. Kennedy and Marilyn Monroe, facilitated the passionate affair and watched it from very close range. Before he died in 1984, although he had previously denied all knowledge of the affair, he confessed his involvement and most of the facts of the secret relationship. Lawford stated that he had been impressed by how different the Monroe affair seemed from Kennedy's usual womanizing. "Of all his 'other' women," Lawford related, "Marilyn was perhaps the best for him. They were good together. They both had charisma, and they both had a sense of humor."

A week after the intimate dinner at Puccini's, Kennedy won the Democratic presidential nomination. As he gave his stirring acceptance speech at the overflowing Los Angeles Coliseum, Marilyn was prominently present to cheer him and coyly offer her own public endorsement of his candidacy. After the triumphant spectacle, Marilyn attended a skinnydipping party at the secluded Lawford beach house, and, then, the following day appeared at a victory dinner Joe Kennedy proudly gave for his son at the very exclusive Romanoff's Restaurant in Beverly Hills.

The presidential nominee arranged to spend an extra day in southern California so that he could devote himself exclusively to Marilyn. They both knew that it would be their last leisurely romantic interlude for some time, and both made the most of every minute they had together, enjoying each other with a carefree, ecstatic abandon. From now on, there would be the added pressure of maintaining total secrecy, for there was greater danger in discovery. It could harm Marilyn's popularity and box-office appeal and do even greater injury to Kennedy's future plans. No one would vote for a man who was caught cheating on his wife and shaming his family. And certainly no one would accept such faithless behavior from the Chief Executive.

———————————

Jack Kennedy returned to Hyannisport and his brooding wife on July 17. Jackie had to be firmly persuaded by his aides to come and meet her husband at the airport. She had heard reports of his romancing Marilyn Monroe during the convention and was feeling more hurt and estranged from Jack than ever.

After Kennedy won the 1960 election and moved into the White House, the affair with Marilyn resumed, taking on an almost easy regularity. Besides staying with Kennedy at his secret suite at the Carlyle and in the secluded Lawford beach house, Marilyn often traveled with the President on *Air Force One*. This was successfully accomplished by a rather simple but effective physical disguise. Marilyn would wear a brunette wig, large sunglasses that obscured most of her face, and unflattering "older" clothing. The crew of the private presidential airliner and others were casually told that she was Peter Lawford's private secretary.

It was, in fact, Lawford who was responsible for arranging many of their secret meetings. On at least one occasion he took photographs of Marilyn performing fellatio on Kennedy while the President was luxuriating in a huge marble bathtub. Evidently, the fun and games were unlimited.

For almost a year and a half, the dangerous and erotic affair between President Kennedy and Marilyn Monroe enthusiastically continued, as if it would last forever. But, by now, it was no longer a well-kept secret. The FBI and the Secret Service both had become aware of Kennedy's sexual relationship with the blond superstar. They also had followed Monroe's personal problems and knew about her recurrent emotional troubles, her dependency on drugs and alcohol, and her futile stays at psychiatric clinics.

Marilyn's deteriorating emotional state eventually began to undermine her relationship with Kennedy. As it became more and more impossible to ignore the obvious—that it was a dead-end affair and would never go anywhere, especially not in the direction she had hoped—the actress began losing touch with reality.

Lawford, by now, was a close friend, and Marilyn freely confided in him. "She was crazy about Jack," he has told. "She devised all sorts of madcap fantasies with herself in the starring role. She would have his children. She would take Jackie's place as First Lady. The fact that he was President allowed her to attach a lot of symbolic meaning to the affair." But Lawford knew the unattractive side of his brother-in-law better than almost anyone else, and he was convinced that JFK was only amusing himself with Marilyn and really had no deep feelings for her. He also doubted whether the heavily drugged actress truly loved Kennedy. She had so lost touch with reality that he suspected she was only imagining the great passion she had always so desperately sought.

Marilyn frequently telephoned Kennedy at the White House and sent a steady stream of gushingly romantic love letters and poems. In a desperate attempt to force things to a climax and make Kennedy divorce his wife, Marilyn foolishly telephoned Jackie. The actress's telephone call to the First Lady helped more than anything to destroy Marilyn's relationship with the President. She had seen it as an attempt to force the stalled situation to a showdown. She wanted Kennedy to have to be in a position to choose between her and his wife. Unfortunately, it was a foolish and impulsive gesture that only served to make things more unpleasant and strained for everyone involved.

Marilyn later told Lawford that Jackie had not displayed any emotional upset at all during the call. She had simply agreed to give her husband a divorce so that he could marry Marilyn, but the First Lady had stressed that Marilyn would have to be willing to live completely openly with JFK in the White House.

Marilyn's self-deception was monumental. She completely failed to see how furious Jackie really was, and she totally misinterpreted the spirit of the First Lady's impossible offer. There was absolutely no way in 1962 that the President could have divorced his wife and had the sexy, unstable Monroe join him openly in the house on Pennsylvania Avenue.

Meanwhile, oblivious to the female contretemps, Kennedy made arrangements to spend the last weekend in March at Bing Crosby's luxurious home in Palm Springs. Marilyn quietly journeyed to the fashionable desert spa and joined the President there for three days. Appropriately, this secret rendezvous in Palm Springs, the happy scene of their first lovemaking, would mark one of the last idylls of their lengthy affair.

On May 19, Kennedy at last exceeded the limit to which he could arrogantly flaunt his illicit relationship with the famous sex goddess. It was a week before his forty-fifth birthday, and the occasion was a festive celebration and fund-raising bash for 15,000 prominent Democrats at Madison Square Garden in New York. Several top entertainers were there to honor the President, and Marilyn was one of them. Dressed, as Adlai Stevenson described her, "in skin and beads," Marilyn slithered up to the microphone and sang, "Thanks for the Memory" and "Happy Birthday, Dear President Kennedy" in a sexy, breathless voice. After she had finished, the President spoke to the boisterous crowd and smilingly told them, "I can now retire from politics after having had 'Happy Birthday' sung to me in such a sweet, wholesome way."

It was, naturally, Peter Lawford who had arranged for Marilyn's surprise appearance at Madison Square Garden that evening. Acting as master of ceremonies, he asked her to perform after discovering that Jackie would not be attending. Because of her delayed arrival, he jokingly introduced her as "the *late* Marilyn Monroe."

After the posh celebration at the Garden, President Kennedy and Marilyn separately made their way to the penthouse suite at the Carlyle. She spent several hours alone with him there, not knowing that it would be their last lovemaking.

They would never meet again. Kennedy had finally decided to end the relationship once and for all. His decision had been based on a recent warning from both his Attorney General brother, Robert Kennedy, and the Director of the FBI, J. Edgar Hoover,

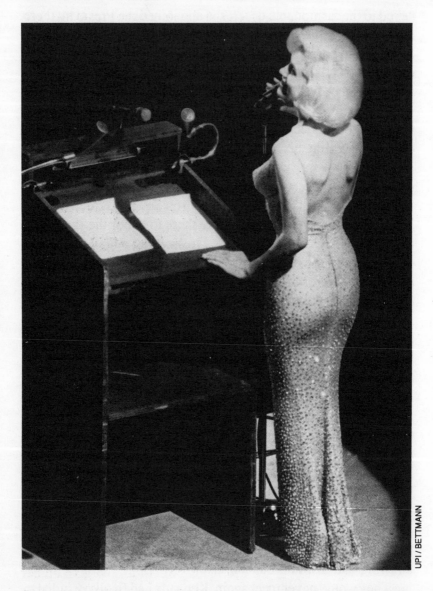

Sex goddess Marilyn Monroe creates a national sensation by seductively singing "Happy Birthday" to her lover, President Kennedy, at Madison Square Garden, New York, in May 1962. Their affair ending, the beautiful actress would be dead three months later.

that the Santa Monica beach house of his brother-in-law had been bugged by the Mafia and that at least one of his sexual encounters with Marilyn had been tape-recorded.

This presented a very real danger to the President. Although he could do nothing about his mistakes of the past, Kennedy quickly concluded that he must protect his future. The first step in his plan of protection was to completely avoid Marilyn—a loss that appears to have meant very little to him.

Predictably, the emotionally ill actress did not take his abrupt withdrawal very well. Not very well at all. Marilyn knew, in her heart, that things were over between her and the President, but she desperately refused to believe it. She continued calling John at the White House and sent him pathetically begging letters. When she finally started threatening to go public and take her case to the press, the President quickly sent his younger brother, Bobby, out to reason with her.

Robert Kennedy was then Attorney General of the United States. He had known Marilyn before. Although several less authoritative sources suggest that Bobby was the first Kennedy brother to be sexually involved with the blond superstar, Lawford insisted that Bobby and she had met at a dinner party at his house which Bobby's wife, Ethel, also attended and that they only saw each other a couple of other times at large gatherings, such as JFK's birthday bash at Madison Square Garden.

Thus, if Lawford is to be believed, Marilyn and Bobby were only nodding acquaintances when he followed the President's urgent plea and flew to Los Angeles to talk to the neurotic actress and make her see reason. Bobby was sensitive and sympathetic, letting Marilyn see that he understood how difficult it was going to be for her to accept the President's dilemma and give up her attempts to contact him. Lawford suddenly found himself watching a new romantic drama unfolding. As he told it:

She took it pretty hard. Bobby felt for her. They met the following day and passed the afternoon walking along the beach. It wasn't Bobby's intention, but that evening they became lovers and spent the night in our guest bedroom. Almost immediately the affair got very heavy.... Now Marilyn was calling the Department of Justice instead of the White House. Angie Novello, Bobby's personal secretary, had long conversations with her whenever Bobby wasn't around. Pretty soon Marilyn announced that she was in love with Bobby and *he* had promised to marry her. It was as if she could no longer tell the difference between Bobby and Jack . . .

Instead of helping the pathetically disturbed actress out of her deep chasm of despair, Bobby Kennedy inadvertently helped plunge her down deeper.

Marilyn was now totally out of control, unable to cope with even the basic essentials of daily life. Desperate, she sought relief by taking more and more drugs. Unable to sleep nights, she staggered onto the set of her current film, *Something's Got to Give*, and could barely remember a single line of dialogue. When she did speak, she slurred her lines to the point of being almost unintelligible. Her co-star, Dean Martin, tried valiantly to cover for her and assist her with her undemanding role, but nothing seemed to work. The movie was Twentieth Century–Fox's most expensive feature of the year. George Cukor, one of Hollywood's most tasteful and brilliant directors, was guiding Marilyn with as much patience and skill as was humanly possible. (Cukor had no equal when it came to handling "difficult" actresses. His skill and empathy with women was legendary. He had made Katharine Hepburn a star, been responsible for Vivien Leigh's and Olivia de Havilland's extraordinary performances in Gon*e With the Wind*, and had firmly steered Ingrid Bergman and Judy Holliday in their Oscar-winning portrayals in *Gaslight* and *Born Yesterday*.)

Now, the incomparable Cukor attempted to direct the masochistic Monroe—and he had finally met his match. Lawford had warned her that her whole career would "go down the tubes" if she didn't "step on the brakes"; but she couldn't. There was no way she could solve her massive emotional problems. "Bobby was gradually retreating from her the same way Jack had retreated," Lawford sadly observed. "She went up the wall. 'They treat everybody like that,' she said. 'They use you and then they dispose of you like so much rubbish.' "

Marilyn's bitter feeling of being discarded like trash was tragically confirmed a few days later from another powerful source. The studio finally could take no more of her unprofessional behavior. Monroe was fired, and *Something's Got to Give* was canceled from production. She thought her career was over.

Deteriorating rapidly, Marilyn was now on the verge of a complete collapse. Taking refuge with the Lawfords, she spent her days and nights either staring off into space or crying. All the time, she kept complaining about how used and abused she had been by the Kennedy brothers. That summer, the Lawfords took Marilyn on two separate trips to Lake Tahoe in an effort to rescue her from her rapid downward spiral. During both trips she drank heavily and took an excess of sleeping pills. Each time, either physical illness or acute emotional distress forced her to cut her vacation stay short and return to Los Angeles.

Several days after her second forced return, during the first week of August and just two days before her tragic death, she found out that Bobby Kennedy and his family were staying up near San Francisco. She immediately called Peter Lawford and tried to get the telephone number by which she could reach Bobby, but Lawford didn't have it; he suggested to Marilyn that she should call his wife, Pat Kennedy Lawford, who was visiting with her family at Hyannisport. Marilyn immediately called, and Pat was able to find Bobby's number in California. She innocently gave it to Marilyn.

Telephoning Bobby, the distraught actress begged him to fly down and meet with her, but he was annoyed that she had called and definitely didn't want to see her. Furthermore, he couldn't just leave his family and fly off to Los Angeles. He already had a tight schedule. But Marilyn wouldn't take "no" for an answer, and she eventually talked him or forced him into it: The next day Bobby Kennedy flew down to Los Angeles and surreptitiously took a helicopter from the airport to the backlot of the Fox studios. There, he was met by Lawford, who cautiously drove him the six miles to Marilyn's secluded home on Helena Drive in Brentwood.

Bobby and his brother-in-law arrived at Marilyn's at two in the afternoon and found that she had already been drinking rather heavily. Lawford proceeded to go outside by the swimming pool so that Bobby and Marilyn could be alone and talk privately. Within a very short time he heard their voices shouting, so he returned to the house. Bobby was yelling at her that he was going to go to Lawford's house, while she shouted back that he had promised to spend the whole afternoon alone with her.

They continued bitterly arguing back and forth for ten minutes as the uneasy Lawford watched Marilyn become almost uncontrollably hysterical. "At the height of her anger," Lawford remembered, "she allowed how first thing Monday morning she was going to call a press conference and tell the world about the treatment she had suffered at the hands of the Kennedy brothers." At this, Bobby completely lost his temper and told Marilyn, furiously, to leave him and his brother completely alone—that they never wanted to hear from her again.

"Marilyn lost it at this point, screaming obscenities and flailing wildly away at Bobby with her fists. In her fury she picked up a small kitchen knife and lunged at him." Lawford grabbed Marilyn's arm and, with Bobby's help, wrestled her to the floor and took the knife away from her. Bobby then suggested that they call the distraught actress's psychiatrist, Dr. Ralph Greenson, who immediately came over to the house.

Bobby Kennedy and Lawford left, and what transpired next remains a mystery to this day. There has been much speculation, both logical and highly imaginative, of how Marilyn Monroe died

44

that evening. Elaborate and fanciful theories have been popular-
ized in which the tragic actress was the victim of murder; but there
is no evidence to sustain such a claim. All of the facts lead to the
overwhelming conclusion that Marilyn died by her own hand, the
result of either an accidental or intentional drug overdose. In all
probability, it was suicide.

Marilyn had of course attempted to kill herself before, in her
own very romantic and theatrical way. Likely, this time it was
simply another well-staged attempt to manipulate those around
her emotionally—in this instance, Robert Kennedy. But so full of
anguish and despair, she doubtless gave in to her ever-increasing
impulse of self-destruction, swept away by the rapidly disintegrating events of the day.

What *is* strongly suspected is that the Kennedy camp carefully
orchestrated a thorough cover-up immediately after her death.
Marilyn's close friend, Ted Jordan, received two phone calls from
her that fatal evening. She fuzzily complained to him of troubles
with Kennedy.

"She said Lawford had phoned her around 7:00 and invited her
over for some Chinese dinner and a little poker with friends,"
Jordan later wrote. "Bobby wanted her to come. But Marilyn
suspected that once the poker game ended, Lawford would invite
a couple of hookers over for Bobby and himself, and they would
expect Marilyn to participate. 'And I've had enough of that stuff,'
she said. 'Bobby promised to stay here, and that's how it is.'

Ted Jordan hung up, but passed the evening uneasily, feeling
that this time Marilyn might be having serious problems. When he
finally decided to call her back later that night, he was startled to
hear Peter Lawford answer the phone. Lawford informed him of
Marilyn's "accident," and Jordan was left with the strong suspicion that Lawford had gone over there to "tidy up" and make
certain that nothing remained that might incriminate the Kennedy
brothers.

The next day, Robert Kennedy spoke before a meeting of the

45

American Bar Association in San Francisco. He then took his family to the World's Fair in Seattle and proceeded to join Supreme Court Justice William Douglas, who was camping in the Washington forests. Showing a ruthless and cool nerve, Bobby callously ignored the fact of Marilyn's death and totally dissociated himself from the events that followed.

When later questioned by the press about Marilyn Monroe's untimely death, First Lady Jacqueline Kennedy only responded: "She will go on eternally."

The illustrious President John Fitzgerald Kennedy had no comment.

*The degree and kind of a man's sexuality reach
up into the ultimate pinnacle of his spirit.*
—Nietzsche

3

THE MISTRESS AND
THE MOBSTER

ohn F. Kennedy's sexual partners were as eclectic as
they were numerous. The affairs that are the best
documented are those that were revealed by the ladies
in question several years after Kennedy's death. The
critical and cynical post–Watergate mood of the country focused
public interest on a thoroughly honest and uncensored investigation
into all aspects of each and every President's life. America was ready
to have its sacred myths exploded and destroyed, and many of the
former Kennedy mistresses were more than willing to oblige.

One of the first to confess was a beautiful, dark-haired woman
named Judith Campbell Exner. During the first years of Kennedy's
Presidency, during his torrid and lengthy affair with Marilyn
Monroe, he was also engaging in a long-term sexual relationship
with Judith. Theirs was the most notorious and potentially dangerous affair in which the President would be involved.

Judith Campbell Exner, today a recluse who is slowly dying
of cancer, tells a fascinating and exciting story of her romantic

47

involvement with Kennedy. It reveals secret ties to the Mafia and organized crime, and provides unique insights into the President's troubled private and professional life.

Judith claims that she functioned as Kennedy's link with the Mob for most of 1960 and 1961. Faithfully following the President's constant requests, she regularly carried sealed envelopes back and forth between Kennedy and the head of the Chicago Mafia, Sam Giancana, and Giancana's Los Angeles lieutenant, Johnny Roselli. Judith arranged ten meetings between the President and the Chicago Godfather and firmly believes that one of them may have taken place in the White House itself.

Although never informed by either of the principals about what took place during these meetings or what was the purpose of them, Judith Exner believes that two of the important issues resolved may have been the rigging of the vital 1960 West Virginia Democratic Presidential Primary and the collaboration of the CIA with the Mafia to assassinate Cuba's Fidel Castro.

For one who played such a sensational role in such a clouded and turbulent episode of history, Judith Exner sprang from an exceptionally proper and conservative background. Born in Los Angeles in 1933 and raised in a wealthy and traditional home in the posh suburb of Pacific Palisades, Judith gravitated toward Hollywood and an acting career that never went anywhere. At age eighteen, she settled on a marriage with an up-and-coming actor named William Campbell. The marriage was not a happy one, and seven years later they divorced, in 1958. With money she had inherited from her family, Judith moved to Beverly Hills and began living a glamorous, carefree life, frequenting the best restaurants and most exclusive clubs and socializing with movie stars. She met Frank Sinatra and had a brief affair with him, and it was on his invitation to see his show in Las Vegas that she made her fateful encounter.

It was at the Sands Hotel in Las Vegas on February 7, 1960, that Judith was introduced by Sinatra to the aspiring presidential candidate. Kennedy was flying from Texas to Oregon and had made a special detour to Vegas to visit his good friend Sinatra. When Kennedy met the stunningly beautiful brunette he was instantly attracted. Perhaps the obvious fact that the young woman was totally charmed and captivated by him made her all the more desirable.

Unlike his usual immediate conquests, the meeting with Judith passed rather properly and romantically. They spent the evening in casual conversation and, quite remarkably, Jack Kennedy made no advances or propositions. He simply invited her to have lunch the following day on Sinatra's patio. During the three-hour lunch, Kennedy and Judith became much closer, but still, according to her, did not make love. He promised to call her and flew off to Oregon.

Throughout the next month, although busily campaigning for the Democratic primaries, Kennedy called her almost every day. He seemed to be taking a very personal interest in all aspects of Judith's life and appeared to be increasingly anxious to rendezvous with her again. Arranging a meeting for the first week in March, they met at the Plaza Hotel in New York and passionately consummated their long-distance relationship on the eve of the New Hampshire Primary.

In an exclusive interview in *People* magazine in February 1988, Judith confessed to Kitty Kelly: "It was a wonderful night of lovemaking. Jack couldn't have been more loving, more concerned about my feelings, more considerate, more gentle. Later, because of his bad back and an arrogance that overtook him in the White House, he developed a cavalier attitude in bed, as if he were there to be serviced. But in the beginning, when I fell in love with him, he was very demonstrative. It was amazing to me that he could be so relaxed on the eve of his first primary of his presidential campaign, but unbelievably, he didn't mention New Hampshire once during our entire night together."

The fact that Kennedy took such an atypical and unusually romantic approach with Judith might be interpreted as his seeing a more important use for her than merely sexual pleasure. Perhaps it was qualities other than her great beauty that appealed to his current needs. He may have viewed the pliant, star-struck young woman as being sensitive, insecure, and naive—qualities that could be easily manipulated, exploited, and controlled. The lovely brunette might well have appealed to John Kennedy because he saw in her someone who would unquestioningly carry out his desires, both in and out of bed. Very soon, it seemed that she was being moved into a unique position to be of such service.

The week after her dreamy encounter with Kennedy at the Plaza, Judith was invited to Miami by Frank Sinatra to see him perform at the Fontainbleau Hotel. It was there that Sinatra introduced her to his Mafia friend, Sam Giancana. Giancana was using the alias "Sam Flood," and this was the innocent identity that Judith knew him by for several months to come.

"I didn't know then that Sam was the Chicago Godfather," Judith told Kitty Kelly, "but I did know he was important to Frank because of the way Sinatra acted around him, bowing and scraping and being so deferential. I feel like I was set up to be the courier. I was a perfect choice because I could come and go without notice, and if noticed, no one would've believed it anyway."

Judith was initiated into her courier capacity only a few weeks later, when she rendezvoused with Kennedy at his home in Georgetown, Washington, D.C., while his pregnant wife was away at Palm Beach. There, she and Kennedy made love in the same bed he shared with Jackie. During a dinner at the house on April 6, 1960, Kennedy spent the entire evening talking with a political lobbyist about his strategy for the West Virginia Primary while his mistress listened attentively.

The election in West Virginia was acutely problematic for

Kennedy because he was a Catholic candidate running in a state whose population was 95-percent Protestant. Kennedy knew that a victory in West Virginia could be a crucial factor in his capture of the Democratic presidential nomination, and he was very worried and concerned. According to Judith, Kennedy and the lobbyist discussed how money could be delivered to those who had influence in the state. JFK turned to her and casually asked, "Could you quietly arrange a meeting with Sam and me?"

When she timidly asked him why, he simply responded that he thought he might need Sam's help in the campaign. He told Judith that he wanted the meeting as soon as possible and gave her several dates on which he would be available. Today, she is convinced that Kennedy was well aware of "Sam Flood's" true identity at the time, as, indeed, he must have been.

Eager to be of help to her lover, Judith called Giancana and arranged to meet with him. She flew to Chicago the very next day and met the incognito Godfather at a popular nightclub. A meeting with Kennedy was arranged four days later at the Fontainebleau in Miami. After Judith telephoned Kennedy and informed him of her success, he talked her into also flying down to Florida because he wanted her to be present.

The meeting took place in Miami as scheduled.

"I was not present," Kennedy's former mistress told Kelly, "but Jack came to my suite afterward, and I asked him how the meeting had gone. He seemed very happy about it and thanked me for making the arrangements. He then stayed with me for an hour or so, and we talked about the campaign." They also talked about Kennedy's marriage, and he matter-of-factly told her that if he didn't win the Democratic nomination for President that coming July, he and Jackie would definitely get a divorce. "He didn't say he was leaving her for me or for any other woman, or that Jackie was leaving him for any other man. He simply said that their marriage was unhappy and the divorce was a mutual decision between them." When her lover left, he handed Judith an envelope with $2,000 in cash inside. It was a gift in gratitude for her services.

Evidently the meeting with Sam Giancana was even more successful than Kennedy had believed. FBI records show that large Mafia donations were made to his state campaign in West Virginia. This and the considerable efforts of Giancana gave John F. Kennedy an easy victory in the May 10 primary election.

As Kennedy progressed closer to the Presidency, Judith became more in love with him. According to Kennedy's brother-in-law and trusted confidant, Peter Lawford: "She began to believe she meant something to Jack. She thought he cared for her. But Jack wasn't the type to confuse sex with love."

The self-deception must have been especially difficult for Judith when Kennedy reverted to his old ways. Such an occasion was the opening night of the Democratic Convention in Los Angeles, when he took her to a suite at the Beverly Hilton and tried to talk her into participating in a ménage à trois with another attractive young woman. Making love with two women at the same time was, of course, one of John Kennedy's favorite recreational activities. But Judith's romantic sensibility couldn't tolerate such a thing and she was deeply offended. She flatly refused to have anything to do with it.

Kennedy slyly insisted, saying, "I know you; I know you'll enjoy it." But Judith stood firm in her refusal.

She also began noticing that Kennedy's favorite way of having sex, lying passively on his back, was not simply a way to accommodate his ailing back. She felt that it was primarily calculated to make the woman feel she was there "just to satisfy the man."

Moreover, with his capture of the Democratic presidential nomination, Kennedy's use of Judith as a courier to the Chicago Godfather was far more important to him than sex.

Between the time he won the nomination and the election five months later, Kennedy asked his obliging young mistress to arrange several more meetings with Sam Giancana. One of these clandestine encounters occurred at the Navarro Hotel in New York four weeks after the Democratic Convention. Judith believes that this meeting, and possibly the others that followed, concerned Giancana's role in helping to secure the upcoming election for Kennedy.

"After Jack was elected," Judith revealed, "Sam kept saying he would never have been President if it hadn't been for his efforts on Kennedy's behalf in Cook County, Illinois." It was a landslide vote for Kennedy in Cook County that barely won him the Illinois election, the crucial factor in his presidential victory.

After moving into the White House, the popular new Chief Executive almost ignored his anxious mistress, until a few months later, when he needed her help again. Following the disastrous Bay of Pigs invasion of Cuba, the publicly humiliated Kennedy telephoned Judith and requested that she fly to Las Vegas and pick up an envelope from Johnny Roselli and take it to Giancana in Chicago. She happily complied, carefully transporting the envelope in her purse to Chicago and arranging another meeting between Sam and the President after she arrived. Kennedy traveled west to Chicago on April 28 and met the Mafia Godfather in Judith's room at the Ambassador Hotel.

Giancana was already in Judith's room when the President finally arrived, and immediately gave her a seductive hug, apologizing that he could not stay on with her that evening. According to Judith, Kennedy shook Sam's hand and they exchanged friendly greetings, Sam addressing the President as "Jack" with a casual, if not bold, informality. Kennedy instructed Judith to leave the room, so she went in and sat in the bathroom while the President of the United States and the Chicago crime lord discussed business.

The next day, Judith flew to Florida at Kennedy's urgent

request and picked up another envelope from Roselli and Giancana and brought it back to Washington five days later. She immediately called the White House and was quickly put through to the President.

Although they had previously made a date to have lunch on the following day, Saturday, May 6, Kennedy told her that the contents of the envelope were urgent and couldn't even wait a day. She immediately took a taxi to the White House, and was taken to the Cabinet Room by one of the President's private staff. Kennedy smilingly took the envelope from her.

The following day, Judith kept her luncheon date with the President and joined him in the family quarters of the White House. They snacked informally on hamburgers, then he led her to the master bedroom. "I saw twin beds," she recalled. "Jack then led me through an alcove to another bedroom with a large double bed and we made love."

Upon leaving at the end of the afternoon, Judith was handed another envelope and asked by Kennedy to take it to Sam Giancana. Again, she was happy to be of such valued assistance to the man she loved, and she promptly did what was expected of her.

During the rest of the spring and summer of 1961, Judith found herself spending much of her time traveling back and forth across the country on planes and trains relaying the unmarked envelopes between the President and Sam Giancana and Roselli. Judith claims that she never opened any of the plain, unmarked envelopes and still has no idea what was inside them. Sensing that the contents were extremely important to her powerful lover, she never let the innocent-looking envelopes out of her sight and scrupulously kept them with her at all times.

After a while, Judith began noticing a change in the way Kennedy was treating her. The romancing disappeared almost entirely and he began displaying an arrogant, imperious manner toward his bewildered mistress. Then, during an August rendezvous with Kennedy in the White House, she was deeply embarrassed and enraged by him when he insultingly accused her in front of presidential aide Dave Powers of having told someone about his suggestion of a *ménage à trois* and her refusal the year before.

But if the sexual romance was seriously deteriorating, Judith was still functioning ably as a secret courier to the Mob. She dutifully fetched one more envelope from Roselli and Giancana and brought it back to the White House in late August. As if to make up for his callous treatment of her, Kennedy used this occasion to take her back down to the large double bed in the family bedroom and present her with a costly ruby and diamond brooch.

Because Judith, by now, was acutely feeling Kennedy's constant neglect, she less than enthusiastically accepted his extravagant gift, realizing that it was inspired as much by guilt as by affection. And gifts or no gifts, their relationship kept moving downhill. As 1962 began, it looked as if things were over between Jack and Judith. By now, she had visited the President many times in the White House. She was beginning to be resentful at having to be totally available for Kennedy and at having to come instantly running to his call. She also felt exploited by the constant courier assignments.

While carrying on her affair with John Kennedy, Judith was intensely lonely and frustrated, but she kept trying to convince herself that Kennedy's marriage was as unhappy as he claimed it was and that his constant promises of a possible future divorce would miraculously come true.

"I was very lonely a lot of the time going with a married man," the terminally ill ex-mistress sadly reflected upon her famous love affair. "Also, I was raised a Catholic and knew that such an illicit relationship was wrong in the eyes of God, but I suppose I rationalized things because Jack had said his marriage was unhappy and divorce was a possibility."

By March 1962, Judith had visited Kennedy about twenty times in the White House and on numerous occasions at different locations across the country. The official White House log from the end of 1960 to mid-1962 shows that more than seventy telephone calls were recorded between Judith and the President. Many of these recorded calls came from the home of Sam Giancana.

There had been lots of little arguments between Judith and the President and their calls to one another became less and less frequent when, suddenly, she discovered to her horror that she was being followed by FBI agents. The federal investigation was centered on Sam Giancana, and Judith's highly visible presence by his side had also qualified her activities for close scrutiny.

When federal agents began thoroughly interrogating the frightened young woman, she immediately called Kennedy and begged for help. "Don't worry," the President confidently told her. "They won't do anything to you. And don't worry about Sam. You know he works for us." Kennedy kept telling her over and over again that Sam was working for him.

But when the FBI increased its hounding of Kennedy's mistress-courier, she became even more unnerved, urgently pleading with him to use his influence to make them stop. His responses were impatient. "He'd say, 'Ignore them. It's just part of Hoover's vendetta against me.' He hated J. Edgar Hoover and called him 'a queer son of a bitch.' As the harassment got worse, Jack lost patience with me. 'You've got to learn how to handle this,' he'd say. 'I've got more important things to deal with.'"

At the end of March, Hoover met with Kennedy at the White House and seriously warned him of Judith's Mafia ties and her telephone relationship with someone at the Executive Mansion. Apparently Hoover did not know that it was the President she was having the "relationship" with, and that she was involved with Giancana and Roselli at the President's request.

The meeting with Hoover was, seemingly, the last nail in the coffin for Judith and Kennedy's affair. When summer arrived it was completely finished. "There was no big argument or anything like that," she stated. "It was just two people no longer willing to put up with each other. The gloss was gone."

From the exalted bedrooms of the White House, Judith found herself drifting into a sexual relationship with Sam Giancana in his more modest Chicago home. It lasted only a few months, until Sam hopefully proposed marriage and Judith rejected the offer. Moving back to Beverly Hills, she tried to cope with the continuing FBI surveillance and pull her life together.

After Kennedy's assassination the following year, Judith had a breakdown and tried to commit suicide. In the years that followed, she gave birth to an illegitimate son and gave him up for adoption. She married for a second time in 1972, and eventually separated from her husband, Dan Exner, in 1985.

Today Judith's life has made a full circle of tragic ruin. The victim of an incurable cancer, she suffered through a mastectomy in 1978 and three years ago had a lung removed. Diagnosed as having deadly metastatic cancer, Judith Campbell Exner, the stunningly beautiful brunette who became one of the most notorious and dangerous mistresses in White House history, has been given only another year to live.

Civilized people cannot fully satisfy their
sexual instinct without love.
                              —Bertrand Russell

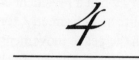

ANY WHICH WAY
HE CAN

After triumphantly attending several gala inaugural balls upon taking office in January 1961, John F. Kennedy said good night to his exhausted wife and went on to a party at the home of Joe Alsop, where a half-dozen Hollywood starlets imported by Peter Lawford were awaiting him. "All six wanted to be with the President," wrote Lawford. "They arranged a lineup as they would at Madame Claude's brothel in Paris, and Jack chose two of them. This threesome brought his first day in office to a resounding close."

The combination of unlimited power, wealth, and prestige created an endless array of opportunities for the new Chief Executive, and Kennedy was eagerly determined to take full advantage of each and every one. The full extent of his sexual activity is almost impossible to document accurately. Many close observers believe that the President was enjoying illicit sex on a daily basis. Now having his absolute choice of anyone he wanted, Kennedy used all of the unrivaled power of the American Presidency to accommodate his insatiable lust. It would appear that romantic conquests generally took top priority during his administration. On numerous occasions, Kennedy placed his personal pleasure ahead of the duties of his office, even to the extent of seriously endangering national security in the process.

The pre-Vietnam era of the early 1960s was perhaps the last time in American history when a President could get away with conducting his private life so indiscreetly, for the sexual revolution that coincided with the peace movement and hippy generation at the end of the decade made personal sex habits an acceptable topic for public consciousness and concern. Because of the huge technical growth of the media industry and the all-encompassing boom of the news business, not to mention its newfound power and independence, political figures for many years now have become subject to the most intense and relentless public scrutiny.

However, when John Kennedy lived in the White House, the press was still subject to considerable censorship and political control. A long-established "gentleman's agreement" with the American press made the sex life of the President a subject that was absolutely taboo. "They can't touch me while I'm alive," Kennedy once said with an arrogant smile, "and after I'm dead, who cares?" Sadly enough, that was very true.

And President Kennedy flaunted the exalted privilege of his sexual prowess whenever he could. Even in the most sensitive and conservative social environments, he took great pains to let people know, at least subtly, that he was better with women than anyone else. This narcissistic need is a key ingredient of the classic "Don Juan" syndrome from which he acutely suffered.

One great change that the Presidency brought to Kennedy's sex life was that he would never again be forced to be a paying customer. At the climax of his previous campaign, Kennedy was not in such a fortunate position. According to his friend Langdon Marvin, who accompanied Kennedy to Chicago for the first of the now-famous debates with Richard Nixon: "The night before the

debate, Jack said to me, 'Any girls lined up for tomorrow?' "
Marvin dutifully made the usual arrangements. Only an hour
before the crucial debate was scheduled to begin, he took Kennedy
to a room at the Palmer House where a dazzling prostitute was
patiently waiting. Marvin introduced the hooker to the future
President, then went out into the hotel hallway and cautiously stood
guard. Only fifteen minutes later, Kennedy quickly came out of the
room with "an ear-to-ear grin on his face."

The sexual performance evidently added an extra glow of
health and confidence that radiated during his TV appearance only
a few minutes later. JFK made a spectacular impression on the
nation during the debate, and, believing it due primarily to his pre-
show sex at the Palmer House, made sure that his aides had a
prostitute waiting for him just before each of the following
encounters with Nixon.

In pleasure-loving New Orleans, Kennedy was introduced to
famed stripper Blaze Starr. While Blaze's politically powerful
fiancé, Louisiana Governor Earl Long, hosted a large party in their
hotel suite, she and Kennedy spent twenty minutes having sex in
a closet. While hidden there with the statuesque stripper, Kennedy
couldn't resist telling her the story of how President Harding had
made love to his mistress, Nan Britton, in a White House closet
forty years earlier.

Although Kennedy zestfully dashed off toward new and
unlimited sexual horizons when he became President, he still
maintained many former romantic relationships besides those
with Marilyn Monroe and Judith Campbell. One such affair was
with a beautiful Georgetown debutante who greatly resembled his
wife. Her name was Pam Turnure and she had been his secretary
and worked in his campaign.

Their liaison was most interesting because of its ironical
repercussions.

Before the presidential election, Kennedy had freely engaged
in late-night rendezvous at Pam's Georgetown apartment and her

strait-laced landlords had angrily taken notice. The offended couple began a crusade to bring swift retribution to the hypocritical and adulterous senator by planting tape recorders and taking photographs.

The couple, Leonard and Florence Kater, took their vivid evidence to every newspaper, TV station, and magazine they could reach. As amazing as it may seem to the sensation-obsessed world of today, no one in the media at that time would have anything to do with the Katers or their concrete and condemning evidence. When all their efforts failed, the tenacious couple followed Kennedy around on the presidential campaign trail holding up large, home-made signs denouncing him as an adulterer. They naively telephoned Kennedy's father to no avail and even complained to Cardinal Cushing of Boston. The Katers' almost holy mission had a rather comical conclusion when, frustrated at every turn, the beleaguered Mrs. Kater ended up picketing the White House.

The other ironic development of Kennedy's lengthy affair with Pam Turnure was the fact that she became his wife's press secretary when Jackie became First Lady. Pam, at her lover's suggestion, had moved in with Mary Meyer, a good friend of Jackie's. Mary knew about Pam's secret affair with her friend's husband.

A little later, when Kennedy became President, he began strongly suggesting that Pam Turnure become his wife's Press Secretary. His suggestion seemed especially awkward because Pam had no experience whatsoever in this field. Jackie eventually gave in and accepted her husband's mistress as her Press Secretary, perhaps mistakenly believing that she would be able to control the situation better between the two illicit lovers. But, then, suddenly, the restless Chief Executive lost interest in Pam and began sleeping with her roommate, Mary Meyer.

The affair with Mary Meyer did not begin until well into Kennedy's Presidency, in January 1962, to be exact, and it continued right up

62

to the time of his assassination in November 1963. It would be the President's last serious long-term affair.

Mary Meyer was also from a wealthy and prominent family. Divorced from a top CIA official, she was an aspiring artist possessed of an unconventional and somewhat wild and free spirit. Blond and stunningly beautiful, Mary was also gifted with a natural charm and elegance. These qualities were interestingly blended with a bold and gutsy earthiness and a restless desire constantly to challenge and explore the forbidden. This must have appealed enormously to a champion iconoclast like John F. Kennedy. During their intense affair, Mary and the President met for amorous encounters about 40 times. These lovemaking sessions took place in her art studio, at the White House, and in the homes of friends.

Experimenting with the recreational drugs of the 1960s such as LSD and marijuana, Mary boasted of a fanciful if somewhat crackpot scheme of using these euphoria-inducing drugs to "turn on" the leaders of the world and make them abandon their hostile practices and passively embrace peace and love.

Evidently the President of the United States was to be her first convert. When Mary visited the White House in July 1962, she and Kennedy retired to one of the bedrooms and she presented him with a package of six marijuana joints. Kennedy enthusiastically shared one with her, laughingly confiding that he was going to lead a White House conference on drug abuse in only a week or so. The President smoked two more joints, but refused a fourth. "Suppose the Russians drop a bomb," he joked, pretending that there had to be a limit to his irresponsible dissipation.

With the always-helpful assistance of Peter Lawford, Kennedy had already used cocaine and hashish several times. Continuing his drug adventures, the President joined Mary in at least two more marijuana sessions and one LSD encounter, taking an acid trip together as they engaged in wild sex.

Mary's bold and reckless affair with Kennedy flourished right up to the time of his assassination. Then, afterward, in one horrible note of final irony, Mary Meyer was shot down herself, mysteriously murdered less than a year later, while strolling in broad daylight along the Potomac in Georgetown near her home. The assailant was never caught and the tragic murder of Mary Pinchot Meyer remains to this day an unsolved crime.

Another long-term relationship that John F. Kennedy brought to the White House involved actress Angie Dickinson. The beautiful, honey-skinned leading lady has never directly acknowledged an affair with Kennedy, but the carefully calculated tone of many of her comments on the subject have left the impression of a coyly oblique affirmation. "He was wonderful," she said during a recent interview. "That's all I'll say. It would be bad manners to say more."

In a magazine interview, Miss Dickinson confessed: "From the moment I met him, I was hooked, like everybody else. He was the sexiest politician I ever met. . . . He was the killer type, a devastatingly handsome, charming man—the kind your mother hoped you wouldn't marry."

The late Slim Aarons, an intimate observer of the relationship, claimed that Angie and Kennedy secretly spent a passionate three days in a Palm Springs hideout just before he accepted the Presidency. According to the late Mrs. Aarons, the newly elected Chief Executive and the actress occupied a small bungalow from which they never once came out.

There are several other convincing witnesses who confirm the existence of a prolonged and serious affair. Betty Spalding felt that the relationship was very intense, indeed, and assumes it didn't progress further because Kennedy wanted the Presidency much more than he wanted Angie, and he knew he couldn't bring her with him to the White House. Nevertheless, when Kennedy was elected President, at the inaugural ball at the Statler-Hilton, he disappeared for a half-hour to meet privately with Angie upstairs.

Once firmly established in the White House, in his relentless effort to get his "daily dose of sex," the President discovered that the safest, easiest, and most ideal way existed right at his fingertips: the Secret Service.

An elite group of well-trained young men, the Secret Service provided the President and his family with full-time protection. Their devotion was complete, and they were with the First Family standing guard night and day. They were also their most intimate associates, existing as a barrier between the Kennedys and the world. Within the larger Service, the President had his own group of agents and, instead of using them primarily for the protective and business purposes for which they were intended, he organized them into a high-living fraternity devoted to partying. While this privileged group of handsome young men shared in Kennedy's hedonistic pleasures, another important duty appears to have been procurement. They were expected to provide their illustrious boss with a constant and steady supply of female sex partners. "He didn't want to know about security but about broads," recalled Marty Venker, one of JFK's Secret Service agents. "The agent was supposed to set up dates for the President. If he was new to the job and wasn't aware of this fact, Kennedy let him know pretty quickly. He'd say something to the effect of 'You've been here two weeks already and still don't have any broads lined up for me? You guys get all the broads you want. How about doing something for your Commander-in-Chief?'"

The Secret Service agents were shrewd enough to know how serious Kennedy really was about their procurement duties. If they wished to stay in the glamorous and prestigious duty of the presidential guard, each one of them fully realized that, first and foremost, he would have to provide Kennedy with a steady supply of beautiful and willing women. Most of the agents didn't find this task difficult at all. "Naturally, every local beauty wanted to fuck the President," Venker remembered. "It was her patriotic duty."

Kennedy also had another important use for his elite Secret Service corps. They helped facilitate his womanizing by offering a second very useful service: faithfully monitoring the daily, minute-to-minute movements of the First Lady. By constantly maintaining radio contact with Jackie's personal Secret Service agent, the President's agents could effectively determine her whereabouts at all times. This was an invaluable advantage for Kennedy. It meant that he could indulge his sexual activities to the fullest possible limits, without any worry of being interrupted by the unexpected return of his wife.

On numerous occasions the President would either be carrying on in bed with his girlfriends or cavorting nude with them down in the swimming pool—right up until the very last minute when Jackie's limousine drove through the White House gates. Thanks to the full-time radio surveillance by his agents, the President never had to waste a precious minute. With split-second timing, Kennedy could artfully dispatch a mistress and hide all tell-tale evidence of his philandering—smilingly greeting his wife a moment later.

The swimming pool at the White House was where all of the President's sex parties took place. From the merely modest and functional convenience it had been in the previous, conservative administration, the pool was totally revamped by JFK and made into a hedonist's delight. Secluded indoors in a huge room in the White House basement, the pool was surrounded with brightly painted walls on which elaborate murals depicted the sultry and exotic landscapes of the French Riviera. The glass door to the area had, now, been carefully frosted so that any intimate activities of the President could not be witnessed from the outside. When Kennedy held a party down at the swimming pool, he would usually have two or three women with him and instruct the household staff to stay away from the area. Any hapless waiter or agent who disturbed one of these parties met with the President's formidable wrath.

Traphes Bryant, the kennel keeper at the White House, remembered seeing a dazzling blonde swimming nude with Kennedy and several other naked men and women in the pool. As the President lounged nakedly on the deck of the pool, sipping a cool drink, the alarm went off indicating his wife's sudden return. The naked bodies and all of the evidence of the wild party had to be instantly gotten rid of. A moment later, when Jackie walked though the door, her husband languidly looked up from the deck and calmly greeted her.

On another occasion, Bryant was routinely heading for the basement when the elevator door suddenly flew open and a naked office girl came running out so fast that she almost knocked him down. She stopped only long enough to ask Bryant if he knew where the President was.

For Kennedy to indulge himself in such a flagrantly philandering lifestyle within his own home, it was necessary that every member of the staff be involved in a relentless conspiracy on his behalf. And apparently that is exactly what took place. The unspoken code of silence regarding Kennedy's ravenous womanizing was upheld by each and every White House worker as far as the First Lady was concerned. To have divulged the President's shocking secret life to his wife would have been perceived by the staff members as being disloyal, if not unpatriotic.

Between his casual sex romps, President Kennedy returned to his favorite hunting ground—glamorous Hollywood—and initiated another highly erotic celebrity affair. Having been so stimulated by his exciting involvement with Marilyn Monroe, Kennedy eagerly anticipated his conquest of America's other great blond sex symbol: Jayne Mansfield. Once again, it was his obliging and swinging brother-in-law, Peter Lawford, who provided the introduction and made all of the arrangements.

Physically, Jayne Mansfield was even more spectacular than Marilyn had been. Her body was so dramatically proportioned

67

that she appeared almost freakish. Tall and vivacious, she proudly displayed an abundant 42-inch bust that seemed miraculously suspended in mid-air over her tiny 18-inch waist. With her perfectly conditioned body, platinum blond hair, and full, sensuous lips, Jayne was sex personified. Unfortunately, her entire acting career had been based solely on this lurid and obvious fact. During the eight years she had been in films, she had made only three or four successful major movies, these coming at the beginning of her career. It had been a downhill struggle ever since. Each year was bringing less offers, and, although the acutely intelligent actress refused to face it, she was being viewed more and more as a vulgar and tasteless joke. Her career was, in fact, almost over. In another year or so, the supremely exhibitionistic Mansfield would be enduring the humiliation of appearing in cheap porno films. (This was only a prelude to Jayne's real tragedy: Only a few years later, she was gruesomely killed by decapitation in a horrible automobile crash.)

However, both of their tragic futures were unknown when the President began a sexual relationship with the voluptuous actress. At the time, Jayne was still married to muscleman-actor Mickey Hargitay, but the marriage was falling apart and headed swiftly toward a divorce court. It is not known exactly how many times Kennedy and Mansfield got together, but Lawford knew of at least three rendezvous that took place in such divergent places as Beverly Hills, Palm Springs, and Malibu. The actress nicknamed the President "Mr. K," and he raved about her sexual talents. Although she was much more matter-of-fact and realistic about men than Monroe had been, Jayne found it difficult to have casual sex with a man unless she was at least partially drunk. For Jayne Mansfield, all men were just alike: They all responded to her in exactly the same way.

At the time when Jayne got together with Kennedy in Palm Springs she was visibly pregnant with her fourth child. Kennedy hadn't known about her condition until he saw her. Later, he told his brother-in-law that it had really turned him on.

But apparently Jayne wasn't as turned on by him as he was by her. She would tell Peter Lawford that there was "a coldness to him, a hard, flat coldness which must make his personal life with Jackie less than satisfactory."

This extreme lack of warmth in Kennedy, plus the inconvenience and arrogance of his demanding courtship made Jayne quickly lose interest in pursuing the affair. A week after having returned from their Palm Springs lovemaking, the statuesque actress was having drinks with her press agent, Raymond Strait, at the Beverly Hills Hotel when a phone call came through to her from the President. Strait remembered that Jayne argued with Kennedy on the phone and abruptly hung up on him, shouting the words,"Look, you'll only be President for eight years at the most, but I'll be a movie star forever!"

Needless to say, the Kennedy–Mansfield affair did not proceed much further. Jayne was as street-smart as Marilyn Monroe had been naive, and she certainly wasn't the willing victim her predecessor was. Mansfield was more interested in where her own life was going than in being a rich man's plaything.

The kind of sex that John Kennedy liked best was provided by a skilled professional. And for the President of the United States, only the best would do. Leslie Devereux, a high-priced New York call girl, was hired by the ever-helpful Peter Lawford and brought to the penthouse suite at the Hotel Carlyle. She was not informed who her client was going to be and was shocked when President John F. Kennedy appeared and smilingly asked his brother-in-law to disappear.

Leslie made a big hit her first night with the President, and returned to the Carlyle suite about four more times to service him. Their initial lovemaking was rather conventional and unimaginative, but after a while their sexual encounters assumed a much more "kinky" flavor. "I'd been with a number of powerful politicians and one thing they always liked was mild S and M," the attractive Miss Devereux recalled. "So we did a little of that—I tied his hands and feet to the bedposts, blindfolded him and teased him first with a feather and then with my fingernails. He seemed to enjoy it."

The playful sado-masochistic games with the President were just "business as usual" for Leslie Devereux. She found it so easy not to become emotionally involved with him. Like so many other women before her, she experienced Kennedy as being completely "mechanized and cold, with hard glazed eyes and a high-powered smile."

When the President's trips to New York became less frequent, he had Leslie come down to Washington. She visited him twice at the White House for exciting sexual adventures. During her first visit, the beautiful call girl was so casually passed in by the secretaries that she had the impression that these unofficial visits by attractive young women were a part of the President's daily routine. She spent 15 minutes of quality time with Kennedy in a small, secluded room right next to the Oval Office.

Her second visit to the White House was much more leisurely. This time, she was taken upstairs by a Secret Service agent and was shown into the historic and imposing Lincoln Bedroom. An elegant butler soon appeared with champagne on a silver tray. It was first class all the way. Eventually, Kennedy happily entered the somber, antique-filled bedroom and undressed, stretching himself out with Leslie on the giant rosewood bed. She told him that it seemed sacrilegious to make love on Abraham Lincoln's bed, but Kennedy laughed and said there was a White House legend that if you made a wish while in the bed, it always came true. She smiled seductively and told him to make a wish. Kennedy shut his eyes and Leslie mounted him. "See," he laughed, "it never fails." They proceeded to enjoy sex for several hours.

Mature, experienced women or prostitutes guaranteed the President some degree of protection against the unwanted complications of illicit sexual intercourse. But his younger, less sophisticated conquests sometimes were left with much more concrete evidence of their liaison than fond memories.

One such girl was the babysitter for the children of a famous newsman. The newsman had brought her and his family to Camp David, where he was interviewing the President for a special article. Once there, he made two discoveries: that Kennedy had created a nude bathing policy for the Camp David swimming pool, and that the President had initiated an affair with his children's babysitter. The girl became pregnant by Kennedy and had to go to Puerto Rico to get an abortion—an abortion paid for by the Catholic President. And it was not the first one he had financed.

Literally every female who crossed his path was fair game for Kennedy, no matter how youthfully naive, conservative, religious, or famous. Celebrities held a special fascination for him; they were certainly more of a challenge. And often the President appeared to be almost searching for failure, or, at least, for the most impossible odds he could find.

His most ambitious and optimistic seduction attempt was made upon the aging movie actress Marlene Dietrich. The sixty-one-year-old Dietrich was old enough to be Kennedy's mother. He invited her to the White House and as soon as he got her alone he made his forceful attack. A woman of the world, the legendary sex symbol easily managed to fend him off. As they parted—on a cordial basis—the President smiled and asked Marlene point-blank if she had ever slept with his father, quickly adding that the senior Kennedy had always claimed she had.

Having already been successfully rebuffed by actresses Jean Simmons and Sophia Loren while he was a senator, Kennedy must have gained even greater confidence with the Presidency. Surely one of his greatest miscalculations was his sexual attack on the incomparably independent Shirley MacLaine.

The spirited actress was staying in Palm Springs in early 1961, when Kennedy visited. She innocently went to the airport in Frank

Sinatra's limousine to meet the President. Kennedy climbed in the car and almost instantly pounced on her. MacLaine was so shocked by the sudden attack that she actually dove out of the moving automobile, suffering some mild cuts and bruises. The limousine stopped and she was sternly placed back inside by some irritated Secret Service agents. But this time Kennedy took the hint and kept his hands to himself: They became friends, but not lovers.

Lem Billings, Kennedy's oldest and closest friend, was omnipresent throughout the White House years and studied at first hand his buddy's romantic techniques. As Billings has put it: "Jack could be shameless in his sexuality, simply pull girls' dresses up and so forth. He would corner them at White House dinner parties and ask them to step into the next room away from the noise, where they could hold a 'serious discussion.'"

During the last year of their marriage, Jack and Jackie drifted so far apart that each was, in effect, going his or her own separate way. Gossip about "other women" in the President's life became more and more frequent. And his behavior was becoming much less discreet. In an era when journalists were restricted in what they could report about a public figure's personal life, Kennedy escaped time and time again with literally flaunting his infidelity and promiscuity to any who cared to stop and take notice.

Robert Pierpoint of CBS remembered a vivid incident in Palm Beach in which he saw Kennedy come out of a cottage with a beautiful young woman very early in the morning. They embraced in front of an awaiting limousine, then the President passionately took her in his arms and disappeared into the darkness of the car. Pierpoint and a group of other reporters then witnessed a flashy convertible drive up with one of the Kennedy sisters in it. She casually called out to the girl to come and get in the convertible. The President emerged from the limousine with the girl, gave her another passionate kiss, and then let her happily join his sister and drive off. He smiled at the reporters and offered no explanations.

Jack and Jackie Kennedy, a very unhappy couple, carefully pose for a glamour PR photo with their children, John and Caroline, at their Hyannisport home on Cape Cod. Only a short time later, little John will be striking his famous salute at his father's funeral—providing an ideal climactic scene for the great hypocritical legend.

Another time, when an attractive *Look* magazine reporter named Laura Bergquist arrived to interview the President, Kennedy sat lounging seductively in his shorts and scratched his genitals. "Hi Laura—getting much?" he smilingly greeted her.

73

Philippe de Bausset, a Washington bureau chief for *Paris Match* magazine, reported:

> The JFK administration was one huge public relations show. I used to think how amazed the country would be to find out that Jacqueline Kennedy, supposedly the most desirable and exciting woman on earth, couldn't satisfy her husband. It wasn't entirely her fault. Kennedy was too intent on enjoying himself. It may not have hindered his ability to run the country, but it didn't help either. Had he lived, many of his indiscretions would have become public knowledge. He would not have been re-elected . . . We were prisoners of a myth we helped to create. Professional image makers built an image; journalists bought into the propaganda and were later forced to go along with it.

Even if the President was, indeed, "getting away with it" for the present, and smoothly manipulating public opinion, there were certain occasions when his irresponsible philandering presented some serious potential threats to the national security. One notable incident took place at his bachelor pad at the Carlyle on Manhattan's exclusive Upper East Side.

Kennedy had impulsively decided to attend a private party in a townhouse across the street that was owned by a famous society woman who had arranged female companionship for him numerous times in the past. That evening, she had promised the President there would be several especially attractive girls at the party. Tired of the inconvenience of being constantly shadowed by the ubiquitous Secret Service agents, Kennedy successfully plotted to elude them this particular night by sneaking out of the Carlyle through its labyrinth-like basement. He made it to the party without being followed and quickly took inventory of the feminine stock. Choosing the woman who appealed to him most, the President immediately went off with her to her apartment.

Kennedy's Secret Service agents showed up at the party just a few minutes after he had departed. They demanded to know where the President was, but no one honestly knew. There was a feeling of panic. It seemed that the Army lieutenant with the crucial little black attaché case handcuffed to his wrist also had been left behind by the President. The unavailability of the attaché case to Kennedy during the subsequent evening meant that if an enemy had staged an attack on the United States, there would have been absolutely no way to do anything about it. The entire security of the nation had been momentarily sacrificed for the President's sexual pleasure.

Not surprisingly, throughout all these recklessly carnal escapades, the Kennedy marriage was rapidly disintegrating. The friction between husband and wife increased and arguments occurred much more often. The President was now openly flirting with women right in front of the First Lady. Jackie withdrew into herself even deeper than before, either pouting or remaining icily distant. How much did she really know about her husband's marathon sexual pursuits?

Probably much more than most people realized.

"Jackie had the whip-hand insofar as she cared little what people thought and could therefore walk out of the White House any day if so disposed," Peter Lawford stated with authority. Lawford was almost positive that Jackie never had extramarital affairs and, although he was sure that she had never cheated on her husband, he was also certain that she knew about the President's numerous sexual infidelities. "She told me she knew. She said once she caught him in the act."

There were at least two young ladies whom Jackie definitely knew about. When showing an Italian journalist through the White House, the elegant First Lady opened an office door and observed two attractive secretaries seated inside. Turning to the journalist, she casually commented: "Those two are my husband's lovers." The two secretaries were known by the humorous nicknames "Fiddle" and "Faddle." They were former college roommates who had joined the Kennedy campaign and then gone to work in the White House.

Always full of fun and high spirits, they tended to dress alike and became known throughout the Washington cognoscenti as Kennedy's two most steady intimates. On call twenty-four hours a day, Fiddle and Faddle alternately accompanied the President wherever he went.

As for the heavy flow of impromptu women in and out of the White House while the First Lady was away, Kennedy began showing some concern. The damaging evidence might be used against him in the next presidential election. He knew that the Secret Service employees were loyal and had sworn never to talk about what they had seen. But the staff and servants of the Executive Mansion were an entirely different manner. To protect himself, the President was forced to use calculated and severe measures.

With a stroke of bold genius, if not striking cynicism, Kennedy legally had a contract drawn up for all White House employees to sign, in which each swore not to write about anything that had happened there. When the newspapers found out about this unorthodox pledge of secrecy, it caused a sensation and Kennedy was eventually forced to deny his involvement and arrange for his chief usher to take the blame for the controversial idea.

The volume of women coming in and out of the White House had been increased by the cooperation of the President's personal staffs. The Secret Service not only actively procured sex partners for Kennedy, but it also operated its own kind of "quality control" by creating files and running background investigations on the numerous women headed for the presidential bed. Most of these reports were of airline stewardesses and models—perennial favorites of John F. Kennedy.

Despite his growing concern for secrecy, the longer Kennedy was in office, the less cautious he was in selecting his paramours. Friends passed along girls by either casual phone call or letter. Soon, almost any beautiful young woman who presented herself at the door of the White House and asked to see the President would be admitted. And often their quick introduction would immediately stretch out into a stay of several hours.

The traffic of women in and out of the White House at times must have been as congested as a Los Angeles freeway at rush hour. Needless to say, security became an important problem. Most of these beautiful, "drop-in" female visitors were neither questioned extensively or searched. They were simply passed on through with a smile, needing only the most informal and vague sources of introduction. With his reckless and self-destructively hedonistic attitude, the President never let himself be concerned with the great danger he was placing himself in. The potential consequences could have had a variety of disastrous scenarios.

One that is definitely known of hauntingly foreshadowed Dallas: A teenage Irish girl presented herself one day and asked to see the President. She was happily taken right up to the Oval Office. Only later, and just in time, was it discovered that she had a butcher knife in her shoulder bag and that she had just been released from a Dublin mental hospital.

Potentially, an even more dangerous episode was JFK's involvement with the wife of a Soviet spy, whose assignment was obtaining information that would compromise top-level American political figures. The spy, Harry Alan Towers, was married to Maria Novotny, who ran the New York headquarters of an international prostitution ring. The President went to Maria's apartment on Manhattan's West 55th Street. Kennedy requested that two other prostitutes dressed as a doctor and a nurse join him and Maria for sex games. The President of the United States played the willing patient.

Luckily, the FBI was on to Towers, and he fled the country before any significant damage could be done. The FBI was also busy investigating Kennedy's involvement with two prostitutes who figured prominently in Britain's notorious Profumo scandal. Had John F. Kennedy not been assassinated in November 1963, many of his more politically dangerous sexual liaisons might well have kept him from returning to the White House for a second term of office.

To fully document each and every one of Kennedy's illicit sexual affairs would require a manuscript of encyclopedic proportions. Even Kennedy must have eventually tired of his own carnal excesses toward the end of his rather short life. As his sexual behavior departed from conventional promiscuity and assumed a more and more jaded and sordid nature, he began showing signs of being bored. At private White House swimming parties where everyone was in the nude, the naked President would wander off from the orgy and concentrate his attention on his daily newspaper.

The most important fact conveyed by Kennedy's manic and compulsive womanizing is that he was a very unhappy and pathetically lonely man, emotionally isolated from everyone around him. The exact source of his psychological problems cannot be known for certain; however, it is likely that they stemmed from the youthful damage done to him by his extraordinarily unsatisfactory parents. A perfect example of the classic "Don Juan" type, Kennedy may even be much more useful to future students of psychology than political science!

Whatever JFK's political achievements may or may not have been, he definitely helped change the moral structure of the nation by the pernicious influence of his blatantly immoral behavior. The truth of his character has also bred in the American nation a profound sense of betrayal and cynicism. Jacqueline Kennedy's cousin, John Davis, may well have expressed it best when he said: "At the time he died I too was idealistic about JFK. Now, whenever I see those old films of Kennedy on television, I have to stop myself from heaving. It's hard to believe that here was this absolute fake, this womanizer and opportunist, coming off like Euripedes. All our dreams invested in that! What a disappointment!"

Love is the child of illusion and the parent of disillusion.
—Miguel de Unamuno

THE BABY BIRD THAT WASN'T LADY BIRD'S

Lyndon Baines Johnson had something of an obsession for feminine beauty and never took pains to hide his intense appreciation of it. When he suddenly became President, following John F. Kennedy's shocking assassination on November 22, 1963, Johnson was instantly surrounded by gossip and rumors concerning his roving eye for the ladies.

Unlike his predecessor, LBJ was not a ruthless womanizer, incapable of love. His need for love was as strong a drive in Johnson's personality as his need for power; sometimes it was even stronger. Throughout his entire life Lyndon Johnson struggled with these two disparate and often conflicting needs. It was the uniquely challenging experiences of his early life that created his desperate pursuit of both love and power.

An intense devotion to his mother was the major force of Johnson's childhood. A very frustrated woman, Rebekha Baines was from a distinguished Texas family and felt that she had made a serious mistake in marrying beneath her when she wed the crude and untalented Sam Johnson. Sam was a poor farmer, and school teacher, who failed to fulfill his cultivated wife's high ambitions. In an effort to compensate for her error, she lavished all of her attention and affection on her promising son.

At first, little Lyndon eagerly responded and allowed himself to be petted and pampered and given the overly refined education of a "mama's boy." But by the time he reached adolescence, he began to rebel against her domination. It soon became very important for him to prove his manliness and deal directly with his abrasive and badgering father.

This strong need to retain the love of each parent and satisfy their conflicting demands may have led Johnson into politics, in which he could be both a manly achiever and a genteel member of the ruling class who could nobly and kindly lead others to prosperity and salvation. This dual personality of conflicting extremes characterized LBJ's entire adult life and political career. It also helped to fuel his boundless energy and his burning, unrelenting drive to power.

However, it would be his mother's influence that would touch him most deeply. Lyndon Johnson always needed to be loved for his kindness and goodness. Struggling mightily against his great desire to be feared and respected for his toughness and power, his need to be loved would always win. As President, LBJ desperately wanted to be loved by the American people. It was perhaps the greatest tragedy of his life that he bitterly felt the almost complete absence of their affection. The public just never really warmed to Johnson's exaggerated "down home" Texas personality. It mistrusted his oily, manipulative manner, and was willing to think the very worst of him when the war in Vietnam became a national disaster—a fact it blamed solely on him.

But if he failed to capture public adoration, then at least he could try to achieve it privately. His relationships with women not only satisfied this overwhelming emotional need, but also proved to be a crucial factor in his greatest political successes.

Beginning with his mother, women were the most important people in Lyndon's world. He genuinely liked women—women of all ages and all types. And women generally liked him, in return. They responded to his naturally affectionate manner, his warm sympathy, and his endless enthusiasm and energy. They fussed over him and spoiled him and helped him whenever they could. From his boyhood days, when Lyndon would artfully charm and sweet-talk a kindly matron out of a batch of cookies or a pie, to his ambitious years in Congress, when he would effectively cultivate the support of his colleagues by skillfully playing up to their wives, Johnson could always count on feminine sympathy and support to get him what he wanted.

But sexual conquest was another matter for Lyndon B. Johnson. Most of his romantic relationships were only solid and comfortable friendships. Merely a few of them became intimate sexual affairs. This may have been due to a lack of confidence that stemmed from his youth in Texas. Physically awkward and unattractive, with a weed-thin, gangling body, huge ears, and coarse, rubbery features, Johnson as a young man also suffered from the inferior social position of his family and the insecurities of the deep emotional conflicts created by his parents' unhappy marriage. Thus, so socially and psychologically disadvantaged, he was neither popular nor successful with women when it came to romance. To cover this painful circumstance—as he camouflaged his several other defects—Johnson assumed a boastful air so exaggerated that it became a source of much amusement to his friends.

Perhaps this severely handicapped early love life led LBJ to frequent prostitutes when he became wealthy and successful. When he was Vice President under Kennedy, Johnson was reputed to have been a regular patron of a call girl service operated through the Quorum Club, a private retreat on Capitol Hill that was visited by members of the House and Senate as well as by lobbyists and congressional employees.

81

In marked contrast with John F. Kennedy, Johnson's main drive can be seen as an eager quest to better himself. Wealth and power were his prime objectives—although he found that they were almost impossible goals for a poor hill-country farm boy in central Texas. He was, however, smart enough to realize the value of a college education, and he acquired a degree and began teaching school. He was also clever enough enough to realize that there was only one sure avenue to wealth: to marry a rich man's daughter. Limited early on by his extremely modest position in life, LBJ was determined to acquire money and social standing through marriage. Thus, he willingly abandoned his courtships of beautiful and desirable young women and searched for the one woman who could bring him the greatest material gain.

In the meantime, he climbed as quickly as he could by himself. Finally leaving his parents' farm in Johnson City, he settled in Houston, where he taught public speaking in high school. After a year had passed, Lyndon was more ambitious and discontent than ever. When wealthy Richard Kleberg, one of the owners of the huge King Ranch, ran for the U.S. Congress, young Johnson jumped right in and worked tirelessly as a speaker and voter contact man. When Kleberg won, he rewarded Johnson with a job in Washington, D.C., as his staff secretary.

Two years later, in 1934, when he was twenty-six, Johnson traveled from Washington to Austin, where he met wealthy young Lady Bird Taylor, who had just turned twenty-one. She was an unusually shy, intelligent girl, and Johnson overwhelmed her on their first date with a non-stop lecture on his illustrious plans for the future. He topped all this off with a sudden proposal of matrimony.

Lady Bird firmly refused, but Lyndon kept pursuing and would not accept her rejection. Returning to Washington, he spent the next six weeks flooding the flattered girl with daily telephone calls and letters. But Lady Bird still resisted Lyndon's relentless

Champion womanizer Lyndon B. Johnson is tenderly comforted by his ever-faithful wife, Lady Bird, while recuperating from a serious heart attack in 1955. The selfless, kindly Lady Bird apparently forgave and forgot each of LBJ'S numerous romantic transgressions and was always there when he needed her most.

campaign. When Johnson finally returned to Texas, he delivered the timid young heiress an ultimatum: Marry him or he would never see her again. Lady Bird anxiously hesitated, then very reluctantly accepted his offer of marriage.

The quiet and selfless Lady Bird Taylor proved to be the most important ingredient in Lyndon B. Johnson's rise to power. Through her, not only did he gain a ready avenue to wealth, he also acquired a remarkable partner in business and at home. Lady Bird centered her entire life on her ambitious husband and gave her full support to his economic ventures and political quests. As Jackie Kennedy once observed, "Lady Bird would crawl on broken glass down Pennsylvania Avenue for Lyndon."

83

Always a devoted husband and father, Johnson still had an intense interest in beautiful women. Because of his extremely boastful personality, which continued to cleverly conceal his deep-seated feelings of insecurity and inadequacy, it is difficult to assess how extensive Johnson's extramarital relationships were. He certainly took not even the slightest care to hide his attractions. In fact, he seems to have almost exaggerated his flamboyant responses to feminine charms. In a way that was similar to his emphatic and overzealous approach as an inexperienced and unsure adolescent, Johnson may well have been covering his early romantic wounds and self-doubts by this display of flirting and attempted seduction.

Where, exactly, the public show ended and the intimate contacts began is almost impossible to determine. His bragging about sexual conquest was a lifelong trait that he indulged in to an extravagant degree with his male friends and associates. LBJ had to establish his sexual superiority over other men. He needed them to acknowledge his power and skill with the opposite sex. This gave him the stature and dominant force that, he felt, would prove his entitlement to leadership and high office. Again, by overplaying the role he had failed even to remotely achieve when it was most important—in his adolescence—the adult Johnson strove to fully compensate for his early lack of power. There were, of course, affairs, but it is extremely unlikely that they even came close to the marathon descriptions with which LBJ regaled his associates. Johnson thoroughly developed the technique of creating his own personal fact from fiction by simply giving a constant and convincing performance. He was talk, talk, and more talk. He established his own reality from talk—to a far greater degree than the average politician.

Johnson's sexual boasting was always of an exceeding crude and coarse nature. While at college, he was in the habit of exhibiting his large penis and calling it "Jumbo." When bragging about his sexual affairs, he gleefully related the most intimate details in the bluntest terms possible: the exact particulars of his partner's anatomy, the blow-by-blow play of the activity, a precise description of his carnal maneuvers. Everything was conveyed with a sense of great relish and delight.

Of the probably many affairs that Lyndon Johnson was involved in, one love relationship has been fully revealed. A long-term mistress has come forth to not only claim LBJ as her lover but also to name him as the father of her son.

The woman, Madeleine Brown, today sixty-five years old, claims that she had a twenty-one-year love affair with Johnson that resulted in the birth of an illegitimate son. She declares that that son, Steven, born in 1950, is Lyndon Johnson's only male heir. Having made the decision to officially claim his patrimony in court, Steven filed a $10.5-million suit against Lady Bird Johnson in June 1987. Alleging that he has been deprived of his birthright, Steven also wants to change his surname to Johnson.

A solidly built man standing six-feet-four, Steven bears a striking resemblance to Johnson. He was thirty-six years old before his mother told him the truth about his parentage. Madeleine suffered a heart attack in February 1987 and, uncertain of her chances of survival, confessed to her son at her hospital bedside. Although Lady Bird and the Johnson family have so far made no comment concerning Steven's claims, Madeleine believes that the former First Lady suspected the affair in the early 1960s.

According to Madeleine Brown, she met Congressman Johnson in 1948, when she was twenty-three. The product of a strict Catholic middle-class home, she was married to a soda jerk named James Brown, who had been committed to a mental hospital. She encountered the charismatic congressman at a reception held by Johnson's Austin radio station and they were instantly attracted to one another. Three weeks later, Madeleine was asked to a party at the Driskill Hotel that Johnson was also attending.

"He looked at me like I was an ice cream cone on a hot day," she fondly remembered in an exclusive interview in People magazine in August 1987. "And he said after a while, 'Well, I'll see you up in my apartment.' He had a certain amount of roughness about him, and maybe that's what I liked, you know. He commanded. I've been told that every woman needs to act like a whore in bed, and I guess that's what I did."

Madeleine confided that Lyndon was a highly sexed, aggressive lover, who liked to play games in bed. "He was a little kinky," she recalled, "and I loved every second of it. So did he. We spent our time *doing*, not talking. Once, after he was through, he went to the window and opened it and bellowed like a bull, yelling, 'My God, I love Texas in the morning!'"

Claiming that they never discussed world affairs or politics, Madeleine emphasizes that her relationship with Lyndon Johnson was a purely physical one. Although she hoped for a future with her lover, she was made to realize immediately that their affair was just something on the side and to be kept as secret as was humanly possible. She still vividly recalls, "He told me from the beginning, 'You see nothing, you hear nothing, you say nothing.' "

To keep their arrangement secret, an elaborate routine was worked out so that they could communicate and arrange to meet without direct contact. Jesse Kellam, a close friend of LBJ's and the manager of Johnson's Austin radio station, served as the go-between. When Johnson returned from Washington and wanted to see Madeleine, Kellam would telephone the young beauty in Dallas and make some work-related excuse for her to immediately journey to Austin. Madeleine would jump on a plane and be there in an hour or two. Arriving at the Austin airport, she would be met by a mobile news unit from Johnson's radio station, KTBC, and taken to the Driskill, where she would surreptitiously go up to the congressman's suite.

Lyndon Johnson was a man with little time—and a desire to protect his reputation at any cost. Therefore, the interludes with his obliging mistress were always of very short duration—usually a half-hour—the longest one once lasting three hours. When Madeleine eventually discovered that her busy lover had the same hit-and-run relationship with other women, she was upset and unhappy. Still, she realized, there was nothing she could do except hope for the best. "Sometimes, when I'd hint around," she says of her attempts at eliciting a commitment, "he'd just say, 'Today's today, tomorrow's tomorrow.'" That was his favorite answer. I guess it could have meant anything. I liked to think it meant someday I'd be in the White House. I would have been like Nancy Reagan. I wouldn't have stood it if he had other women."

Their affair reached a serious crisis in the spring of 1950, when Madeleine discovered that she was pregnant by then-Senator Lyndon Johnson. Far from being happy at the prospect of fatherhood, LBJ exploded with fury when she told him the news. He called her a "dumb Dora" and, initially blamed her for the unwanted complication. When his rage finally subsided, Johnson promised Madeleine that he would take care of her. Through Jesse Kellam, he arranged to have a Texas attorney, Jerome Ragsdale, handle the financial and legal details.

A baby boy was born in December 1950. Madeleine named him Steven. Because she was still technically married to the institutionalized James Brown, she was able to put his name on the baby boy's birth certificate as father. To set her up in comfort, attorney Ragsdale was instructed to purchase for Madeleine and her new son a six-room house and hire a live-in maid. All her bills and expenses were paid for by Ragsdale, even though she continued to work her job as media buyer for a Dallas advertising agency.

Meanwhile, she continued carrying on her affair with Johnson whenever he came to Texas. They usually followed their old routine of meeting secretly at the Driskill Hotel in Austin, but on several occasions they rendezvoused in Houston and San Antonio. In the interims, gifts and flowers would periodically arrive via Kellam. A mink coat was the most extravagant item she received. Proudly wearing it to her office, she bluntly confessed to her fellow workers, "I got my minks the same way minks get minks."

_____

During the early 1960s, Madeleine entered into a marriage of convenience with a Dallas businessman. She claims that she did so at Kellam's instructions. Although she never lived with her new husband, she continued to have her sexual rendezvous with Johnson. The marriage lasted five years, when she finally obtained a divorce. Madeleine was driving to Austin to meet the Vice President for one of their love sessions when she heard the announcement of John Kennedy's assassination on the car radio. She immediately turned around and drove back home.

Only a few weeks later, Madeleine was instructed by Kellam to meet the new President of the United States at their old hideout in the Driskill.

Lyndon Johnson continued his passionate and intermittent affair with his red-haired mistress until 1967, when she was seriously injured in a car accident. Madeleine's face was severely scarred and she was forced to endure several plastic surgery operations. It seemed to her that she would never be able to see Lyndon again. She confesses, even, to being afraid of her powerful lover, who was becoming more and more worried of having his illicit relationships discovered. Historians credit Johnson during these, the final, months of his Presidency with the development of a full-blown paranoia caused by the failures of his administration and the Vietnam debacle. Thus, it is easy to comprehend how this profoundly paranoid state of mind would also extend to the irregularities of his private life.

As Madeleine slowly and painfully recuperated from her physical injuries, the only correspondence from Lyndon was the telephone calls from Jesse Kellam, subtly reminding her to keep quiet about the President and reenforcing her silence by constantly complimenting her for being a "good girl." However menacing Madeleine felt Johnson to be, she also believed that he must have been especially plagued by guilt and sadness over their secret relationship because of the only son and heir—by then in his late teens—that he could never publicly acknowledge. It was perhaps these hidden sentiments that finally prompted the ex-President, in late 1969, to send word through Kellam that he wanted to see Madeleine one more time.

With heart problems and failing health, Johnson arranged secretly to meet Madeleine in Houston, when he went there to participate in a parade honoring the *Apollo 11* Astronauts. She flew to Houston, took a room at the sumptuous Shamrock Hotel, and patiently waited for her old lover to arrive. When he showed up a few hours later, she was shocked by his worn and tired appearance. As his Secret Service bodyguard waited out in the hallway, Johnson sat down with Madeleine on the sofa and began talking. It was, she says, the first time the two lovers ever had a true conversation.

"There comes a point in the lives of two people," Madeleine Brown wistfully concedes, "when they have to face reality. I think that's what we did. We talked for almost two hours. I cried. We kissed. But we didn't even try to make love. He had always seemed to me like an iron man. But he knew more than I did, I realize now: I think he knew he was going to die before long."

She urged LBJ to publicly acknowledge Steven as his son, but he said, "Oh, I can't do that. I've got the girls [his daughters] to consider, and Lady Bird."

"And I thought what a fool I had been to take seconds," Madeleine tearfully remembers. "But that's what I did."

6

MY FAIR LYNDON

adeleine Brown was not the sole important extramarital relationship in Lyndon Baines Johnson's life. Although his excessive boasting may well have exaggerated his illicit sexual behavior, there were nonetheless many women who shared his bed. Because of the paranoia Johnson showed during his long affair with Madeleine, it is very doubtful that his great fear of discovery would have allowed him to have entered into many other liaisons of such serious duration. The ladies who were sexually involved with him were either dealt with so casually or semi-anonymously that they are almost impossible to document. As one of American history's shrewdest politicians, Lyndon Johnson covered his tracks magnificently.

George Reedy, LBJ's White House Press Secretary, wrote that the President was relentlessly seeking new additions to what his staff privately referred to as "the Harem." The Johnson obsession for beautiful women was legendary, and he never took pains to hide it. According to Reedy, "He may have been 'just a

91

country boy from the central hills of Texas,' but he had many of the instincts of a Turkish sultan in Istanbul."

President Johnson matter-of-factly once turned down an excellently qualified woman who applied for a position on his staff because, as he said, "She's got everything but good looks." Another time, when the President spotted an unusually attractive journalist at a press conference, he told her, "You're the prettiest thing I ever saw!" The next day, he hired her as one of his office staff.

This very special interest of Johnson's in pretty female journalists was noticed by everyone. The men of the press corps dubbed him "The Lochinvar of the Pedernales" (the latter is the valley homestead of LBJ). Toward the end of his administration, gossip began to circulate that he was having a serious affair with a blond Harvard graduate student named Doris Kearns, who had written a famous "Dump Johnson" article for *The New Republic*. When Doris came to Washington, the President immediately took a keen interest in her and they spent much time alone together. Kearns would later innocently explain their relationship by saying that Johnson had identified her with his mother.

After he left office, Johnson worked with Kearns on his memoirs, and she would eventually write her own book about the highly complex and misunderstood President.

———

The surrounding of himself with attractive women was, in many cases, much more innocent and harmless than it looked to even the most intimate observer of Lyndon B. Johnson. Very few people at the time fully comprehended the radical contradictions in Johnson's psyche and the true reasons motivating his behavior. It is reasonable to assume that he was engaging in illicit sexual relations on a fairly regular basis, but of even more importance to him may have been his deep friendships with women.

One particular friendship made early in his career led to a sexual affair of many years standing. It was perhaps the greatest love relationship of his life, and the influence of it on his personal development was extraordinary. And, indeed, the woman involved was no less than extraordinary. As Professor Henry Higgins created a polished human gem out of the raw Eliza Doolittle in *My Fair Lady*, so Alice Glass took the crude and awkward young Congressman from the dusty hills of Texas and carefully fashioned him into a worldly and sophisticated national leader.

Lyndon Johnson and Alice Glass may have seemed like complete opposites, but, surprisingly, they both began life in remarkably similar surroundings. Each was the product of a very modest family in a very small Texas country town. Lyndon, however, grew to be purely a creature of his primitive and limited environment, whereas Alice, even as a child, dramatically appeared out of place in the drab country landscape. Regal-looking and possessing a natural elegance and cool grace that would have been distinctive in the major cities of the world, she swiftly departed from her shabby home town just as soon as she could smoothly arrange to do so.

Her first stop was the Texas state capital, Austin. Working there as secretary to a legislator, Alice Glass confidently avoided the pitfalls of the average girl in her position: She declined all offers of an "easier" living and remained aloof from trifling romances. Alice quietly bided her time, patiently waiting for what she wanted.

She didn't have to wait long. What she wanted walked right up to her during a loud party at the Driskill Hotel. His name was Charles Marsh, and he was one of the richest men in Texas. The owner of dozens of newspapers, the fabulously wealthy and powerful Marsh was more than twenty years her senior. That very first night they met, they became lovers. Marsh was in the habit of acting as rapidly and decisively as Alice, and only a month after having taken her as his mistress, he walked out on his wife and children and took Alice to Washington and New York.

In the mid-1930s, Alice established herself in a very unique position as Charles Marsh's mistress. Instead of conforming to either the flashy or the sequestered role of kept woman, Alice availed herself of her lover's great wealth and position to reign almost like a queen. And a stately, dazzling, benevolent queen she was. Aloof, six feet tall, and possessing the clear features and golden coloring of a Nordic goddess, Alice's beauty therefore derived as much from her impressive physical appearance as it did from her superior demeanor.

Alice's meticulously crafted main stage matched the splendor and elegance of her performance. It was a magnificent mansion named Longlea a hundred miles from Washington, D.C., at the foot of the Blue Ridge Mountains. Alice had helped design every aspect of the house and supervised the dramatic landscaping of the immense estate. Her unrivaled taste and aesthetic sense guaranteed a home that was unsurpassed in exquisite beauty and palatial grandeur. Longlea existed as a dream of perfection for the great and famous of the world who would often come to enjoy its hospitality. And a young Congressman named Lyndon Baines Johnson would be one of them.

Alice was twenty-six years old when, in 1938, Johnson arrived on the scene, and she was in the midst of maintaining an incredibly intricate equilibrium. A woman many years ahead of her time, Alice didn't believe in marriage and had steadfastly refused to marry Charles Marsh, even though she had given birth to two of his children. Her greatest desire was to be free and independent, but there was a strangely contradictory nature in her personality that often made her seek two seemingly opposite and conflicting objectives at the same time. While striving toward complete independence, she was the totally dependent love object of an all-powerful protector. And in as much as she prided herself on boldly flaunting all of the strict moral rules and conventions of society, she was deviously presenting an elaborate lie to her parents and family back home in Texas.

For the very conservative and puritanical folk she left behind, Alice carefully maintained the fiction that she had married a very wealthy English nobleman. She named him "Lord Manners," and, thus, she became "Lady Manners." Whenever her relatives came visiting from Texas, her noble husband would always be away in England on important business. This creative charade worked quite well for Alice for a long time, but when the pressure of prolonging it proved too intense, she decided to have poor Lord Manners killed off while fighting for the Loyalists in the Spanish Civil War. In the process, as an added bonus, Alice became a respectable widow.

It was not her great shining beauty that drew Alice Glass to Lyndon Johnson. It was her equally outstanding attribute: her voracious intelligence. She was an unrelenting idealist with an intellect that was seldom matched. Sincerely devoted to the mission of relieving the sufferings of the poor and the plight of the common man, Alice showed an unfailing interest in anyone and anything that might achieve this altruistic goal.

In 1938, Alice had a foreign friend who was having visa problems. A thirty-year-old Congressman from Austin named Lyndon Johnson was consulted for help. So effectively did Johnson come to the rescue that a solid friendship was instantly formed. Lyndon became a frequent visitor at Longlea. Alice soon came to view him as a selfless idealist who was primarily interested in helping the insignificant and disadvantaged. So impressed and captivated was she but the energetic young Congressman's ideas and enthusiasms that she truly believed "he was a young man who was going to save the world"—as her sister later stated it.

Progressing rapidly from the role of champion and confidante, Alice comfortably became Johnson's patroness. She was in a perfect position to mold and sculpt and polish and refine. Worldly and sophisticated and naturally gifted as she was, Alice quite logically took the crude and gangling young Texan under her protective wing and masterfully taught and gently shaped him. And the deeply infatuated and star-struck Johnson was a very willing subject. He sought her advice on everything, and the coolly elegant Alice was only too happy to comply.

She gave her most immediate attention to Johnson's rather haphazard appearance. No detail escaped her tasteful gaze. His casual speech pattern began showing a greater respect for proper grammar; his manners also acquired a finer polish. Because she possessed an incomparable sense of style, Alice was skillfully able to dress Johnson to his best advantage. His least attractive physical features, such as his long neck and thin wrists, were successfully minimized with expert tailoring and elegant styling. Alice even took charge of the way he was photographed. Astutely observing that the left side of his face photographed far better than the right, she encouraged the future President to pose only in this limited profile. He strictly followed this suggestion for the rest of his life.

Once his "surface" had been smoothed over, Johnson's inner self received something of an overhaul. All of Alice's great culture and learning descended upon him like a melting caress. Longlea became Johnson's "Versailles." It was the glittering royal court, the artistic and cultural center of his universe, to which he returned again and again to nourish his mind and soul. His queenly hostess instructed him in literature and music and poetry. She taught him all the social graces and inspired him to develop his aesthetic sensibilities. He learned to appreciate what *she* appreciated. And, after long poetry-reading sessions on the terrace and concerts on the phonograph in the drawing room, they would take evening walks down by the mist-covered Hazel River and plan and dream of how they were going to save the "little people" and restructure their Depression-plagued nation into a perfect Utopia.

And before long, they fell in love.

Not a conventionally handsome man by any standards, Lyndon Johnson possessed other attributes that mesmerized Alice Glass. What attracted her most was the intense idealism and the sincerity and selflessness that she thought she saw in him. There was much for them to share together in planning for the future. it was perhaps this shining future that they were both so devoted to that gave them such an overwhelmingly mutual interest and unshakable bond.

But there was also an incredible sexual attraction between the two lovers. Alice loved Lyndon's expressive, flashing eyes and found herself totally seduced by his dynamic personality, his great energy. According to Alice's cousin and closest friend, Alice Hopkins, and her sister, Mary Louise Glass, Alice Glass and Lyndon Johnson sometime in late 1938 or early 1939 became lovers.

During Charles Marsh's frequent trips away from Washington, his luxurious apartments at the Mayflower Hotel and the Allies Inn were occupied in the afternoons by Lyndon and Alice alone together. Lyndon also became a constant weekend guest at magnificent Longlea. As incredible as it may seem, Johnson many times brought his unassuming wife, Lady Bird, with him on his visits to Longlea, and sometimes spent weekends there while Marsh was in residence.

This alone may be the ultimate testimony to the deep extent of Johnson's feeling for Alice, for Marsh held the power to either make or break the eager young Congressman. So far, he had been one of Johnson's most helpful and influential supporters, and Johnson had skillfully made the older man feel he was mentor by carefully assuming an almost slavish deference to him. Indeed, there was unparalleled danger for Johnson in carrying on a love affair with the mistress of his most powerful ally. But he couldn't help himself: His passion was too strong. He proceeded to risk everything by continuing to make love to Alice behind her wealthy lover's back.

"Lyndon was the love of Alice's life," her cousin has stated. And Mary Louise Glass fully agreed: "My sister was mad for Lyndon—absolutely mad for him." What's more, Alice Glass firmly believed that Lyndon felt as passionately about her as she did about him. She told several of her closest friends and relatives that she and the Congressman had discussed marriage plans.

97

Alice had perhaps not considered that there were any serious problems to this. In those days a divorced man was something of an outcast. There was no way that Lyndon could divorce Lady Bird and continue to pursue a political career. However, he did tell Alice that he was willing to sacrifice his ambition: He informed her that he was going to get a divorce and accept a job offer as a corporate lobbyist in Washington.

This plan was never carried out. Perhaps LBJ's ambition proved to be even more consuming than he himself believed it was. His single-minded climb toward power certainly eventually eclipsed the finer feelings of his heart. As his secret affair with Alice moved forward on the continued cautious course and lost nothing of its intensity, she became more and more determined to become Lyndon's wife. Meanwhile, although Charles Marsh, continuing to be effectively deceived, was applying greater pressure than ever on his mistress to finally marry him, she calmly resisted his constant proposals and patiently waited for Lyndon to clear the way. It was to be a long wait.

Alice not only had to exercise the ultimate in discretion in the conduct of her secret love affair, she also had to maintain her awkward position as the kept mistress of a man she no longer wanted to live with. And, if this wasn't enough, she also had to sit back and witness, day after day, the friendship between Lyndon and Marsh grow warmer and closer and their political partnership become even more successful. It was enough to make even the most extraordinary of women crumble. But Alice cooly waited.

If there was one person who showed an even greater degree of patience and self-discipline than Alice, it was the equally re-markable Lady Bird Johnson. Most intimate observers of the time definitely believe that Johnson's docile wife had full knowledge of the torrid affair that was taking place right under her nose.

"The thing I could never understand was how she stood it," mused Mary Louise Glass. "Lyndon would leave her on weekends, weekend after weekend, just leave her home. I wouldn't have stood it for a minute. We were all together a lot—Lyndon and Lady Bird and Charles and Alice. And Lady Bird never said a word. She showed nothing, nothing at all."

While the smart, sophisticated set at elegant Longlea were laughing at her behind her back, Lady Bird Johnson may well have been the cleverest of the lot. Whatever transpired between husband and wife, Lyndon Johnson decided not to divorce her and the marriage continued for another thirty years. It was Lady Bird who would eventually become First Lady of the United States; Alice Glass changed her mind and finally married the faithful Charles Marsh. Then, she soon changed her mind again and divorced him. She went on to marry several more times, still dedicated to her search for independence and freedom from the social conventions.

However, the one thing that did survive was Alice and Lyndon's friendship. They remained devoted to one another for the next twenty-five years. Lyndon, progressing dramatically up the political ladder, still made regular visits to Longlea. And Alice still subtly shaped him and coached him in the finer things in life— the ideals close to her heart. It was only his perceived transgression against one of her highest ideals—peace—that finally destroyed their relationship. Alice blamed Johnson for the disaster of Vietnam and was so unforgiving of his failure to end the war that she cut him dead and refused ever to speak to him again. So bitter was she that she burned all of his love letters and tried to completely erase him from her memory.

Poor Lyndon Johnson not only lost the love of the woman who may well have been the passion of his life, but he also lost the love of the American people, who, as well, placed the blame of Vietnam on his shoulders. When LBJ left office and quietly crept back to Texas, he must have gazed often at the vacant landscape and been struck by the supreme irony of his fate. He had always sought love above all else, even power. And now, his quest for power had cost him the affection that he most wanted.

Perhaps he thought often about the other two-term Presidents who preceded him—one of them a man of war who almost effortlessly captured the love of the entire nation. Perhaps he also was aware of the fact that this man, Dwight D. Eisenhower, had once decided to divorce his wife and marry his true love, but likewise had sacrificed his sweetheart and exchanged her for power.

The bitter irony of the comparison could not have comforted the disillusioned Lyndon.

You shall have joy, or you shall have power,
said God; you shall not have both.
                    —Ralph Waldo Emerson

7

ALIBI IKE

An autobiographical memoir in 1976—*Past Forgetting*—informed the American public in detail about a love affair between Dwight Eisenhower and his personal assistant during World War II. The author was Kay Summersby, a frail, sick woman who was dying of cancer. It caused a storm of protest. A legion of defenders quickly and bitterly dismissed the book as totally untrue. Kay Summersby died shortly after, and a debate continues as to its veracity.

Dwight David Eisenhower was one of the most popular and respected Presidents in recent history. Winning fame as a military hero while serving as the commanding general of the European Allied troops, he seemed to secure a place in America's heart throughout his entire public career. His two terms in the White House from 1953 to 1961 were characterized by his conservative, modest, easy-going personality. An honest, personable man with a talent for making people like him. Eisenhower always struck the congenial note.

Learning to be a team player while growing up in a large family in Kansas, Eisenhower decided early in life on a military career. After attending West Point, the handsome young soldier was serving duty in Texas when he met eighteen-year-old Mamie Doud, the petite and pretty daughter of a wealthy Denver meat packer. Strongly attracted to each other, "Ike" and Mamie were married in 1916 and immediately began the gypsy-like existence of an army family. The constant moving from one army post to another put a tremendous strain on the marriage. And then, quite suddenly, their first child died.

The death of their three-year-old son was a tragedy from which they never recovered. Eisenhower would later write that it had been the greatest disaster of his life. The sad couple began drifting apart. Ike escaped into his rising career.

When World War II arrived and he soared meteorically from the rank of colonel to that of commanding brigadier general, Ike traveled to Europe, where he would remain for more than two years. The separation greatly jeopardized his marriage and bitter letters were written back and forth, especially from the unhappy wife who jealously watched and waited as her dashing husband appeared in photos everywhere standing close to his assistant, Kay Summersby.

There was widespread gossip during the war that Ike and Kay were in love and having an affair. There was also talk that he would divorce Mamie and marry his beautiful young companion. However, Eisenhower returned home and the marriage continued, outwardly, as smoothly as ever. There was never any public mention of the affair and when the revelation of it was threatened in the 1952 presidential campaign, Harry Truman gallantly destroyed all the incriminating letters which were to be used as ammunition.

According to Summersby in her book, the gossip was true. There had been an affair.

Kay Summersby was a beautiful divorcee when she met Eisenhower in May 1942. An Irishwoman with bright, sparkling eyes, a vivacious smile, and a bubbly manner of speaking, she was at first in awe of the general, who was old enough to be her father. She was a driver in the British Army and assigned to Ike. A very close working relationship followed in which they were constantly together. Before she realized it, Kay was falling in love.

And, for Eisenhower, a growing affection was obvious to all of those around him. He responded intensely to Kay's beauty, her winning charm, her warm nature, and her playful flirtatiousness. She was exactly what he needed in order to escape the hard, ruthless life of combat and death, generals and politicians. Kay Summersby's soft, thoughtful touch and constant laughter provided Ike's only solace from the almost unbearable pressure of his critical job.

Kay was soon both his driver and his personal secretary. They were with each other nearly every hour of the day. After work, she would join Eisenhower and his friends for dinner and often partner him in a game of bridge. Many of Ike's fellow generals foresaw a scandal involving the two. During one evening when Ike was enjoying Kay's company so sublimely, he later discussed her with another brigadier general. Ike assured his colleague that he just wanted to sit with her and hold her hand but not sleep with her. The brigadier thought Ike might be alibiing.

Back home, the gossip reached all the way to Washington. Mamie grew sick and angry at the endless stream of photos of her handsome husband accompanied everywhere by the stunning young woman. Rumors flowed freely concerning the illicit nature of the relationship. Because of the fact that Kay was officially engaged to be married to another officer, there was some defense to the gossip. But, then, in June 1943, Kay's fiancé was killed by a land mine.

The young woman was devastated and Eisenhower did his

best to comfort and console her. Ironically, the tragedy brought the two even closer together. Ike thought that Kay should return to London, but she bravely insisted on staying with her job. He happily complied. Their relationship, personal and professional, continued. In the spring of 1944 they returned together to London. Accompanying the famous general to meetings with Churchill, the King, and many other illustrious figures, Kay was by now hopelessly in love with him.

Kay was a British subject by birth, but Eisenhower was arranging to have her commissioned in the U.S. Army as a WAC lieutenant. According to Kay in her memoirs, it was at this time that they both realized how much they were in love. Finally having a little privacy at Eisenhower's residence, Telegraph Cottage, they attempted to consummate their affair. They failed, because Ike was impotent. Another attempt also culminated in failure, and Kay quoted Ike as saying that his marriage "killed something in me" and that for years "I had never thought of making love, and when I did—I failed."

When Kay got around to writing her book decades later, she confided to her collaborator, Sigrid Hedin, that Ike had not been totally impotent and that she had had to teach him about lovemaking very patiently. In her book she gushingly confessed to being totally "unraveled" by his kisses and characterized them as "hungry, strong, and demanding." She admired his broad shoulders and lean, hard body, and she wanted to constantly hold him and fantasized about lying on a grassy lawn with him above her.

When the war finally ended, Ike wrote to his immediate superior officer, General Marshall in Washington, and formally requested to be relieved of duty so he could return home and divorce Mamie and marry Kay Summersby. Marshall was absolutely outraged by Eisenhower's request and wrote back a bitterly emphatic denial in which he swore to personally "bust" Ike out of the army and make his life a living hell if he attempted to follow through with such a plan.

Kay Summersby, the loser in Dwight D. Eisenhower's battle between passion and power, sits wistfully alone on vacation in London several years after the end of World War II. Unlike the lucky Duchess of Windsor—whose lover had traded a throne for her—Kay was quietly dropped by Ike when he returned to America from Europe to concentrate on higher ambitions.

The episode was kept so secret that when Harry Truman revealed it in his autobiography, *Plain Speaking*, in 1973, even Kay Summersby had not known of Eisenhower's aborted efforts. She admitted to being both surprised and pleased by the discovery of Ike's initial intention of divorcing his wife and marrying her. Truman went on to reveal that he had personally destroyed the incriminating letters between Eisenhower and Marshall to protect Mamie's feelings and Ike's reputation, and also to avert their use as a dirty campaign tactic.

With this alternative placed in limbo, Kay entered into a dilemma of her own at the conclusion of the war. She could no longer retain her commission as a WAC and work for Eisenhower. Going briefly to America, she applied for citizenship, then returned to work as a civilian in an army office in Berlin.

This must have been a great help for Ike in his efforts to shift his interests back towards his wife. Separated from Kay now permanently, he wrote to her a long, businesslike letter thanking her for her work and loyalty and advising her to keep up her optimism. To an associate, Eisenhower confessed how badly he felt about Kay because he realized how deserted and alone she felt.

During Ike's postwar rise to national glory with his smiling wife at his side, Kay became a United States citizen and moved to New York. In 1947 she planned her wedding to another man, then abruptly broke it off. The following year she wrote a circumspect book about her public adventures with Eisenhower. It was a huge success and in 1952 she finally married a stockbroker. Years passed, and she never saw Ike again. After his death, when she was ill and dying of cancer, she decided to tell the story of their romance.

Although Kay Summersby's testament is denied by many persons who are not in any position to know the whole truth of the affair, it challenges credibility to think that her book, which amounts to almost a deathbed confession, could be anything other than completely true. The lifelong character of the woman plus a total lack of motive for deception leads any logical reader to accept her version as the absolute truth.

Like hatred, sex must be articulated or, like hatred,
it will produce a disturbing internal malaise.
—George Jean Nathan

8

THE LONELINESS OF
THE MAD MONK

n his 1976 book *Nixon vs. Nixon*, Dr. David Abrahamsen concluded that the thirty-seventh President of the United States possessed "a basic inability to express and give love and to receive it." Abrahamsen went on to qualify Richard Milhous Nixon as a psychopathic personality suffering from a severe character disorder, orally and anally fixated.

While the world of today seems dominated by the nihilistic, destructive acts of the unloved products of broken homes, who have grown up to loath themselves and hate others, it is significant that our most self-destructive Chief Executive was raised, himself, in an unhealthy environment. Nixon's harsh, joyless parents unintentionally molded the emotional disturbances of the future President. By the violent influence of his bitter, rejecting father and the impossibly high standards of conduct of his unhappy, hyper-manipulative mother, the little boy surely developed a deep rage and an inescapable feeling of worthlessness and self-hatred.

But, most of all, he must have suffered from acute guilt and insecurity, and the unaffectionate nature of his austere family, together with tragic upheavals in their living conditions, left him with only one unshakeable conclusion: He would always be unloved. And it was a painfully gnawing sensation that would never leave him.

Justly or unjustly, these feelings must have nurtured the negative components of Nixon's personality and fatally harmed the development of his moral character.

A wealth of detailed psychiatric profiles have been written on Richard Nixon. Their common themes are his extreme narcissism; his compulsive obsessive, secretive, and paranoiac orientation; and his profound sense of insecurity and need to be universally loved. Love, indeed, seems to be the most critical and paradoxical element of Nixon's troubled life. The overwhelming need for love and the overwhelming absence of it not only created a severely stressed man, torn by conflicting opposites, but also an incredibly lonely individual, whose emotional isolation in life has been nothing less than pure tragedy.

Of all the American Presidents, Richard Nixon presents the most enigmatic sexual subject. The nature of the man almost precludes the existence of love and romance, and yet they have played a significant part—although as twisted in shadow and confusion as the other elements and areas—in his life.

Nixon's public presentation of a perfect marriage has always been a political necessity, but his slavish maintenance of it has been motivated by far more than the ambition for power: The search for true love and the quest for an ideal relationship have always been Nixon's greatest need and desire. In fact, the need was probably so immense and the expectations so high that the impossibility of their fulfillment must have sunk all chances for a union of any lasting happiness.

Richard and Pat Nixon were the dream couple of the cozily plastic 1950s. The dream continued right into the White House in 1968, but, then, as Nixon began crumbling as a man and as his Presidency failed, even the meticulously crafted and cared-for charade of a warm and happy marriage could no longer be effectively sustained. The truth about Watergate brought out the truth about Richard Nixon and, in turn, the true nature of his "happy" marriage.

The very peculiar circumstances of how Richard Nixon and his future wife first came together indicate a great deal about his psychological makeup. The very first time he saw Patricia Ryan at the rehearsals of an amateur theatrical group, he took her aside and, after a short conversation, asked her to marry him. She "thought he was nuts," but his ensuing single-minded campaign to win her eventually made an impression. Pat consented to see him, but it was a very long time before they even established a firm friendship. "He would drive me to meet other beaux, and wait around to take me home," she later recalled.

As intimidated as she was by Nixon's determination and intensity, the beautiful and popular Pat Ryan admired it all. He was definitely a young man who was going to get what he went after in life! After more than two years of this rather strange courtship, the reluctant Miss Ryan finally gave in to Richard's constant proposals and agreed to marry him.

The marriage appears to have been a relatively happy one in its early years. But it was also an unusual partnership. What they both had in common seems to have been, simply, the need to struggle and work. Each was something of a workaholic, programmed by years of adversity and poverty.

Certainly no one could have considered marrying Richard Nixon as an "easy way out." Pat's Dickensian childhood of extreme deprivation and her full-time nursing of one dying relative after another may have, in effect, led her directly to a personality like Nixon as a natural extension of her suffering and tribulations. Whatever it was, precisely, that motivated their partnership, it appeared to work fairly well for several years. The birth of two adored daughters undoubtedly provided a "center" and helped it survive.

However, Nixon's sudden rise in politics was paralleled by the apparent declines in his own personal happiness and the health of his marriage. Whatever the correlation between this acquisition of power and evaporation of love, the public performance of marital bliss was never quite convincing to any close observer: toward each other, the Nixons always seemed stiff and uncomfortable; there was an awkward and almost up-tight feeling to their relating; behind the broad smiles and tender looks, they conveyed the impression of being individually isolated and emotionally disengaged.

Members of the media constantly commented on Nixon's complete lack of physically affectionate displays toward his spouse. Even an occasional kiss on the cheek or a casual hug had always been totally missing. When Frank Gannon asked Nixon point-blank in a 1984 interview why he had never said publicly that he loved his wife, the ex-President very impatiently replied:

> When I hear people slobbering around ... "I love her" ... that raises a question in my mind as to how much of it is real. We just don't go in for those public declarations of—of love . . . We never held hands in public. She isn't a public kisser; I am not either. Sometimes love . . . is much greater when you don't make a big point of showing it off.

The illogic of such a statement may reveal much more of Nixon's true feelings than he probably intended. If he, indeed, perceives even the slightest display of affection as being too extreme, then there can be serious doubt that any such true affection is sincerely felt at all.

An old friend of Pat Nixon's, Robert Pierpont, a CBS White House correspondent, noticed a dramatic change in her formerly outgoing and spirited personality when he encountered her again several years after her marriage. He found her to be extremely nervous and ill-at-ease, and strangely silent. Having observed the Nixons during the 1960s, Pierpont later commented: "I felt strongly that Nixon and his wife were trapped in a situation where the best she could do was not to hurt him. They tried to play the game of being the perfect husband and wife, but it came through as transparent. It looked phony, so unrealistic."

For a very long time it was all too apparent that Richard Nixon considered his wife to be something of a non-person. He dominated her, took her completely for granted, and had her obediently perform in his campaigns as if she were in a trained-animal act. While in office, he relegated her to the role of silent shadow. Her job was to buttress his fragile ego and provide relentlessly unquestioning support. And, as if born to be the perfect martyr, Pat Nixon readily accepted every insensitivity and slight.

"He abused her perpetually but not physically," remarked Richard Bergholz of the *Los Angeles Times*. "She was just a stick of furniture sitting on a stage. She was just someone who smiled and had that adoring look on her face when she'd heard the speech for the fiftieth time. We all suffered when she suffered."

There had been rumors of a complete break in their marriage sometime in the early 1960s. But, as with many unhappy couples who together have forged a difficult adjustment to the world, they chose to preserve the security of their relationship. Pat Nixon must, too, have found it impossible to confront her husband's potential fury, and she probably concluded that her personal unhappiness was a fair price to pay for the great protective shield of her home and the comfort of emotionally withdrawing from life. The children were also a very important consideration.

It has been written that Pat Nixon, while First Lady, admitted to her physicians that she and her husband had not been close since the early 1960s. She had wanted to divorce him, but couldn't go through with it. She simply became more and more silent, more and more devoted to seemingly pointless tasks requiring rigid discipline.

In the White House the Nixons lived in different wings and led almost totally separate lives. The President, on the average, never spent more than an hour a day with his wife, generally seeing her only at their stiff, silent dinners and talking to her for a few minutes during the early afternoon. Those on the staff who came in daily contact with the lonely couple felt uncomfortable when they saw them together. They also felt sorry for the First Lady. A member of her private staff, Kandy Stroud, later confessed to Lester David, the author of *The Lonely Lady at San Clemente*: "She gave so much and got so little of what was really meaningful to a woman— attention, companionship, consideration. Sometimes he was so brutally indifferent I wept for her."

Whatever Richard Nixon's emotional and human needs were at the time, the only person who appears to have been meeting them was a wealthy and remarkably passive Cuban emigrant named Bebe Rebozo.

Of all the people who had ever entered Nixon's lonely life, Bebe Rebozo was the only one who seemed to offer him exactly what he needed and wanted from an intimate relationship. For many years, this submissive and incredibly good-natured bachelor had been the President's closest and most constant companion. Rebozo had selflessly centered his entire life around the whims and requirements of Richard Nixon.

There was endless speculation on the precise nature of the Nixon–Rebozo friendship. Gossip often assumed a most vicious tune. Those who were well associated with the President's unique personality held the belief that the man was basically asexual; they believed that his only passion was politics. Nixon had always shown a profound disinterest in women: He either ignored them or was openly contemptuous of their intellectual aspirations and their active participation in public life. In a sexual or romantic context, he had always seemed oblivious to their existence.

UPI / BETTMANN

Richard M. Nixon (at right) enjoying life with his closest companion, Bebe Rebozo (center), on Rebozo's houseboat at Key Biscayne, Florida. Robert Abplanalp, another friend, is at far left. The rather intimate Nixon–Rebozo friendship remains a great mystery of the ex-President's life.

Furthermore, when he was forced to deal with women in public, he always seemed terribly uncomfortable.

The legendary journalist Adela Rogers St. John recalled seeing Nixon at a Republican rally at which he was surrounded by some of Hollywood's most gorgeous actresses: "You never saw such beautiful flesh. And he acted like a man utterly unsexed. It was as if he didn't know they were there."

Whereas Nixon was willing to use the threat of sexual exposure against his political enemies—ordering his staff to impose round-the-clock surveillances on suspected subjects in order to uncover any possible scandal—he was fanatically protective of his own private life. While President, he strictly forbad any and all investigations into his personal affairs and was vengeful in his punishment of even the slightest transgression.

His relationship with Bebe Rebozo was one of the most

sensitive areas of his privacy. Publicly, Nixon played down the friendship, and deceptively minimized it whenever he possibly could. In fact, he seemed constantly to go out of his way to avoid making any reference whatsoever to his dearest friend. He also took pains to see that Bebe was not made to officially log in on his frequent visits to the White House—thus eliminating any possible documentation of his almost constant presence. Nixon's closest aide, H. R. Haldeman, noticed that he was always "edgy when Bebe's name was mentioned."

Another close aide, General Alexander Haig, told Henry Kissinger that the President was basically a weak man who lacked guts. Haig also joked about Nixon and Bebe Rebozo having a homosexual relationship, imitating what he considered to be the President's limp-wrist manner.

Several of the hyper-aggressive men with whom Nixon surrounded himself on his private staff were disparaging, if not completely contemptuous, of him behind his back. Haldeman and John Ehrlichman nicknamed Nixon "the Mad Monk." During their years at the White House they watched as their Mad Monk descended deeper into emotional isolation and loneliness. The only exception to his bitter estrangement from the human race seemed to be the unassuming Bebe Rebozo.

From 1954 until the time of his resignation from office in 1974, Nixon had Rebozo close at his side during almost every important decision he had to make. After Nixon lost the California gubernatorial race in 1962 and had his painful emotional breakdown in public, he told the world that he was going to go home and spend some time getting to know his family again. But, instead, he went off to spend three weeks alone with Bebe on Paradise Island in the Bahamas. Before that, Bebe had moved to California from Florida and had suffered a financial loss, friends have reported, just so that he could be close to Nixon while he lived there.

Rebozo lived on Key Biscayne in Florida, and Nixon's frequent rest and relaxation sojourns there during his Presidency were for the specific purpose of being with his friend. What the public didn't know was that Nixon's special friend was visiting the White House much more often than the President was officially flying down to Florida. Bebe was with the Nixons on every important family occasion, and he participated in the functions of their daily life as if he were a member of the family.

The intensity and exclusiveness of the Nixon–Rebozo relationship created a great deal of malicious gossip and uncharitable speculation. Although very few intelligent observers would attribute to them an overtly homosexual affair—this being highly inconsistent with the characters and sensibilities of both men—there were many who certainly saw heavy psychological elements at play in their devoted partnership that were typical of the average marriage. In fact, many witnesses described their rather strange mutual attachment as being like a "good marriage."

Ironically, Nixon had always publicly shown a most pronounced contempt for homosexuality and those suspected of it. For him, the accusation of being gay was the ultimate weapon that could be used to destroy a man, and during his opportunistic career he had often tried to successfully employ it. Part of his "dirty tricks" of the 1972 presidential campaign had been to smear his Democratic opponents, Senators Humphrey and Jackson, with the tag of homosexual. Nixon had also engaged in a long, concentrated effort to prove that one of his most ardent critics, popular journalist Jack Anderson, was gay.

It was Nixon's greatest fear that he might be thought of as even the slightest bit weak or unmanly. His very fragile masculine self-image made him try relentlessly to identify himself emphatically with super-macho types; and the men he chose to surround himself with in his private little "palace guard" all reflected the aggressive, fearless power he so desperately admired and attempted to obtain by association. With his habit of anal expletives and his constant castration threats, Nixon may have been revealing what his inner thoughts were most focused upon. Anything less than overtly macho was looked on with complete aversion. Once he even made official reference to "all those impossible fags in the State Department."

The only soft and gentle man who seemed to have escaped the President's contempt and derision was Bebe Rebozo. Nixon was so sensitive about his friendship with Bebe that for years he managed to keep it completely secret from the press. The first specific reference to Rebozo did not occur until 1968 in the *New York Times*.

At this time, there is only so much that can be known about the Nixon–Rebozo friendship. It will not be until the subjects themselves have passed on that any complete investigation into the relationship can be made. Meanwhile, in the words of White House political observer George Reedy, it "remains the most important unsolved mystery in Nixon's life."

*Is it not strange that desire should so many
years outlive performance?*

—Shakespeare

9

LUSTING HEARTS AND
PROUD PASSIONS

ollowing the catastrophic Watergate scandal, the public perception of the moral character of the American Presidency fell to an all-time low. When Nixon resigned in disgrace, he was succeeded by his Vice President, Gerald Ford. In startling contrast to his predecessor, Ford had a public and private life that was beyond reproach. The private lives of the three Presidents who followed Ford in office have been equally as circumspect. If these last four Chief Executives have, indeed, engaged in extramarital affairs, they have done so with such caution and cunning that their secret liaisons may never be known, or at least not uncovered until long after their deaths.

Although there are, as yet, no illicit passions to report in the lives of Gerald Ford, Jimmy Carter, Ronald Reagan, and George Bush, it is interesting to analyze the sexual character of each man.

With his exceedingly dull and physically clumsy public image, Gerald Ford scarcely seems to be the romantic type, yet it was during the Ford Presidency that the private sexual aspects of the

First Family were publicly discussed both honestly and candidly for the very first time in American history. The source of the outspokenness was not the mild and good-natured President; it was his impulsive and talkative wife.

Betty Ford quickly established a reputation for being one of the most direct and honestly straightforward First Ladies ever to have dwelt in the White House. A gracious and charming woman, she was gregarious to the point of being indiscreet when plainly answering all questions put to her by the press. It is through the no-nonsense and unpretentious Mrs. Ford that the world finally learned of the exact sexual status of a President and First Lady and the sexual mores of their family.

When Betty Ford was showing reporter Sheila Weidenfeld around the White House for the first time, she opened the door to her bedroom and casually remarked:

> Something else no one seems to expect is for a First Lady to sleep with the President. This is *our* bedroom, and that is *our* bed. We are the first President and First Lady to share a bedroom in an awfully long time. To my great surprise, though, people have written me objecting to the idea of a President of the United States sleeping with his wife.

Soon after having moved into the White House, Betty confided to writer Myra MacPherson that she had been asked everything by reporters except how often she slept with her husband. "And if they'd asked me that," she laughingly added, "I would have told them."

"What would you have said?" MacPherson curiously inquired.

"As often as possible!" the First Lady exuberantly replied.

Evidently the President enjoyed the spontaneous boldness of his wife's remarks, for they only increased and became directed at a national audience as his administration progressed. Betty Ford eventually became a figure of controversy when she agreed to be interviewed on the popular CBS Sunday-night show *60 Minutes.*

On the show, Morley Safer surprised the First Lady by asking her how she would react if her daughter Susan came home and told her that she was having an affair with a man.

Without the slightest hesitation, Mrs. Ford calmly replied, "Well, I wouldn't be surprised. I think she's a perfectly normal human being, like all young girls. If she wanted to continue it, I would certainly counsel and advise her on the subject. And I'd want to know pretty much about the young man."

The First Lady also told Safer that she approved of premarital sex, arguing that it might be beneficial in lowering the divorce rate, and that she was in favor of legalized abortion.

Whereas no President's wife had ever ventured any opinions on sex and its consequences before, suddenly a soft-voiced, sweet-looking woman was almost single-handedly challenging the silent status quo of the establishment. A storm of protest ensued, but the President very admirably stood behind his wife and refused to either publicly or privately censor her opinions and remarks. Since then, Betty Ford has been as equally outspoken about the most intimate problems of her own life, including her now-famous struggle against alcoholism and drug addiction, her cancer operations, and her emotional breakdowns.

Thus, President Ford and his wife revealed themselves as not only a very happily married couple, but also as a man and a woman who enjoyed a very active sex life with one another. With the possible exception of the Trumans, it was probably decades since the occupants of the White House master bedroom had engaged in a completely happy and exclusive sexual relationship together.

As if they had suddenly established an entirely new trend, the devoted and passionate Fords were immediately followed in the White House by the honeymoon-happy Carters. Jimmy and Rosalynn Carter presented the nation with not only an unusually solid and happy marriage, but also with one of the most sincere and committed examples of Christian morality that has ever been

121

displayed by a Chief Executive and his wife.

For many, the devout and kindly Carters appeared almost too good to be true, especially in an age in which corruption and politics were cynically viewed to be one and the same. There had never been even the slightest hint of scandal in the Carter's private lives. In fact, when Jimmy became the Democratic presidential candidate in 1976, his overpowering commitment to the fundamentals of the Christian way of life and his ultra-square image were viewed as possible liabilities in his quest for the White House. Therefore, it came as a total shock to the nation when quite suddenly he, of all people, unleashed a violent explosion of sexual controversy.

Rosalynn and Jimmy Carter were one of the nation's most openly affectionate presidential couples. Jimmy's perhaps too honest admission, publicly, of "lusting in his heart" after other women created a sensation, but here it's a love pat for the Chief Executive.

As with First Lady Betty Ford, it was not an illicit action that caused the furor, but simply very intimate opinions offered honestly and spontaneously to the press. However, instead of innocently consenting to an interview on a major network TV show, Carter had agreed to an in-depth session with *Playboy* magazine. His consent to be interviewed by such a prominent source of sexual exploitation was enough to raise eyebrows in the Christian community. But when the November 1976 issue of the magazine hit the newsstands, eyes blinked in astonishment at its contents.

In talking about the concept of sin, the saintly Carter boldly confessed that he had sinned by "lusting in his heart" after women during most of his adult life. The remarks were made at the end of a long interview and came as a response to the question whether his strict religious beliefs would make people think he would be a rigid, inflexible President. After a long discourse on his personal relationship with the Baptist Church and his own spiritual beliefs, Carter talked specifically about the almost impossible rules of Christianity and the great difficulty in not breaking them and committing sin. He cited Christ's declaration "I tell you that anyone who looks on a woman with lust has in his heart already committed adultery."

Then, Carter matter-of-factly admitted:

> I've looked on a lot of women with lust. I've committed adultery in my heart many times. This is something that God recognizes I will do—and I have done it—and God forgives me for it. But that doesn't mean that I condemn someone who not only looks on a woman with lust but who leaves his wife and shacks up with somebody out of wedlock.
>
> Christ says, Don't consider yourself better than someone else because one guy screws a bunch of women while the other guy is loyal to his wife. The guy who's loyal to his wife ought not to be condescending or proud because of the relative degree of sinfulness . . .

123

Earlier in the same *Playboy* interview Carter had also candidly and specifically revealed his deep feelings about his wife and his marriage:

> Well, I really love Rosalynn more now than I did when I married her. And I have loved no other woman except her. I had gone out with all kinds of girls, sometimes fairly steadily, but I just never cared about them . . .
>
> When I was in the Navy, I was at sea most of the time and I'd see her maybe one or two nights a week. Now, when I'm home in Plains, I see her almost every night. And if I'm elected President, I'll see her *every* night. So there is obviously a time to be together and a time to be separated. If you're apart three or four days and then meet again, it's almost—for me, its a very exciting reunion. I'll have been away from Rosalynn for a few days and if I see her across an airport lobby, or across a street, I get just as excited as I did when I was, you know, 30 years younger.

By all accounts, the marriage of Jimmy and Rosalynn Carter has lived up to their high Christian ideals. Although many took issue with his lusting-in-his-heart remarks in the *Playboy* interview, and viewed it as tactless or naive, no one has doubted his sincerity. While adhering to a strict moral code of sexual conduct, Jimmy Carter was nevertheless a man with a healthy sexual appetite and was exceedingly honest and comfortable in publicly acknowledging it.

In direct contrast, Ronald Reagan—the only Hollywood actor and only divorced man to ever become President—has always been circumspect almost to the point of being prudish, when it comes to sexual matters. Although the marriage of Ronald and Nancy Reagan achieved something of a legendary status as one of the greatest prolonged love affairs of modern times, it is very interesting to consider the love-history of this paradoxical movie star from the Midwest who turned to politics late in life and became our nation's oldest Chief Executive.

The most important influence in Ronald Reagan's youth and early adult years was his mother, an extraordinary woman who appears to have possessed only positive traits. She was an almost ideal mother in her ability to healthfully nurture her son and bring out his best qualities while at the same time instilling in him her own high values and principles. Reagan's mother encouraged her naturally good-natured boy to be the kind, gentle, and caring man that he became. A deep and sincere love existed between mother and son, as well as a mutual understanding and respect. The great success of their relationship set a very strong pattern for the way Reagan would relate to women in the future. Straightforward, uncomplicated, and optimistically happy, Reagan's attitude toward the opposite sex was always one of complete ease and comfort. He automatically saw women as friends, and he respected them, looking to them for both approval and emotional support.

It would appear that the positive experience of his mother's unfailing love and acceptance brought Ronald Reagan to view all women with much of the same affection and appreciation. Women were valued individuals, if not exalted human beings, and it appears that Reagan never allowed himself to perceive them simply as sex objects. In fact, Reagan was a pure romantic when it came to love and sex; he seemed only interested in sex when it was placed in the context of a true love relationship. It was good, solid, enduring relationships that Reagan searched for throughout his life. Casual sex for pleasure never seems to have been of value to him.

This fact was quickly noticed by several beautiful young starlets when the handsome twenty-six-year-old actor arrived in Hollywood in 1937. Given the loose morality of the occupational environment, pretty actresses were used to having at least some sexual advances made toward them by the males they encountered. They were pleased to discover that the newcomer was anxious first to establish a friendship, and only then proceed cautiously on to romance.

Reagan's first real girlfriend, fellow Warner Bros. contract player Jane Wyman, experienced quite a bit of frustration in establishing reciprocal feelings of romantic passion in her easygoing beau. Friends, too, noticed how casually he treated his "pal" Jane. After they had been dating exclusively for more than a year, Wyman assumed that they were headed toward something permanent. However, Reagan still was proceeding so relaxedly that it appeared he was taking her companionship for granted. The crisis in their relationship came when she was hospitalized for minor surgery and he responded with a rather formal and noncommittal get-well card. Wyman refused to see him when he showed up at the hospital to visit—and her gambit worked. Reagan was disturbed by her rebuff and went on in to see her anyway. When he came out, they were engaged to be married.

That same year, 1939, Reagan, after struggling for two years in minor B movies, landed his first role in a top-notch grade-A production. The film was called *Dark Victory*, and it was Warner Bros.' finest effort in a year of magnificent movies. *Dark Victory* would win several Academy Award nominations and be especially remembered for Bette Davis' arguably greatest screen performance and Max Steiner's superb musical score. The film's director, Edmund Goulding, was an experienced veteran who had made some of the most successful pictures of the 1930s.

Ronald Reagan was given the important supporting role of "Alec Hamm." He was billed just below Humphrey Bogart, and it was to be his big break, his first big chance to show the studio that he was capable of portraying a complex character and able to "deliver" as an actor. If Reagan passed that test, he would instantly be saying goodbye to the low-budget Warner programmers that seemed to be spelling a dead-end to his career. Reagan attempted the role, and failed miserably. His inability to play the part well was not due to any lack of technical skill; it was primarily the result of his very unsophisticated attitude toward sex and his extremely narrow sexual sensibility.

His ambiguously written character, Alec, was a perennially drunken playboy. Alec drank because of some secret sorrow and he spent all of his time hopelessly pursuing the Bette Davis character, and her constant rejection of him seemed to motivate his confused obsession. Although not overtly homosexual, Alec Hamm was obviously agonized by his hidden homosexuality and losing his desperate struggle to come to terms with it. Even for the very rigid censorship standards of the time, the character's sexual problem was treated in an extremely discernible manner and could be fully understood by any mature adult in the audience.

But Reagan's understanding of sexuality was exceedingly simplistic: For him, sex was either black or white, so that sexual feelings of a highly complex or conflicting nature were both threatening and incomprehensible to the young actor. He adamantly resisted any understanding of the part and played the agonized Alec as superficially and one-dimensionally as he could. Complicating matters somewhat was the homosexuality of director Edmund Goulding, who felt a deep kindredness for the character and knew better than anyone how Alec should be played. But Reagan seems to have sensed the similarities between his director and his role as Alec, and he not only resisted exploring either one of them, he adopted an almost hostile attitude toward the entire proceedings.

In his autobiography, *Where's the Rest of Me?*, Reagan inadvertently revealed his true insecurities of having to identify with such a sexually ambivalent characterization:

> I was playing, he [Goulding] told me, the kind of fellow who could sit in the girls' dressing room dishing the dirt while they went on dressing in front of me. I had no trouble seeing him in that role, but for myself I want to think I can stroll through where girls are short of clothes, and there will be a great scurrying about and taking cover.

Reagan's attitude is all that more remarkable for coming from an actor—whose craft and profession it is to pretend to be what, in fact, he is not. His distaste in doing so displays not only his limited views on sex, but also explains his failure to have ever developed significantly in the film industry. For years to come, Ronald Reagan would only show enthusiasm for roles that were an idealization of his self-image.

———————

The inflexibility of Reagan's narrow sexual sensibilities is perhaps best seen in his unchanging attitude toward homosexuality. Working for decades in a business that is home to a very high percentage of gays and bisexuals, Reagan has remained intimidated by the prospect of sexual diversity. More than forty years after confronting the role of Alec Hamm in *Dark Victory*, Reagan took great pains to emphasize to the press that he had raised his son to be "all man," when the junior Reagan decided to pursue the career of ballet dancer. His remarks were as embarrassingly unnecessary as they were inappropriate, and they served only to emphasize the senior Reagan's continuing discomfort at any hint of sexual ambiguity.

Perhaps Ronald Reagan's conservative view of sex would not have appeared out of place had he remained in his original small-town, Midwestern environment. His years in Hollywood apparently left his rather prudish character untouched, although he had relaxed enough by 1946 to smilingly confide to his *Night unto Night* co-star Viveca Lindfors that he enjoyed having sex best in the afternoon after coming out of a shower. His observation was simply a casually stated preference to a friend and co-worker, not an invitation to an illicit encounter. In fact, only two years later, after Reagan had separated from Jane Wyman, he was in England sharing an adjoining suite with beautiful actress Patricia Neal at London's Savoy Hotel while making *The Hasty Heart*, and she was disappointed at his total lack of romantic interest. "Although I was a young, pretty girl," Neal says, "he never made a pass at me."

Eddie Bracken, Reagan's co-star in his next film, *The Girl from*

Jones Beach, probably understood him as well as anyone. He later commented on Reagan's attitude toward women: "He was never for the sexpots. He was never a guy looking for the bed. He was a guy looking for companionship more than anything else."

THE BETTMANN ARCHIVE

Newlyweds Ronald and Nancy Reagan forget about the popcorn and feast on each other at the 1953 Paramount Theater premiere of the first 3-D film, *House of Wax*. Reagan wasn't the star of this Warner Bros. picture—although if he had been, it might have helped his then badly sagging acting career.

And, only two years later, Reagan found the great love and companionship he had always been searching for: He met actress Nancy Davis and married her after a brief courtship. Proving that passion was as much a part of their initial attraction as companionship, Nancy was already pregnant with her first child at the time of their wedding. And, by all accounts, they lived happily ever after.

At the end of his eight-year stay in the White House, Ronald Reagan paid his wife one of the greatest compliments a husband can make after thirty-seven years of marriage. He referred to his happiness with Nancy as being nothing less than the glowing, idealized love that young boys dream about.

The only personal drawback to the intense love affair of Ronald and Nancy Reagan appears to be the alienating affect it had on their children. For while the President and First Lady stared into each other's eyes with worshipping adoration and presented America with an image of honeymoon bliss, the well-recognized hostility toward them from their own children, and the obvious family estrangements, have provided the nation with an unattractive and unsettling picture of parental failing.

In startling contrast is the very warm and affectionate current First Family. George Bush and his wife, Barbara, have been married for forty-five years and have five happy, loving children and numerous grandchildren. The family is unusually united and close-knit, sharing a high degree of mutual respect and cooperation.

The First Lady proudly confesses that she married the first boy she ever kissed. The Bushes' romantic marriage has withstood a constant shifting of homes and the tragedy of losing a daughter to cancer, and has gracefully evolved into a loving and comfortable partnership. In his mid-sixties, the President is in perfect physical condition, the result of a slavish devotion to diet and regular exercise. With exceptional vitality and enthusiasm, George Bush appears to be a man many years younger than his age. Someday, after he has left office, it will be very interesting to gain access to the intimate particulars of his private life.

Meanwhile, the public portrait of a large, happy, and active First Family is a most welcome sight. The informal yet aristocratic George and Barbara Bush—both of them products of East Coast wealth—bring to mind another privileged couple of similar background: Franklin and Eleanor Roosevelt. However, in their case, the Roosevelts, who presented an equally perfect marriage to the nation, led shocking secret lives behind the facade.

*A god could hardly love
and be wise.*
—Publilius Syrus

10

MISTRESS "HIS"

ossip and rumors have circulated for the past few
decades concerning some of the most unconventional pre-Kennedy sexual behavior to have occurred
during an American Presidency. The President
involved was Franklin Delano Roosevelt, the most loved/hated,
controversial man to have ever held that office. He also had the
longest term of office, more than twelve years. Roosevelt's social,
political, and economic impact on the United States was immense.
However, as with all great men, his private life remained obscured
and carefully fabricated to create a comfortable and inspiring
myth. This was especially true of his romantic relationships.

The Roosevelt marriage was as complex and fascinating as the
two characters involved. Enjoying every superior advantage of
the aristocratic class, Franklin and his wife, Eleanor, did not even
pay lip service to the strict rules of middle-class morality. They
were both laws unto themselves, and they conducted their marriage and ventured into alternative relationships exactly as they

pleased, discreetly, but with a thrilling courage that challenged public censure.

The spoiled and adored only child of wealthy parents, Franklin Roosevelt was always the confident center of his own world. As an uncommonly handsome young man, he seemed quite indifferent to women, until his junior year at college. Then, quite unexpectedly, he fell in love with his shy, introverted, awkward cousin Eleanor. An orphan who had had a traumatic and unhappy childhood, she was the classic wallflower, exceptionally plain and ungainly. It seemed a strange and inexplicable match, this friendly, popular young Adonis and his withdrawn, unattractive fiancee. Most likely, Franklin was captivated by Eleanor's brilliant intellect and her deep social conscience and high ideals. Idealism was romanticized to the zenith during that era, and sex was so zealously repressed that its existence was a complete mystery to the genteel rich until after marriage.

Franklin and Eleanor were perfect representatives of their class and time. In love with love and high-minded about all aspects of life, they nurtured their affection on platonic dreams and hoped-for heaven. When they married in 1905, reality dealt them a swift and cruel blow. Two discoveries were immediate: First, for Eleanor, sex was an ordeal that she did not enjoy at all; second, for Franklin, sex was the heaven he sought. The marriage began. Before the honeymoon was over, the new husband had already grown tired of his frigid and grimly serious bride. He began innocent flirtations with other women. Charming and attractive, he had no problem gaining feminine response. Eleanor grew jealous and sulked. Adding to the tension when they returned home with the ubiquitous presence of Franklin's domineering mother, who would live with them and control their household for the next three decades.

———

For the first eleven years of their marriage, Franklin obviously had his way more often than not. Six children were born. But in 1916

134

Eleanor went on permanent strike. She informed her husband that there would be no more children. And to ensure this, she refused to ever share a bed with Franklin again.

For the remaining thirty years of their marriage, they maintained a friendly, intellectual partnership which was completely devoid of any physical intimacy. This suited Eleanor perfectly, but Franklin had to make other plans. Quick, impersonal encounters may have been sexually satisfying for him, but they left him emotionally unfulfilled. He needed a mutually committed long-term love relationship.

And he found it.

Lucy Mercer was a beautiful young socialite whose family had lost their fortune. She was even more charming and personable than Franklin was. She was also Eleanor's social secretary. The affair began in 1916, probably not too long after the sexual boycott was announced. It must have added to the excitement of the illicit union to conduct it right under his wife's nose in their very home.

The elegantly seductive Lucy Mercer was soon deeply in love with her employer's husband, and he was equally in love with her. They started taking short trips together, once on a naval yacht cruise up the Potomac where Franklin and Lucy registered as husband and wife at a Virginia Beach motel. When Eleanor went north to escape the Washington heat to their summer home in the cool Canadian woods, Franklin began staying behind in Washington, secretly visiting Lucy and making excuses to his suspicious wife.

The affair became stronger and stronger. Caught up in their happiness and great love, Franklin and Lucy lived for the moment and didn't think of the future. Not until 1918 when a crisis occurred that forced them to.

Returning from a trip to Europe as assistant secretary of the navy, he became chilled on the ship and came down with pneumonia. While he was seriously ill, his wife took charge of his mail. She also looked through his personal papers and found the love

135

letters from Lucy. After the shock had softened somewhat, Eleanor dried her tears and angrily confronted her husband and Lucy. She half-heartedly offered to give him a divorce, but sadly predicted an inevitable disgrace for their six children. The total ruin of Roosevelt's future political career was emphasized. Then, to make certain that he would have no other choice than to continue the marriage, Eleanor brought in her most devastating weapon—Franklin's mother.

Sara Delano Roosevelt sternly informed her son that she could not stop him from divorcing Eleanor and marrying Lucy, but if he did, she would completely cut off his generous allowance and disinherit him. This spoke to him the most eloquently. Totally enslaved to the habits of luxurious living, he was unable to face the loss of his fortune. Franklin gave in to his mother's demands. He stayed married to Eleanor and gave his solemn word that he would never see Lucy Mercer again.

There is a good chance that he might have divorced Eleanor and married Lucy if he could have retained his mother's support. Evidence suggests that he was not fully committed to a political career at this time, and the loss of speculative political offices in the future were probably not as drastic as most historians have concluded. Roosevelt was a man deeply in love. His marriage was over, for all practical purposes. He clearly saw his happiness in being married to Lucy. But economics, the bottom line for most human behavior, dictated his choice. And money combined with his career plans and the future of his children left him really with only one intelligent choice. Being an intelligent man, he made it.

Awkwardly, the marriage went on, but Franklin and Eleanor went their separate ways, each having his or her own private life. The public never knew that they no longer lived as husband and wife. They presented a smiling, happy partnership, especially where the children were concerned, and they were devoted to one another, but there was never again a display of affection between them, although it surely existed on a platonic level.

Before too much bitterness or regret had set in, Franklin developed a bad case of polio in the summer of 1921. Struggling for his life at first, he slowly recovered but permanently lost the use of his legs and became a cripple for the rest of his life. This tragedy brought the couple more closely together than ever before. Eleanor stayed by her husband's side and fought as hard as he did in conquering the disease.

This struggle gave their marriage the structure and substance that it had previously lacked. Importantly, it also gave it a new purpose. It necessitated these two widely different personalities working together as a team.

But Franklin Roosevelt was the same man as before and with the same needs. And still with the same ability to fulfull them. The doctors had examined him thoroughly after his recovery and found that only his legs had been paralyzed, not the lower trunk of his body as many people had assumed. Medically they had pronounced him "without symptoms of 'impotentia coeundi' "; or in plain English, he was still perfectly capable of sexual intercourse.

In 1920, Lucy Mercer had married Winthrop Rutherford, an elderly and wealthy North Carolina socialite. However, the most intimate and reliable sources indicate that Lucy continued to see Roosevelt during her marriage. The two married lovers would meet intermittently through the years. Usually it was on neutral ground during travel that was calculated to exclude Eleanor. The homes of his close friends were the most convenient sites for these romantic encounters. The celebrated fiancier Bernard Baruch lent his South Carolina estate to Roosevelt for this purpose. The Baruch estate was most often used because its thousands of acres ensured complete privacy and also because Lucy vacationed nearby in Aiken and could easily commute without attracting attention. Roosevelt's personal physician, Dr. McIntire, would cooperate by saying he had ordered the southern trip for the

President's sinus trouble. Things would really get interesting on the occasions when Eleanor would decide to pay a visit and the two women would have to be kept hidden from each other.

When Roosevelt attended his first inaugural in March of 1933, he secretly sent for Lucy and placed a limousine at her disposal.

Governor Franklin D. Roosevelt, of New York, hears news of his presidential victory, November 1932. After fathering six children by his wife, Eleanor, the politician was denied further intimacy with her and sought his pleasures elsewhere—most notably with the young socialite Lucy Mercer.

She was unable to come to the White House reception because of Eleanor, but FDR managed to meet with her in private.

Throughout the White House years, Lucy Rutherford was a steady and secret visitor. The servants witnessed her frequent clandestine comings and goings, but they kept their mouths shut. Sometimes, in fact, they would even participate in executing the illicit deception. Grace Tully, one of Roosevelt's private secretaries, later admitted having slipped Lucy through her office several times to meet with the President. Lucy often had lunch there. And when Eleanor was away on one of her numerous jaunts, Lucy would have dinner and stay overnight.

The visits were not confined only to Roosevelt's home turf. He would often go to see Lucy at her country home on the Hudson, Tranquility Farms. This was possible because of the war. A blackout was placed on the President's movements for security reasons, and, thus, the press pool which always surrounded Roosevelt was left behind on his journeys. Meetings with Lucy at her home were made even easier because Tranquility Farms was fairly close to his own estate, Hyde Park.

When Lucy came to Washington while Eleanor was at home in the White House, she would wait out in the nearby country and Roosevelt would have his chauffeur drive him to the secluded place and then slowly tour the vacant landscape. When Lucy's husband finally died in 1944, her visits became much more frequent. Those who saw them together were struck by the almost sad, bittersweet quality of the relationship. It was obvious that each had been the true love of the other's life.

The end of their affair came only with his death. In April 1945, Roosevelt had gone south to Warm Springs, Georgia, for a rest. He was with Lucy Mercer Rutherford there when he suddenly died of a stroke. Lucy was quickly spirited away by the time Eleanor arrived. The world would be told that the President had been alone when he died. The truth would not be made known for several years.

But Lucy was not the only love of Franklin Roosevelt's later life. There was another woman whom he was just as devoted to and enamored with. Her name was Marguerite "Missy" LeHand.

Missy LeHand loved Roosevelt almost beyond reason and gave up her entire life for him. While he was President, FDR lived with Missy at the White House and treated her as his real wife. The arrangement was made as official as possible, with the servants and staff being instructed to treat Missy in exactly the same manner they treated Eleanor.

Tall, good-looking without being a beauty, Missy had gentle gray-blue eyes and prematurely gray hair. It was her unfailing sense of humor and kindly nature that appealed most to FDR. She had been working for him for several years in one of his offices when she became his mistress. For whatever reason, Eleanor seems to have gracefully accepted the arrangement and never showed any jealousy towards Missy. She treated Missy like a member of the family and gradually the gentle young secretary assumed most of the other duties of the wife and mother.

In the White House Missy lived in a bedroom suite on the third floor. While Eleanor took on the "chief executive" role by assuming a large share of FDR's leadership duties, Missy became the unofficial First Lady. It was her voice that ran the household. It was Missy who wrote Roosevelt's checks and paid the bills. She gave the Roosevelt children their allowances and took care of their expenses. She even controlled Eleanor's spending money, and it was to Missy that the children would come with their troubles and problems. While Eleanor traveled the country and even went her own separate way when in residence at the White House, Missy shared almost every aspect of the President's daily life. She swam with him when he took his exercise, she dined with him, she shared his hobbies with him, and, most importantly of all, she had fun with him and made him laugh, something Eleanor was never able to do.

And Roosevelt relaxed and enjoyed life with Missy in the White House as best he could. Although sexually circumspect, he didn't go to the bother of pretending that the intimate relationship didn't exist. In the evening Missy was seen by everyone in her nightgown in Roosevelt's bedroom sitting on his lap. She would also sit on his lap at other private occasions where friends and family were present. When traveling by car with his wife and Missy, he always sat next to his mistress, surprising most people who didn't suspect the relationship.

For the Roosevelts' children, the marital situation of their parents was just a fact of life that they had accepted without question. Nothing else about the family was average or "normal" by conventional standards, so it was understandable that the love lives of the mother and father should be so different and eccentric. However, the uniqueness of the parental relationships must have quietly taken their toll on the youthful psyches, if the later spectacular lack of matrimonial success of the children is used as a measure.

In the spring of 1941, Missy's health suddenly broke and a brain tumor was diagnosed. She was confined to her bed and grieved over her inability to take care of the President. She then suffered a stroke and became totally incapacitated. Taken from the White House and hospitalized, she grew hysterical and began losing her reason. She wanted the President to remain by her bedside, but he couldn't spare the time and didn't want to be around her irrational and pathetic condition. She despaired and tried to commit suicide by setting herself on fire. First, FDR sent her to Warm Springs, and when that didn't work out, he sent her home to her own family in Massachusetts to recover.

Although to some he seemed callous in his treatment of Missy, Roosevelt changed his will at this time and left half of his entire estate to her. The other half went to Eleanor.

However, Missy did not survive the President. She suffered another stroke and died in the summer of 1944. Because Roosevelt was attending a conference in the Pacific when it happened, only Eleanor attended her husband's mistress' funeral. The White

House issued a formal statement about how President Roosevelt had lost a fine, devoted secretary.

FDR never changed his will back, and when he died the following year, he still declared in the document that he was leaving half of everything to the deceased Missy. It may have been his safe and sentimental way of finally giving public recognition to the true nature of their relationship.

Although Lucy Mercer and Missy LeHand were the great loves of Franklin Roosevelt's life and his two long-term romantic relationships, he was so attracted to women that there were other serious flirtations which may have become affairs. Liking tall, blue-eyed, aristocratic ladies who dripped with glamour, Roosevelt was more than susceptible to the glittering charms of the Crown Princess Martha of Norway.

Martha was a married woman in her early forties, with small children when she arrived in Washington as a royal refugee at the beginning of World War II. When she arrived on her first visit to the White House, she and the President seemed instantly attracted to each other. Possessing a flirtatious charm of her own to match FDR's, the Crown Princess played up the the President and began a very close friendship that many observers suspected had a sexual basis. At the very least, it was an ultra-romantic relationship. It was also one which outraged Eleanor more than any other.

Whether it was the intensity of the President's infatuation or simply the First Lady's jealousy, brought to fever pitch by the princess' superior social status, Eleanor Roosevelt was almost visibly ill when forced to witness her husband and his royal "friend." She grew so angry and upset that Martha eventually was bounced from White House functions when the seething First Lady was there.

Martha continued visiting the President on a regular basis, only carefully scheduling her stays to coincide with Eleanor's absences. Roosevelt, usually hating the use of nicknames for himself, smilingly told the Crown Princess to call him "Godfather." She willingly obliged and added a "dear" to the name. Associates couldn't fail to notice the extra passion with which Roosevelt kissed her on every occasion possible.

As the war progressed and Martha's husband remained with his government-in-exile in London, Martha settled in more permanently in Washington. Roosevelt took her house hunting in the country and helped her find a lovely estate in nearby Maryland. He would surreptitiously slip out to visit with her as often as he could. After the death of his mother, FDR took the Crown Princess to Hyde Park and made her his long-term house guest. He also went house hunting in the Hyde Park area to see if a place could be found for her near him.

Crown Princess Martha was still living near Washington when Roosevelt died. No one knows for certain the extent of their affair, but it seems highly unlikely that it ever became sexual. Evidence for this conclusion is simply the outward display involved in the relationship. The constantly exaggerated flirtation between the President and the princess never lost its intensity, thus logically indicating that this social "foreplay" never progressed to its next step. Had their love been consummated, they would not have continued putting the bulk of their energy into the fine art of verbal seduction.

After the President's death many ladies came forth with stories of torrid and tender affairs. The most notable was Dorothy Schiff, a successful publisher, who waited until the 1970s to announce her Roosevelt romance to the world. Most of these claims lack reliable substantiation. What remains is a simple fact which is echoed by a chorus of observers who knew the President best: Mr. Roosevelt certainly did like the ladies.

There is probably no sensitive heterosexual alive who is not preoccupied with his or her latent homosexuality.

—Norman Mailer

11

MISTRESS "HERS"

If Franklin was allowed to have a mistress, then in all fairness, Eleanor could have one too. And she did.

Homosexuality in the White House has, most likely, occurred as often as in the general population. Perhaps more often. Those in high places, especially elected office, are forced to cover their tracks and keep their unorthodox affections a secret. Speculative and creative gossip always puts forth a variety of interesting theories. Facts of this most private nature are much more difficult to determine and establish. If the First Family of the land truly wishes to keep the fact of a homosexual relationship a secret, it can do so very easily. The public at large finds it extremely distasteful to draw this conclusion regarding the Presidency, so the evidence must be rather overwhelming and the subject must be willing to have it discovered.

Both are the case with Eleanor Roosevelt.

Had this gallant First Lady wanted to keep her illicit relation-

145

ship from public knowledge, letters would have been burned, behavior would have been more guarded, and an entire lifestyle would have been tactfully altered. It was almost as if Eleanor wanted posterity to discover the truth about her hidden sexuality.

Even given such indisputable evidence, there are many who still refuse to accept the obvious. These persons have the typical "defense attorney" mentalities, operating out of one prejudice or another with an absolute commitment to avoid accepting the unacceptable conclusion. They resist at all cost the undeniable facts. Until they witness them with their own eyes, they will never believe.

However, to all open-minded and logical observers, there can be only one reasonable conclusion: Eleanor Roosevelt was primarily a lesbian personality who carried on at least one long-term lesbian relationship. And during all twelve years she lived at the White House!

Eleanor and Franklin had made their marital adjustment back in the 1916–18 period. They no longer slept together and remained husband and wife in name only. Eleanor confessed many times to various people that she had never liked having sex with a man, that it was an ordeal for her and she had grudgingly performed it only as a "wifely duty."

After they drifted to separate beds and went their own romantic ways, Eleanor did not find the solace of an extramarital love relationship as quickly as did her husband. Perhaps because she was seeking a much more socially taboo arrangement, it took her longer.

Finally, during the first Presidential campaign of 1932 she was introduced to Lorena Hickok. Lorena was a large, mannish-looking woman with a jovial, straightforward personality. She was always overweight, wore her hair in a bun, and dressed in very masculine clothing. Perhaps what the two women shared initially was their pronounced lack of attractiveness. They each possessed a brilliant intellect and were both interested in a wide variety of topics. Totally independent and liberated during a time when most women weren't, they were both deeply committed to humanitarian causes.

UPI / BETTMANN

Bosom buddies First Lady Eleanor Roosevelt and Lorena Hickok delight in each other's company in a modest, out-of-the-way San Francisco restaurant in 1934, where a photographer stumbled upon them by chance. Recent evidence indicates that the two unattractive women may have enjoyed a lesbian relationship.

The friendship between them was immediate, and it quickly became intense. Hicky, as Eleanor affectionately called Lorena, was with her on election night when FDR won his first landslide victory. She was also with the new First Lady on the eve of the Inauguration at the Mayflower Hotel in Washington. By this time the two women had become inseparable. They spent Inauguration Day in each other's company, and it went without saying that Hicky would also be taking up residence in the White House when the Roosevelts moved in.

Hicky was assigned a small sitting room to sleep in in the northwest corner of the Executive Mansion, directly across the hall from Eleanor's suite in the southwest corner. It was a most convenient arrangement. Many nights Hicky slept on the daybed in Eleanor's bedroom suite. At least that was where the servants would find her in the morning.

At first, Hicky was an accepted guest and was welcomed by the President. She would join the family for dinner and other private activities. But, then, FDR seems to have suddenly changed his opinion of the awkward woman and was heard yelling at his wife that he wanted "that woman kept out of this house." After that, it became Hicky's chief job to stay out of his sight. On a more or less permanent basis, Hicky lived in the White House full-time for four more years.

Periodically, Hicky was sent off on investigative trips especially designed for her by Eleanor's government friends. One of her most important and lengthy assignments was to see how relief was being administered nationwide under the Federal Emergency Relief Administration. It was her heartbreaking reports to Eleanor of the pathetic living conditions of the poor that were responsible for galvanizing the First Lady to full-steam-ahead in her charitable programs.

The two women soon sought out more private places beyond the confines of the White House. They would drive to favorite spots, such as the cemetery in Rock Creek Park, where they sat and meditated on a graceful statue entitled "Grief." Adamantly refusing the protection of the Secret Service, so that they could move freely about together, Eleanor and Hicky enjoyed each other's company as often as they could manage. Wearing suits so masculine that they could stylishly fit a man, flat shoes, and dark cotton stockings, Hicky even walked like a man. It's a wonder that her close relationship with Eleanor did not raise more eyebrows than it did.

The First Lady seems to have been oblivious to Hicky's complete lack of beauty and style. She did, however, gradually develop the habit of passing down all of her clothes to her lover. Soon Hicky would be reluctant to admire a dress the First Lady was wearing for fear the generous Eleanor would have it tailored to fit her.

Generous in many other ways, Eleanor saw to it that Hicky had everything that she needed. She got her lucrative jobs and gave her considerable financial assistance. She even bought her a new car. But there were things the kindhearted First Lady could not give her. Because of her husband's strong feeling against Hicky and other obviously lesbian women who, FDR felt, were giving the White House a potentially bad reputation, Eleanor could never invite her to any of the Presidential functions.

It was a continuous problem keeping Hicky hidden from FDR. She was confined more and more to the seclusion of her small sitting room. It was Eleanor now who would sneak across the hall to visit as often as possible. With the help of loyal servants, the two women would slip in and out of the White House while FDR was in his office.

One of Eleanor's most cherished possessions was a sapphire ring that Hicky had given her for her birthday in March of 1933. The ring was one which Hicky, in turn, had received years before from an opera singer. Eleanor rarely wore jewelry of any kind, but almost always wore Hicky's gift. Eleanor wrote her: "Hick darling . . . Oh, I want to put my arms around you. I ache to hold you close. Your ring is a great comfort. I look at it and think she does love me, or I wouldn't be wearing it."

During the thirty years of their intimate relationship, Eleanor wrote Lorena Hickok more than 2,300 letters. All of them were exceptionally affectionate, and many were extremely passionate. Lorena kept them and stipulated in her will that they not be made public until ten years after her death. When they were published in part in a biography of her in 1980, they caused a sensation. Defenders sprang forward and tried to create a smoke screen by arguing that Eleanor's era was much more romantic and sentimental than the current age and that feminine friendships often assumed an intensely lovestruck tone which could easily be misinterpreted as sexual in nature.

These explanations and excuses are so false as to be patently absurd. When Eleanor and Hicky were lovers in the 1930s and '40s, they were not delicate relics from the Victorian past. They were both thoroughly vital and modern women who not only were fully adjusted to their times, but eagerly anticipating the sweeping changes of the future.

Eleanor Roosevelt was not, by nature, a sentimental and emotional woman. All of her family, friends, and associates universally testify that she was an extraordinarily reserved and emotionally withdrawn personality who rarely gave the slightest sign of affection even to her own husband and children. She was never casually romantic towards anyone or anything. She almost never engaged in verbal endearments with those closest to her, and she seldom kissed anyone. Eleanor, herself, complained her whole life about her inability to relax and be comfortable with people.

Therefore, given her nature and habits, the letters to Hicky are an astounding revelation. The intensity of their passionate sentiment only proves how overwhelming Eleanor's deep love and sexual feeling, at last found, must have been for this woman.

In one early letter Eleanor wrote: "I can't kiss you so I kiss your picture goodnight and good morning! Don't laugh! This is the first day I've had no letter and I miss it sadly but it is good discipline." On November 27, 1933, she wrote: "Dear one, and so you think they gossip about us, well they must at least think we stand separations rather well! I am always so much more optimistic than you are—I suppose because I care so little what they say."

A short time later Eleanor wrote Hicky another letter:

Dear, I've been trying today to bring back your face—to remember just how you look. Funny how even the dearest face will fade away in time. Most clearly I remember your eyes, with a kind of reassuring smile in them, and the feeling of that soft spot just northeast of the corner of your mouth against my lips. I wonder what we'll do when we meet—what we'll say. Well, I'm rather proud of us, aren't you? I think we've done rather well.

While the First Lady ruled almost as Chief Executive, Hicky always remained in her shadow. As a top reporter, Lorena had had a most promising future, but she eventually gave it up completely to be with Eleanor. She lived part of the year with the First Lady at a cottage on the Hyde Park estate in New York. Their life retained its very private and secluded character.

After FDR died in 1945, instead of finally enjoying the freedom to live together openly, they began going their own separate ways. Eleanor became even more involved in humanitarian causes and devoted most of her time to public service. She and Hicky lived near New York City, but in separate houses some distance from one another. When Hicky contracted diabetes and her eyesight began failing in 1955, Eleanor invited her to come live with her at her small home, Val-Kill, on the Hyde Park estate. It was not a mutually satisfactory experience and lasted only a little more than a year. Some said that the older, more conservative ex-First Lady was put off by Hicky's sloppy masculine appearance and her inability to stop calling her "darling" in front of visitors.

Hicky was moved to a spare room in the big house and was still living there when Eleanor died far away in the hospital in 1962. Hicky died six years later. Thus, one of the most complex and unorthodox of illicit affairs in the history of the Presidency finally came to a quiet conclusion.

> *With love one can live even*
> *without happiness.*
> —Fëdor Dostoevski

12

A PARAGON OF
PROMISCUITY

*T*he most infamous sex scandal involving a United States President is the dubious legacy of Warren G. Harding. What's more, the record of Harding's public administration contains an unparalleled amount of corruption, dishonesty, and misuse of power. Although historians have placed most of the blame on the President's weak and ineffectual leadership and generally rank him as the worst Chief Executive, Harding himself was an honest and conscientious public servant. It was his private life that has placed him in such ill repute.

Illicit sexual affairs, blackmail, adultery, illegitimacy, and suspected murder—these were the ingredients of Warren Harding's personal life which made it resemble the breathless episodes of a bizarre soap opera.

A country boy from Ohio, Harding was the product of a poor farming family. Growing up to be superbly handsome with a tall, well-built physique, piercing blue eyes in a bronze-tanned face, and the classical features of a Greek god, he was made instantly popular by his appearance. His exceptionally amiable and affectionate nature also increased his great personal magnetism. It also created most of his problems. Harding's father once took a shrewd look at the young man's character and smilingly informed him: "If you were a girl, Warren, you'd be in the family way all the time. You can't say no." And his father was right!

Ambitious and with a talent for dealing with people and cultivating friendships, Warren made his own way in the world, first obtaining a college education and becoming a school teacher, then buying a local newspaper and running it at age nineteen. The paper prospered and success seemed to come almost effortlessly.

However, there were hidden flaws of perilous magnitude in his shining facade. In direct contrast to the handsome, smiling appearance of this much-admired young Adonis, there were deep emotional problems and personality defects that would plague him his entire life and eventually destroy him. Before taking office, Harding innocently made a sincere statement that revealed the true source of his emotional weakness: "I cannot hope to be the best president in the country's history, but I hope to be the best loved."

Harding genuinely needed affection all of his life. Affection meant more to him than anything else. Wealth, achievement, and power were always secondary goals for this acutely insecure man. A childhood of poverty and inadequate parental affection had left Harding with an intense need to capture love and respect at any cost. Further traumatizing his early years was the local rumor that the Harding family had mixed blood. The allegations of Negro ancestry had no basis in fact, but the gossip and the derisive cries of "nigger" from his boyhood companions and even from his contemptuous father-in-law haunted Warren until his death. Eventually it would be scurrilously used against him in the 1920 election for the Presidency, but to no advantage to his opponents.

These elements had a brutal effect on Harding's delicate nervous system. He suffered his first nervous breakdown when he was only twenty-two. It was necessary for him to go to Dr. Kellogg's famous sanitarium in Battle Creek, Michigan, for several months to recover. During the next thirteen years of his life, Harding would have four more breakdowns which would force him to return for even longer convalescences at the Battle Creek clinic. Most of these psychological crises were caused by Harding's troublesome sexuality and the unsatisfactory emotional character of his marriage.

In May 1921, only a few months into his Presidency, Warren G. Harding stands arm in arm with Madame Eve Curie, who with her husband had won the Nobel Prize in 1903. Harding has presented her with a gram of radium, but, true to form, his attentions have been diverted to a younger lovely nearby.

Warren Harding felt a deep sense of sexual inadequacy throughout most of his life. As a young man he was irresistibly attractive to women, but he does not seem himself to have been that attracted to them. Modest and unassuming, his greatest drive was towards reliable affection and acceptance, the dividends of friendship, rather than the confusing gambits and potential threats of sex and romance. Even with the willing assistance of available women, he found it nearly impossible to enter into a serious relationship. Romance was something that he felt very uncomfortable with.

His marriage was a curious affair which took place after his wife had assumed the male role of pursuer and literally courted him and dragged him to the altar. There is little to explain why he so willingly entered this loveless union except that his wife had been the first woman to turn the tables on him sexually and assume a masculine dominance. When the couple were unable to have children, doctors told Harding that he most likely was sterile due to a case of childhood mumps.

Thus, an insecure, inadequate, and frustrated man discovered his sexuality late in life and indulged it to excess without judgment or propriety. Harding's sexual anxieties combined with his overwhelming need for love and affection produced an exceptionally promiscuous personality. But the affairs would not come until later in the Harding marriage, a partnership which somehow seemed to work, though no one knew why. The pairing of Warren G. Harding and Florence Kling De Wolfe was a phenomenon that appeared to be beyond any understanding.

Amos Kling was the richest man in Marion, Ohio. A Mennonite of harsh, unyielding principles, he had only one daughter, Florence, whom he raised as strictly as possible. However, dominating the high-spirited girl was no easy matter, and Florence grew up to be more than a match for her father. Awkward and unattractive with a pointed nose and a comically puffy face, Florence made up for whatever grace she lacked by developing an almost frightening firmness and resolve. Nothing could stop her from getting what she wanted. At first, when she was nineteen, it was young Henry De Wolfe. She became pregnant by him and they secretly eloped.

A son was born, but after a few months the alcoholic De Wolfe deserted his family and Florence was forced to support her infant by giving piano lessons. Her bitter father forgave her and adopted the boy and raised him. Several years passed before Florence decided what she wanted next.

It was handsome young Warren Harding, the editor of the Marion *Star*. She saw him and relentlessly pursued him until he agreed to marry her. This time her father refused to forgive her. He cut her out of his will and didn't speak a word to her for eight years. Then, he waited another seven years to recognize her new husband.

Although Florence Harding was always obsessed with her dazzling husband and worshipped him like a god, there is no doubt that Warren did not love her. He certainly never had a physical attraction to her and the nature of their marital relationship was more like one of brother and sister. Why he ever married her in the first place has remained an unanswered question. It is true that her advances were so determinedly persistent that it was easy for someone as mild and tender-hearted as Harding to give in. It was the easiest course to follow, and he might have been unable to hurt her feelings by emphatically rejecting her. He also may have been canny enough to sense that he would progress towards his illustrious goals in life much more rapidly with a dynamo like Florence behind him.

Literally, her pushing and shoving became the theme of their marriage. Taking charge of the business dealings of the newspaper office, Florence Harding put it on a solid basis and gradually it became the most successful paper in the state. She also guided her husband into local and state politics, constantly shoring up his fragile ego and feeding his self-esteem. Her belief in his exalted destiny was indestructible. His success was her divine mission in life. And succeed Harding did.

However, the more successful her husband became, the more he sought the satisfaction of a true love relationship. In response, his wife, whom he smilingly called "the Duchess," grew more resentful and jealous. She was suspicious of his every move and spied on his private routine. Because of his tranquil personality and aversion to any type of confrontation or conflict, Harding usually let the Duchess have her own way.

Warren Harding endured the loneliness of his marriage of convenience for fifteen years before he found what he had been looking for. He was Lieutenant Governor of Ohio in 1905 when he began an illicit affair with one of his wife's good friends, Carrie Phillips.

Carrie was the uncommonly beautiful wife of Harding's own close friend, Jim Phillips, the owner of a local department store. Together, the two couples had traveled and socialized extensively. Then, suddenly, circumstances allowed Carrie and Warren to come to terms of sexual intimacy. First, the Philips' son died and Jim went off to the clinic in Battle Creek for a prolonged medical treatment. The Duchess simultaneously was confined to a hospital for the treatment of one of her chronic ailments. Thus, Warren and Carrie were alone. The affair began.

The passionate union would continue for more than fifteen years. It remained a total secret from everyone, expecially the respective husband and wife. Through constant cunning and sheer luck, almost no one found out about the affair—not until almost a half-century later when 250 handwritten love letters from Harding to his mistress were discovered. These passionate letters fully documented the illicit affair. Carrie and the future President met often and enjoyed an exciting love life, probably made even more stimulating by the close proximity of their spouses and the immediate danger of discovery.

The two couples took a cruise to the Mediterranean and toured Egypt in 1909 and a few years later made a trip to Bermuda. They went to the theater together, played cards, had dinner parties, and attended moonlit dances at the country club. All the time the unhappily married Carrie and the equally dissatisfied Warren were sleeping together on a regular basis.

Three years into the relationship, Carrie began pressing Harding to divorce his overbearing wife and marry her, but Harding was just beginning his political career and he had his eye on the Senate. He realized that to divorce and remarry would automatically terminate his ambitions. Also, of perhaps equal magnitude for him was the painful prospect of emotionally confronting his wife and seeing her suffer. Weak-willed and tender-hearted, Harding always avoided hurting anyone, whether it was the right and honorable thing to do or not. Thus, he stalled Carrie and the affair continued.

A woman of some determination herself, Carrie kept after Warren to get rid of the Duchess and marry her. She finally delivered an ultimatum and forced him to make a choice. In perfect character, Harding refused to give her an answer, and, with hurt frustration, she left him and took her daughter to Germany where they remained for three years. On returning home, she quickly took up with him again and began making the same demands, although less vigorously than before. Carrie, most likely, had now gained a more realistic knowledge of her lover's character. She might reconcile herself to the unofficial role of mistress, but she decided she wanted at least some of the Duchess' influence and power. She was willing to provide a little of the domination that her paramour so obviously craved. And he was now in a position where it could count for something: Warren Harding was a senator in the United States Congress.

The risk, now, was greater than ever. Harding was a national figure, the World War had begun in Europe, and his mistress was very pro-German and constantly being followed by Secret Service agents. Carrie did everything she could to make Harding vote for the nation's entry into the war on the side of Germany. Adding to the senator's discomfort was the fact that his angry wife had finally found out about his relationship with Carrie.

The Duchess had always suspected her handsome, younger husband of having romantic flings and discreet sexual affairs, but the revelation of this genuine love relationship with one of her best friends must have had a devastating effect on her. The Harding marriage from this time on disintegrated into one long argument after another with much open resentment and bitterness on both sides. The Duchess became obsessed with tracking down and exposing her husband's endless infidelities. Although still remaining smilingly at her husband's side and praising him for all to hear, she made their private life an arena of continuous warfare.

Their spouses' discovery of Warren and Carrie's affair doomed it once and for all. Jim Phillips took the news almost as badly as the Duchess had. When Harding opened his presidential campaign in Marion, Phillips' downtown store was the only one that didn't drape itself with banners and celebratory slogans. Since everyone's reputation was involved, no mention was ever publicly made about the embarrassing affair.

It was the 1920 presidential campaign that put an absolute finish to Warren and Carrie's romantic relationship. When Harding was offered the Republican nomination, the party bosses had asked him point-blank if there was anything in his private life that could cause a scandal and be used against him. Meditating alone for ten minutes, Harding returned with the simple answer "No."

Wishful thinking, no doubt, but the new candidate was determined to break off forever with Carrie and placidly bring his wife to the White House without scandal or upset. However, Carrie was not as pleased by the turn of events as her ex-lover was. She had saved all of his love letters and hinted that they might possibly have more value than the cost of the stationery.

The Republican National Committee needed little convincing. They paid Carrie $20,000 for the letters plus a monthly stipend of $2,000 as long as Harding was President. Not letting it go at that, the Republicans made sure that the former mistress and her cuckolded husband did not fall into the hands of the deadly Democrats. Jim and Carrie were given a free trip around the world and they remained out of the country until after Harding's death.

Harding won the greatest victory in history at the polls and gracefully assumed the Presidency, but it was at a severe personal sacrifice. Carrie Phillips had been the love of his life and it must have caused this affection-starved man acute pain to give her up for good. There was only one compensation now for his loveless marriage—the other steady sexual affair he had been carrying on with a much younger girl.

Her name was Nan Britton, and Harding had known her since she was a child. Nan was thirty years younger than Harding and was the daughter of a Marion doctor who regularly submitted articles to the *Star*. The fourteen-year-old girl was hopelessly infatuated with Harding. She followed him around town and pasted his campaign-poster portraits all over her bedroom. The Duchess was quick to notice the physical precocity of the blond, voluptuous child and she asked Nan's mother to keep her from climbing up on Harding's bulging lap.

Nothing came of her adolescent adulation until she moved to New York City in 1916, when she was twenty. Nan wrote to Senator Harding in Washington asking for his help in finding a job. He answered her immediately and promised to see her the next time he came to New York.

He arrived in Manhattan much sooner than he had planned.

Meeting with his beautiful young constituent, he was not able to offer her a job at the time, but after retiring to her hotel room and making love to her for several hours, he did manage to tuck $30 into her silk stocking. Later he got her a clerical job at the United States Steel Corporation and privately contributed to her support. They became lovers. The long-distance affair was difficult to maintain, but obviously worth the effort. Harding visited Nan in New York as often as he could, and she traveled down to Washington. Their rendezvous grew dangerously indiscreet. They made trips to the Midwest together, Nan usually masquerading as the much older man's niece, and in the nation's capital they made love in apartments borrowed from Harding's friends and the

UPI / BETTMANN

The first presidential mistress to take her story to the press and the bookstores was Ohio-born Nan Britton. Thirty years younger than the Ohioan President, and the mother of Harding's love child, she wrote boldly of their affair—and made a mint!

palatial Rock Creek mansion of the wealthy eccentric, Ned McLean. Harding wrote her numerous love letters on official Senate Chamber stationery, and even used the privacy of his

Senate office for their romantic sessions. It was on his uncomfortable office couch that Nan conceived a child in 1919.

The twenty-three-year-old Nan gave birth to a daughter in October of that year. She was named Elizabeth Ann Christian. As he prepared to run for the Presidency, Harding privately acknowledged paternity of the child and began making payments for her support.

During the Republican convention in Chicago in 1920, Harding saw to it that his mistress was given a minor job. He slept with her several times at her sister's apartment there before and after he won the presidential nomination. Managing a bit more caution during the campaign, the two lovers remained apart for several months before finally meeting secretly in Marion just after Harding's triumphant election victory.

Typically kind and generous, President Harding promised to always support Nan and their daughter, and he regularly sent them $500 or more each and every month. However, the pomp and power of the White House must have made his barren emotional existence with the Duchess even less bearable than before. Within a few weeks of going to the nation's capital, Harding took a great gamble and began sending for Nan.

The gorgeous young mother started spending most of her time in Washington. Flirting with disaster, the President would meet her at Ned McLean's (made even more deliciously perilous by the fact that Ned's wife was the Duchess' best friend) and all the other old trysting places, plus a new secret space—the large coat closet in his White House office. In fact, the secluded closet became their favorite location for having sexual intercourse. The Duchess almost caught them in flagrante delicto on one occasion when she angrily suspected what was going on and tried to burst into the office. Fortunately for Harding, an agile and loyal servant ran offense and temporarily blocked the First Lady's entrance while Nan was spirited out a side door.

The Duchess probably knew much more than she said, even in

her daily screaming marathons at the President. Both she and her busband were in ill health and spent a great deal of time fulfilling the duties of their positions. Unfailingly gracious and genial in public, they retired to a private life of bitterness and exhaustion. To help compensate for the pain and humiliation of her empty marriage, the Duchess turned to the occult and brought a horde of psychics and mediums into the White House. Her skeptical husband even attended a few of the seances. But the spirit world could offer no miracles for the Harding marriage or the avalanche of corruption which was beginning to saturate his weakly directed administration.

Nan was the only bright spot in the President's increasingly darkened life. There were most likely other women used for much briefer sexual encounters, but Nan held Harding's deepest affections now that Carrie had long since disappeared from the scene. Proud of having finally fathered a child, it must have been agony for him to realize that he could never rescue her from the stigma of illegitimacy.

By 1923, the world of Warren G. Harding was poised at the precipice of total collapse. Gradually, he had become aware of one betrayal of his trust after another by the friends he had so generously divided his power with. Cheating and dishonest financial gain were the hallmarks of his friends' professional behavior. Scandal of immense proportion lurked menacingly on the horizon. There seemed no way out, and Harding tried his best not to confront the complete disgrace and ruin which was inevitable.

Always facing life more honestly and pragmatically than her romantic husband, the Duchess did her best to defend their reputations at all cost. She tackled the Nan Britton affair first. More outraged than ever, she yelled at and hounded the President until the servants at the White House were embarrassed to be near them. Nan must go away—this the First Lady definitely insisted. The affair must end. Harding, threatened with immediate exposure in all aspects of his beleaguered existence, reluctantly agreed and sadly sent Nan off on an extended stay to Europe, that popular place of exile where his other mistress, Carrie Phillips, was living in banishment.

Next, the clever First Lady saw the necessity of capturing the immediate support of the country. Her husband would have to get out of the White House and go out to the people and win their devotion and suppport before any of the government irregularities became public knowledge. To accomplish this, a long, cross-country trip to Alaska was planned. Almost prophetically, one of Harding's guilty administrators committed suicide just before the presidential party departed on their trip.

Everything was all right until, sailing south from Alaska, the President suffered a serious physical breakdown. The party hurried on to San Francisco where Harding, his remaining tour and speech schedule cancelled, was confined to his bed at the Palace Hotel with what was diagnosed by his doctor as food poisoning. In a few days, he seemed beter, but then one evening after the Duchess had been alone with him, he collapsed and died.

The official cause of President Harding's death was listed as a stroke. However, his widow refused to allow an autopsy. She also wouldn't allow a death mask to be made, and she ordered that the body be embalmed immediately. Rigid and as commanding as ever, the Duchess escorted her husband's body back to Washington. She never cried or showed any emotion, even in private with her closest friends.

The rumor soon spread that she had poisoned her husband. It increased in strength when the following year the personal physician of the late President, Dr. Charles Sawyer, died in a similar manner when the Duchess was visiting him alone in his home. However, before the suspicions reached printed form, she died a few months later.

Both Hardings had just missed the sensational storm of the greatest political scandal in American history. Years passed as one corrupt member of Harding's administration after another was brought to justice and found guilty. But the most damaging personal injury came shortly after in the form of literature.

Gaston Means, a former detective and convicted swindler, published *The Strange Death of President Harding* in 1930. In his book he obliquely claimed that Mrs. Harding had murdered her husband by poisoning him in the San Francisco hotel room. He implied that her motive had been revenge for her husband's many infidelities and, most especially, his affair with Nan Britton. Others who picked up this theory have explained the Duchess' suspicious behavior during Harding's death by giving her a far nobler motive. They claimed that she poisoned the President because she knew of the scandal that was about to break and she wanted to spare him the disgrace and the torture that he would have to suffer. Without any concrete evidence either for or against, the rumor has persisted to this day. Another book that had seriously defamed Harding's reputation had been published three years earlier by Nan Britton.

When the President suddenly died, Nan had returned from Europe and married a Swedish ship captain. The marriage quickly collapsed and she was left penniless. Since Harding had left her nothing in his will, she approached his family for support, but they refused to recognize paternity and would not make any payments. Nan hinted blackmail and the family called her bluff. She responded with a book unsubtly titled *The President's Daughter*. Publishing it herself because no company would dare touch it at that time, the book was her life story, with a heavy emphasis on her involvement with Harding. Within a month it had sold over 100,000 copies and became the country's bestselling book.

Nan cloyingly had the last word in her written dedication: "With understanding and love to all unwedded mothers and to their innocent children whose fathers are not usually known to the world."

> *There is always some madness in love. But there is also always some reason in madness.*
>
> —Nietzsche

13

THE BEAST OF BUFFALO

Ironically, one of the greatest sex scandals ever to have rocked the American Presidency involved the son of a devout Presbyterian minister. Grover Cleveland, a thoroughly decent and scrupulously honest man, engaged in a rather wild and sexually loose lifestyle while he was the sheriff of Erie County, New York. It was his unyielding honesty and sense of honor that originally helped create the great scandal which almost deprived him of his chance to become President.

A courageous and pragmatic young man, Cleveland had to make his own way early in life. Of great bulk and sporting a walrus moustache, he was generally considered to be an ugly man, but one of high character and genial personality. During his years as sheriff in Buffalo in the early 1870's, he found that his job placed him socially with the uncouth, easy-living saloon crowd and he found relaxation and diversion from the tensions of his work in their fun-loving company. Respectable ladies were excluded from these social gatherings, but women of easy virtue were most welcome. One of the prettier and more refined of these women was Mrs. Maria Halpin, a thirty-five-year-old widow from New Jersey.

Maria Halpin was bright and vivacious, even though her life had been a difficult one, and she was now working as a collar marker in a factory to support her two small children she had left behind. Hard-working and ambitious, Maria obtained a better job in a department store and quickly rose to a management position when suddenly she was fired. The reason for her swift dismissal was that she was pregnant. She gave birth to a healthy son in September 1874. She named the baby Oscar Folsom Cleveland.

She also named Grover Cleveland as the father.

As determined as ever, Maria lost no time in demanding that the astonished sheriff marry her. Cleveland honestly did not know for sure if the child was his, but since there was the definite possibility that it could be, he stepped forward and acknowledged paternity. However, not being in love with Maria Halpin, he refused to marry her. He did promise to support her and the boy, and he kept his promise. But things did not work out as smoothly as he had hoped, and within a short time any satisfactory arrangement seemed impossible.

Maria was drinking to excess and neglecting the baby. Feeling his full responsibility and realizing that something had to be done, Cleveland had two detectives go to the Halpin house and forcibly take the boy from his mother and place him in a Protestant orphanage until a good family could be found to adopt him. Maria was quickly committed to a Catholic insane asylum without the proper legal proceedings. She stayed only a short time, then was released, and demanded more than ever that her ex-lover support her. Cleveland already was paying her son's fees at the orphanage, but he generously set her up in a small business enterprise in the neighboring town of Niagara Falls and gave her a small sum of money.

This arrangement didn't last either, and Maria was soon back in Buffalo making Cleveland's life miserable again. She hired an attorney and started legal action to regain the custody of her son.

Before the case came to trial, the impetuous woman even attempted to kidnap the child. Cleveland had finally had enough. He offered her a small fortune if she would drop her lawsuit and leave town. Maria eagerly accepted the money and left Buffalo. Cleveland would not hear from her again for almost twenty years.

The boy was quietly adopted by a rich family, and he eventually became a respected doctor in upstate New York. The scandal and gossip rapidly evaporated after Maria disappeared from the scene, and Grover Cleveland was able to be elected mayor of Buffalo and governor or New York without any public mention being made of the illicit incident. But, then, Cleveland ran for President in 1884.

This presidential campaign would win the distinction of being the dirtiest in American history. James G. Blaine was Cleveland's Republican opponent. A charismatic, experienced statesman, Blaine was implicated in several unethical dealings that misused the power of his office. When the Democrats mercilessly pressed their attacks on his character, the Republicans dug deep into Cleveland's clouded personal past and ruthlessly retaliated. Like a thunderbolt from nowhere, the *Evening Telegraph* in Buffalo ran the headline: "A Terrible Tale—A Dark Chapter in Public Man's History." The article with it stated that Maria Halpin gave birth to Cleveland's illegitimate child and that the father abandoned the child in the orphan asylum after stealing him away from his heartbroken mother.

Every paper in the country picked up the story and it caused a sensation throughout the entire population. Before Cleveland had a chance to reply to the sordid accusations, civic leaders and most church groups immediately condemned him and warned voters not to elect him President. The delighted Republicans quickly coined their campaign cry: "Ma! Ma! Where's my Pa?"

The Democratic campaign staff panicked and ran to Cleveland and asked him what they should do. Cleveland calmly responded: "Tell the truth!" And that's what they did. Not only refusing to deny the affair, Cleveland openly admitted it and offered no explanations or apologies. He firmly believed that it was important to establish the truth by confessing to the accurate parts of the news stories so that the even more damaging and sensational falsehoods attached to it could be quickly disproven and set to rest.

When the Democratic Party press sought to exonerate Cleveland by printing a story based on popular gossip that their candidate's late friend and partner, Oscar Folsom, had really been the illegitimate child's father and that Cleveland, a bachelor, had generously claimed paternity to protect the honor of his married friend, Cleveland exploded with outrage and sternly wrote the editor:

> I learned last night that McCune had started the story and told it to newspaper men that I had nothing to do with the subject of the *Telegraph* story—that my silence was to protect my friend Oscar Folsom. Now is this man crazy or does he wish to ruin somebody? Is he fool enough to suppose for one moment that if such was the truth (which it is not, so far as the motive for silence is concerned) that I would permit my dead friend's memory to suffer for my sake? And Mrs. Folsom and her daughter at my house at this very time! I am afraid that I shall have the occasion to pray to be delivered from my friends. . . . This story of McCune's must be stopped. I have prevented its publication in one paper at least.

As the volatile campaign progressed, the issue of Cleveland's moral character assumed an almost hysterical importance. Dubious witnesses stepped forward from every quarter to testify against him with imaginative narratives about his dissipations and debaucheries. The slander reached preposterous proportions. When the beleaguered Democrats sought to defend themselves by collecting as much documented gossip about Blaine's personal life as they could get their hands on, they gathered it together and presented it to Cleveland. He took it and tore it to bits and burned it without even looking at it, quietly announcing: "The other side can have a monopoly on all the dirt in this campaign."

Cleveland maintained a confident dignity throughout the campaign and ignored the malicious attacks as best he could. Week by week as the election drew nearer, condemnation of him intensified and became more severe. It seemed that almost every segment of "decent" society was loudly speaking out against him. The Halpin Affair refused to die down. Maria Halpin even surfaced momentarily in New Rochelle to demand more payments from Cleveland or she would present more embarrassing information. He didn't respond to her and she was never heard from again.

Fortunately for Cleveland, it turned out that perfect timing saved the day. As damaging as the story of the affair was, it ended up doing very little harm to his election. Had it become public knowledge during the Democratic convention, there is no possible way Cleveland would have ever been chosen as the candidate. And had the charges been brought against him just a little later in the campaign, he would not have had enough time to impress the public with his completely honest and straightforward admissions and his maintenance of personal dignity.

Eventually, the passion of the illicit discovery burned itself out and the majority of voters came to an unexpectedly sound and logical conclusion. One political observer of the time accurately summed up popular feeling by saying: "We are told that Mr. Blaine has been delinquent in office but blameless in private life, while Mr. Cleveland has been a model of official integrity but culpable in his personal relations. We should therefore elect Mr. Cleveland to public office, which he is so qualified to fill, and remand Mr. Blaine to the private station which he is admirably fitted to adorn."

It was a close contest, but Grover Cleveland was victorious and won the election. Thus, the jubilant Democrats loudly chanted: "Ma! Ma! Where's my Pa? Gone to the White House, Ha! Ha! Ha!"

As soon as the controversial bachelor President arrived in

Washington, he was besieged by a barrage of matrimonially ambitious matrons who eagerly paraded their nubile daughters for his inspection. To their great surprise, the man with the notorious womanizing reputation politely turned away and showed no interest whatsoever in seeking female companionship. What they didn't know was that the new President, who had only recently been dubbed "The Beast of Buffalo" by a hostile press, had a deep secret: He was already in love.

And an even greater shock to the public would have been the discovery of his beloved's identity. She was the extraordinarily beautiful Frances Folsom, the young daughter of Cleveland's late friend and former law partner, Oscar Folsom. Ever since Oscar's untimely death, Cleveland had faithfully cared for his widow and adolescent daughter. He had brought Frances toys and even went as far as to be declared her legal guardian. She had affectionately responded by calling him "Uncle Cleve." Theirs was a tender and devoted relationship. The tough-as-nails bachelor worshipped the soft, pretty child, and to his sister he secretly confided that he was "waiting for my wife to grow up."

Away at college when Cleveland became President, Frances had her dormitory room constantly filled with lush bouquets of flowers from her "Uncle Cleve." It was of vital importance, however, for Cleveland to keep this romantic attachment totally hidden. After his savage treatment by the press and public opinion during the recent campaign, he did everything in his power to protect Frances' reputation. Whatever the cost, he did not want her involved in a fresh scandal.

With great care, Cleveland covered his tracks and kept the whole country guessing. Even after he had proposed to Frances and she had accepted him, he maintained the total secrecy of their romantic relationship. To the eyes of the eagerly watching public, he was merely a kind and conscientious guardian selflessly seeing to the needs of his pretty young ward. This charade was success

172

Grover Cleveland, known as the notorious "Beast of Buffalo," put his sordid past behind him when he married a lovely teenager named Frances Folsom. The nation's press went berserk, following the newlywed presidential couple on their honeymoon. The private life of an American Chief Executive would never be "private" again.

fully played out all the way up to five days before the White House wedding when the first formal announcement was made to the nation.

The news of the surprise marriage caused a fantastic sensation. Most of the reactions were extremely unfavorable. The fact that the President was forty-nine and the bride twenty-two prompted outraged and sometimes obscene comment. Many newspapers again ran stories about the Halpin Affair and insinuated that Frances' father might have been more actively involved in the illicit hijinks than previously thought. The long-suffering President wearily witnessed just what he had expected. Again he kept his dignity and remained silent.

The wedding took place in June in the East Room of the White House. It was as private as Cleveland could make it. Only thirty-one guests attended the brief ceremony. But when the press got hold of the bride's photograph, a tidal wave swept over public opinion. The statuesque, raven-haired beauty with perfect, classic features, flawless white skin, and flashing dark eyes instantly captured the nation's heart. Within days it became fashionable to see the marriage in terms of a great and good romance, an idyllic dream come true. Sympathy now, at last, was completely with the new President and his stunning bride. Perhaps too much sympathy.

As the Clevelands departed on their honeymoon to a remote resort in the western hills of Maryland, the nature of the American press was suddenly transformed forever. From that time on, it became imperative for the public to know as much as humanly possible about every aspect of the Chief Executive's private life. The newlyweds woke up on the first morning of their honeymoon to discover a flock of newsmen surrounding their lodge and spying on them with field glasses. Never again would any President be able to escape from the full-time, telescopic gaze of the entire American population.

Returning to Washington, President Cleveland finally lost his cool and made a public statement for the New York *Evening Post*:

> They, the journalists, have used the enormous power of the modern newspaper to perpetuate and disseminate a colossal impertinence, and have done it, not as professional gossips and

tatlers, but as the guides and instructors of the public in conduct and morals. And they have done it, not to a private citizen, but to the President of the United States, thereby lifting their offense into the gaze of the whole world, and doing their utmost to make American journalism contemptible in the estimation of good breeding everywhere.

———————————

So resentful was Cleveland towards his brutal treatment by the press and the intense passion and fickle loyalty of public opinion that he built a home in the country near Georgetown and practically refused to live in the White House, moving in only during the winter months for the social season. However, he and his gorgeous wife charmed all of society and became an exceptionally popular couple.

Failing to be re-elected, Cleveland waited four years and then became the first and only President to be returned to a second non-consecutive term of office. By then the Republican opposition had fully exhausted the sensational mileage of the Halpin scandal, so they became more creative in their attacks and spread the word that the President was a drunk who beat his wife. Mrs. Cleveland, used to the character of American politics, smiled tolerantly and gracefully replied: "I could wish for American women no greater blessing than that their lives be as happy and their husband may be as kind, attentive, considerate, and affectionate as mine."

And one look at the supremely happy marriage of the adoring husband and devoted wife put a swift end to this new gossip. Soon, further proof came forth to testify to the happiness of the Clevelands: a daughter was born to them—the first baby ever born to a President in the White House.

*There is no remedy for love but
to love more.*
　　　　　　—Henry David Thoreau

14

MR. PRESIDENT AND HIS
SLAVE MISTRESS

The most shocking and controversial illicit presidential affair ironically involves one of the nation's most esteemed and respected Chief Executives, Thomas Jefferson. This multi-talented Renaissance man who is credited with being the intellectual father of the American democratic system and the leading spirit behind the founding of the new country is also credited with being the lover of one of his beautiful black slaves, fathering several illegitimate children by her, and keeping her as his secret mistress for the entire length of his residency in the White House.

Like Washington and Adams, Thomas Jefferson also possessed an extraordinary passionate and romantic temperament. His early home life was also very similar to that of our first President. Jefferson lost his father when he was a child, and his relations with his mother were problematic and charged with much hostility. This love-hate relationship between mother and son produced in Jefferson a pronounced need for feminine affection

177

and companionship throughout his entire life. He would always be attracted to very soft, feminine, subservient women who never challenged his role of complete mastery.

Although forever concerned with the philosophical constructs of moral and ethical questions, Jefferson seems to have been both adventurous and pragmatic about his own sexual morality. Before his marriage he pursued several young women and even once tried seriously to seduce the attractive wife of his close friend, John Walker. When Jefferson did finally marry in 1772 when he was twenty-eight, he chose a pretty young widow five years his junior named Martha Skelton. The marriage was an exceedingly happy one and produced six children, two of whom survived to reach adulthood. However, Jefferson's joyful union was to last only ten years. After a difficult labor, Martha gave birth to another daughter and then lapsed into a prolonged illness from which she never recovered.

During her final days, Martha Jefferson whispered to her devoted husband that she could not stand the idea of another woman ever coming into the household and taking her place with the children. Jefferson gave his wife his sacred pledge that this would never happen—that he would never remarry.

He kept this promise. He never married again. But only a few years were to creep by before he would realize the inescapable need for what was so vital to his nature.

The premature loss of his young wife only further intensified Jefferson's insecure personality and produced a greater need to compensate through extreme possessiveness and complete dominance in his personal relationships. At first, this was focused on his two young daughters with whom he was neurotically concerned. Then, in 1784, he was sent to France where he remained for several years as American ambassador. Not a Puritan like John Adams, Jefferson would discover the sensuality of Parisian society to be a totally liberating influence.

Walking the stately avenues and strolling through the delicate gardens of the French capital, Jefferson soon found his vibrant romantic soul soaring with hope once again. He objected almost as strenuously as Adams did to the gross sexual immorality of the French. But a true and deep love attachment was a necessity for any man, he thought, and a sincere romance was a good and noble thing.

Jefferson quickly fell in love. She was Maria Cosway, the wife of an effeminate English portraitist. Unhappily married, Maria and her husband had an understanding that not only gave the beautiful young blonde the freedom to pursue a serious flirtation, but also permitted Jefferson to remain close friends with both. The affair with Maria Cosway lasted for more than a year. Of an ultra-romantic nature, their relationship seemed doomed almost from the beginning. Not only was the lady married, but she was emotionally unstable and with too much independence and spirit for Jefferson's tastes. After a series of tempestuous quarrels and misunderstandings, the two lovers eventually separated for good. Maria later abandoned her husband and child and retired to a convent.

Just before the final break with Maria, Jefferson entered into one of the strangest and most sensational relationships in Presidential history. His daughter, Patsy, arrived from Virginia to keep him company. Accompanying Patsy was a fifteen-year-old black slave named Sally Hemings. Within a short time, Sally would become Jefferson's mistress, and she would remain so for many years.

That this affair took place is the most controversial and hotly debated issue among Jefferson's many biographers and historians. Because the illicit relationship came to light during Jefferson's Presidency and was used by his political enemies against him in the most vulgar and ruthless personal attacks, it has consequently been suspect to scholars who could not help questioning its truth because of the vile character-assassinating motives behind it. Also there have been staunch defenders of the Jeffersonian image who seem to argue from a clear point of prejudice. These researchers usually are from the South and undoubtedly have biased opinions and moral judgments concerning the delicate matter of miscegenation. They argue as defense attorneys rather than as objective historians willing to accept valid evidence and piece it together to form logical conclusions.

In the case of Thomas Jefferson and Sally Hemings, the evidence and conclusions are unmistakable to any logical, open mind. There was most definitely an affair of considerable duration, although the details of it remain sketchy and vague.

Before going to Paris with Patsy Jefferson, Sally Hemings was one of several hundred black slaves that Jefferson owned at Monticello. Jefferson had inherited Sally and her family and more than a hundred other slaves from his father-in-law, John Wayles, upon his death in 1774. Wayles had been a slave trader, a profession which Jefferson thoroughly detested, and had kept as his concubine one of the most attractive of his "properties," Betty Hemings. Betty was the mother of fourteen children—seven fathered by white men, and seven fathered by black. Sally was the light-skinned mulatto daughter of Betty Hemings and John Wayles. Thus, she was the half-sister of Jefferson's beloved wife, Martha.

The Hemings family became firmly established at Monticello and received unusually special treatment from the Jefferson family. Granted uncommon rights and privileges for slaves, they were given highly favored positions as household servants. Martha Jefferson showed great kindness and concern for her father's former mistress and her mulatto half-sisters and brothers during her lifetime, and she even had Betty Hemings in attendance upon her when she was dying of her lingering illness. This full acceptance of John Wayles' sexual indiscretion by his daughter and the strong and vivid model of Wayles' miscegenation itself were important factors for what Jefferson would later initiate in France.

When Jefferson had left for Europe, Sally was only a child of twelve. The somber widower had always shown a fatherly interest in this special slave. But two and a half years later, when Sally entered his home in Paris, Jefferson was shocked speechless.

Sally Hemings had sexually blossomed into a woman. And the beautiful woman she had become was a dusky mirror-image of Jefferson's dearly-loved wife, Martha.

Sally had a gorgeous, olive-colored complexion and long, straight auburn hair. She also possessed a beautiful profile, sensuous lips, and the elegant bearing of a refined lady. It was the great similarity of looks and personality between Sally and his late wife that must have moved Jefferson so profoundly on so many different levels.

He had promised Martha never to remarry. He was still the same insecure personality who constantly craved total dominance and control over his relationships. And he was now fully returned to his passionately romantic disposition, thanks to the previous interval of Maria Cosway. Thus, circumstances combined to move Jefferson easily towards the decision he was about to make.

As the affair began, it caused Jefferson a great deal of guilt. It involved all that had been alluring and forbidden in the world of his past. Out of necessity to his social position, political aspirations, moral conscience, and refined sensibilities, he adopted a theme of complete and utter secrecy surrounding his involvement with Sally. No direct mention of it was ever made by him in written statement or spoken word to anyone. And when later charged publicly with the illicit affair by his enemies, he remained consistently quiet, never making the slightest effort to defend his reputation and deny the accusations.

In Paris, Jefferson employed Sally in a privileged position in his mansion and separated her from the other servants. He hired a tutor to teach her French and spent large sums of money buying her dresses and fashionable apparel. Jefferson was falling deeply in love. By the end of her first twenty months abroad, Sally Hemings was pregnant with Jefferson's child. Six months later plans were made for a sudden return to America. There was a serious complication. In France, Sally was a free woman, as

Thomas Jefferson, one of the nation's most illustrious Founding Fathers, led a dangerous double life following the death of his-wife. Among other indiscretions, the writer of the Declaration of Independence was the secret father of several children by one of his black Virginia slaves, Sally Hemings. Sally lived on, at Monticello, for two years following Jefferson's death.

French law forbade slavery. If she were to return to the Jefferson home in Virginia, she would lose her freedom and become re-enslaved. Sally had grown to enjoy her liberty and she had just begun to understand the French language. To Jefferson's great surprise, she refused to return home with him.

Jefferson took Sally in his arms and tried to change her mind with tender, passionate words. But this did no good. He, then, tried to plead with her, but this also didn't work. At last, desperate, he made extraordinary promises to her, granting great privileges. He gave Sally his sacred word that any children she might have would be freed at the age of twenty-one. Sally must also have had a sincere love for Jefferson. She agreed to return home to Virginia.

They immediately sailed home. Arriving at Monticello, Sally watched the humble slaves worshipfully greet their master. She could not fail to notice more acutely than ever the meaning of the institution of slavery. She most likely doubted her decision to come back voluntarily to her enslavement. She must have loved Jefferson a great deal to have made such a sacrifice.

Within a short time, Sally gave birth to Jefferson's son. She appropriately called him Tom. Tom would grow up to look so much like his father that many visitors to Monticello commented that he was often mistaken for him at a distance. It would be this remarkable likeness that in the future brought about the great scandal concerning Sally that plagued Jefferson's stay in the White House.

Installed firmly into the household of Monticello, Sally personally conducted the duties of taking care of Jefferson's private chambers and his wardrobe. She also undertook light work such as sewing, and when she gave birth to more children she would take charge of them and spend much time in maternal cares. This would be Sally's entire life for the next thirty-five years until Thomas Jefferson's death. Perhaps to show her that he intended to keep his promise and free their children when they became adults, he freed her older brother Robert four years after they returned from France, and her brother James two years later.

Sally's own family grew rapidly. In 1795 she had another

child, a daughter she named Harriet, and she gave birth the following year to another little girl she called Edy. These pregnancies occurred during the three-year seclusion of Jefferson at Monticello, a mysterious period of his life during which he received very few visitors and intended to retire permanently from public life. Both daughters died in infancy, and in April 1798 Sally gave birth to another child, a boy whom she named Beverly.

While Jefferson was fathering these children by Sally and simultaneously freeing her brothers, the question of her own freedom must have caused a constant problem. Today it seems incredible that such an obviously sincere and committed love relationship could have endured so long on the barbaric master-slave level. However, at the time, for Jefferson to have freed Sally would have meant he would lose her. In the South it was relatively common practice for a master to carry on a liaison with one of his slaves. It was easily accomplished by means of a relentlessly mutual denial in an atmosphere of secrecy. But to carry on the same affair with free black woman was a very dangerous and difficult matter. If it were to become public knowledge, it could ruin a man's reputation totally. And the closer Jefferson came to the Presidency, the more he worried about his public image and the more he feared the discovery of his involvement with Sally Hemings.

As long as Sally remained a slave, she would not be a serious threat to his career. If he were to set her free, he would be forced to give her up and end the relationship. The hypocrisy of such a decision was a terrible thing for the conscience of an honest and liberal man like Jefferson. He was opposed to slavery, in general, and found many conflicting aspects of his life difficult to justify. But he was also an ambitious man, and he would not ever seriously consider jeopardizing his social standing and political ambition for a futile confrontation with his moral beliefs.

In May 1801, only three months after his inauguration as the third President of the United States, Jefferson was a father once again when Sally gave birth to another daughter. At this same time a political enemy of Jefferson's named James Callender was snooping around the Charlottesville countryside collecting damaging information on the President's liaison with the beautiful black slave. The "yellow children" of Monticello, Sally and Jefferson's offspring, had long been an object of curiosity and whispered speculation. No one had ever dared confront Jefferson with direct questions about it before, and the new President was notorious for never talking about any subject he did not wish to speak about. But now Callender threatened to make the affair public and tell the world.

At first, hoping to profit privately, Callender, an unscrupulous man, tried to blackmail the President and his friends. When this didn't work out to his satisfaction, he took his facts to the press. On September 1, 1802, Callender wrote a shocking, scandalous article in the relatively new Federalist newspaper, the *Richmond Recorder:*

> It is well known that the man, whom it delighteth the people to honor, keeps and for many years has kept, as his concubine, one of his slaves. Her name is SALLY. The name of her eldest son is Tom. His features are said to bear a striking resemblance to those of the President himself. The boy is ten or twelve years of age. His mother went to France in the same vessel with Mr. Jefferson and his two daughters. The delicacy of this arrangement must strike every portion of common sensibility. What a sublime pattern for an American ambassador to place before the eyes of two young ladies! . . .
>
> Some years ago, the story had once or twice been hinted at in *Rinds Federalist.* At that time, we believed the surmise to be an absolute calumny . . .
>
> By this wench Sally, our president has had several children. There is not an individual in the neighbourhood of Charlottesville who does not believe the story, and not a few who know it . . . Mute!

Mute! Mute! Yes very Mute! will all those republican printers of biographical information be upon this point.

This was the first public attack on the private life of an elected American President. The article created a sensation. Three weeks later Callender wrote another in which he corrected the factual error he made regarding the sailing arrangements of Jefferson and Sally to France. As the storm of controversy raged, Jefferson maintained a total silence. He let his supporters and enemies furiously battle it out. He never acknowledged, let alone answered, the charges against him. While most of Jefferson's friends defended his reputation and refused to believe the story, John Adams, the former President under whom Jefferson had served as Vice President, was a notable exception. He had seen Sally Hemings in London and he knew Jefferson's character very well. He believed Callender's story.

Every newspaper in the country picked up and reported the story of Jefferson and Sally Hemings. Some held Callender's story in total contempt, while others seemed to rejoice in it and add rumors and speculations of their own. Within a month of its first appearance, the topic had gained such heated strength that many popular verses and ballads began circulating in society. One of the more popular ballads appeared first in the *Boston Gazette* and then in the Philadelphia *Port Folio* on October 2, 1802. It was set to the tune of Yankee Doodle and went:

> Of all the damsels on the green,
> On mountain, or in valley,
> A lass so luscious ne'er was seen,
> As Monticellian Sally.
>
> Yankee doodle, who's the noodle?
> What wife were half so handy?
> To breed a flock of slaves for stock,
> A blackamoor's the dandy.

Search every town and city through,
Search market, street, and alley;
No dame at dusk shall meet your view,
So yielding as my Sally.

Yankee doodle, who's the noodle?
What wife were half so handy?
To breed a flock of slaves for stock,
A blackamoor's the dandy.

When press'd by loads of state affairs
I seek to sport and dally
The sweetest solace of my cares
Is in the lap of Sally.

There were much more profane sayings that appeared in print and were recited and sung by a large segment of the American populace. The irreverent and vulgar jokes and parodies of modern-day stand-up comics are mild in comparison to the brutal popular humor of early American life. Jefferson secluded himself at Monticello as much as he could during the storm of personal attacks. Young Tom, Sally and Jefferson's eldest child and the most damaging evidence of their liaison, either slipped away or was sent off to live somewhere else shortly after. For more than two years the scandal raged at fever pitch. Then it gradually began dying down. By 1805 it still occasionally found its way into the papers, but the highly emotional reaction of the public had subsided and the affair was considered a dead issue.

A third son, Madison, had been born to Sally and Jefferson, and later in his life he was to write of his famous white father: "He was uniformly kind to all about him. He was not in the habit of showing partiality or fatherly affection to us children. We were the only children of his by a slave woman. He was affectionate toward his white grandchildren, of whom he had fourteen, twelve of whom lived to manhood and womanhood."

This rejection was to be expected of such a situation. Part of the result of miscegenation in the rural South was a cool behavior towards the offspring which functioned as a constant and silent denial of parentage. Jefferson was no different from the others who worked within such a strict code.

Although the public accusations and resulting scandal might have convinced Jefferson of the necessity of sending Sally and their children away to live somewhere else, he refused to do so. He never could bring himself to abandon his slave family. After the scandal broke, Jefferson's two oldest daughters pleaded with him to do this very thing, but he still refused. They would not visit him at Monticello for some time because of it. One of Jefferson's granddaughters, Ellen Randolph Coolidge, remembered seeing the "yellow children" at Monticello and described one or two of them as "white enough to pass for white."

In 1807, during Jefferson's second term in office, Sally gave birth to their last child, a son who would be named Eston. As time passed and Sally matured to middle age while Jefferson approached old age, the sexual passion of their relationship diminished and a calmer affection took its place. Thus, the troublesome question of illicit miscegenation became largely one of the past and Jefferson's conscience seems to have been quieted somewhat. Leaving the White House and returning to his beloved Monticello, Jefferson enjoyed an active retirement surrounded by both his black and his white family. And, true to his word, he kept his promises to Sally Hemings regarding the future of their children.

These children were separated from the other slaves at Monticello and given special duties. They were permitted to stay around the mansion and required to do very light work such as going on errands. At age fourteen they were given schooling in some mechanical trade, usually carpentry for the boys and weaving and gardening for the girls. They also received a considerable amount of academic schooling, possibly with Jefferson's white grandchildren.

Madison Hemings wrote later of his older brother: "Beverly left Monticello and went to Washington as a white man. He married a white woman in Maryland and their only child, a daughter, was not known by the white folks to have any colored blood coursing in her veins. Beverly's wife's family were people in good circumstances."

Of his sister Harriet's fate, he wrote:

> Harriet married a white man in good standing in Washington City, whose name I could give, but will not, for prudential reasons. She raised a family of children, and so far as I know they were never suspected of being tainted with African blood in the community where she lived or lives. I have not heard from her for ten years, and do not know whether she is dead or alive. She thought it to her interest, on going to Washington, to assume the role of a white woman, and by her dress and conduct as much I am not aware that her identity as Harriet Hemings of Monticello has ever been discovered.

All of the five children were allowed to quietly slip away from Monticello and no attempts ever were made to find them once they were adults. But Sally Hemings remained with the elderly ex-President and loyally took care of him in his declining years.

Thomas Jefferson died in 1826 when Sally was fifty-three. In his will he freed the entire Hemings family—except Sally. As incredible as it may seem, Sally was left as inherited property along with the other ordinary slaves at Monticello to Jefferson's daughter Martha. This must have been deliberately done by him as a further protection for his past and her future. The great humiliation of the scandal that rocked his first Presidency was enough to prompt Jefferson to keep Sally as much out of the public eye as possible, even after his death. To have freed Sally with the others would have forced her to leave Virginia, in compliance with the state law, or seek residency through a special petition, one that would rekindle the personal attacks and vicious debates.

Thus, Sally lived on at Monticello for two years after Jefferson's death. Then, as had been previously planned, Sally was quietly given her freedom by Martha Jefferson. She joined the other members of her family living in a small house beneath the hill. She died there in complete obscurity in 1835 at the age of sixty-two. So ended one of the most extraordinary chapters of private presidential history.

Let the dead have the immortality of fame,
but the living the immortality of love.
                              —Rabindranath Tagore

15

CALM WATERS

erhaps because of the furor created by the Sally Hemings scandal, the personal lives of the American Chief Executives for the next several decades following Jefferson's term of office were unusually free from rumors of illicit secret relationships. Jefferson's unfortunate experience at the ruthless hands of the press must have been a vivid lesson well-taken by his fellow Southerners who would succeed him to the White House.

The next President was James Madison, a close friend of Jefferson's and his protégé. Madison was a talented little man, standing only 5'4" high and weighing less than 100 pounds. Boyish and delicate of health, he was an extremely hard worker. A form of epilepsy in his adolescence had made Madison insecure and hesitant in his love life. Already unpopular with the ladies because of his unimpressive stature, he unsuccessfully attempted a romance or two with results so disastrous that his ego forced him to withdraw into a lonely isolation for several years.

Madison remained an introverted bachelor until he was forty-four. It was then that he married the remarkably vivacious and warm-hearted Dolley Todd, a young widow of twenty-six. They became a devoted couple and Madison loved his wife with the fervor of a sacred worship. There was never a hint of scandal during their marriage, and, by all reports, it was an unusually happy and satisfying one, even though they never had any children. Dolley won the reputation of America's most popular and best-loved First Lady.

Another Jeffersonian disciple was handsome James Monroe, who became the fifth President of the United States. Of humble origins, Monroe fell in love with and married Elizabeth Kortwright, the beautiful and haughty daughter of a wealthy New York merchant. Elizabeth was an exceedingly elegant and stylish woman, the center of family attention, and the dominant force in Monroe's personal life. High-handed and regal, she took a great interest in her husband's advancing career and saw to it that his two terms of office had the pomp and glamour of a royal court.

Monroe was a faithful and attentive husband and unfailingly indulged the aristocratic tastes of his queenly wife. This eventually resulted in so much free spending on her part that they constantly had serious financial problems after leaving the White House.

The illustrious Adams family returned to the Chief Executive's office again when John and Abigail's pride and joy, their brilliant son John Quincy, became a one-term President in 1825. The focus of his dynasty's entire hope and ambition, John Quincy had started life a high-spirited and personable young man of great charm and intellectual gifts who won all hearts around him. The much-admired youth had an eye for the girls and entered one juvenile romantic infatuation after another. However, his ultra-strict, Puritanical parents saw to it that business always came first. Abigail constantly interfered in her son's love life and turned thumbs down on each and every marital candidate in whom he showed any serious interest.

John Quincy Adams seems to have finally fallen victim to his parent's rigid code of self-denial and material ambition. Serving in Europe as a diplomatic representative to Holland, Adams courted Louisa Johnson in a very cool and business-like manner. Louisa was the daughter of an American merchant living in London. She was both confused and somewhat tortured by Adams' casual and sporadic pursuit of her. They were finally married and spent the first years together in various royal courts of Europe. The marriage soon cooled to a functional partnership and Louisa was forced to reconcile herself early in life to a passionless union with a man who lived only for his work and his material advancement.

The difficult partnership lasted for more than fifty years. By the time he became President, John Quincy Adams was a cold and forbidding man. Plump, bald, and generally unattractive, his name was never mentioned in any kind of romantic or sexual association. His long-suffering wife, after the suicide of their drunken, poetic, eldest son, would write: "As it regards women, the Adams family are one and all peculiarly harsh and severe in their characters. There seems to exist no sympathy, no tenderness for the weakness of the sex."

Following Adams to the White House was Andrew Jackson, the subject of a legendary personal scandal that threatened the entire prestige of the Presidency, and one which is treated fully in the next chapter. His successor was even more staid and asexual than John Quincy Adams. He was a New Yorker of Dutch parentage named Martin Van Buren. Van Buren was twenty-five when he married his cousin, Hannah Hoes, in 1807. During the twelve years of their marriage she gave birth to four sons and devoted herself entirely to being a conscientious homebody. The dull, plain woman died in 1819, when Van Buren was thirty-six. He never remarried, nor did he become involved with another woman. Every ounce of his tepid passion was poured into his political ambitions. Women held little position or interest in Van Buren's life, even during his tranquil, somber marriage. When he wrote his autobiography in his later years, he never even mentioned his wife's name—not once!

Almost as if to make up for the romantic bankruptcy of the Van Buren administration. the Vice President of the United States provided an even greater scandal than the Jefferson–Hemings affair. The man's name was Richard Johnson and he showed a personal courage and sense of honesty higher than any national leader before or since. Johnson openly and freely admitted that he had two daughters by a black slave named Julia Chinn. He not only acknowledged these children, but he also publicly paid for their support and saw to it that they were given excellent educations. When Johnson attempted to introduce his mulatto daughters into white society, they were savagely snubbed. However, the politician never gave up his efforts and eventually he saw to it that his girls married white men and that his property was inherited by them. The scandal shocked the whole country like no other ever had, but Richard Johnson ignored the vicious attacks of public opinion and refused to give up his career. Thus, he finally succeeded in defeating the scandal and became Vice President during the quiet Presidency of Martin Van Buren.

William Henry Harrison was the next Chief Executive in the White House, but he had a very short stay—only thirty-one days. Harrison's term was the briefest in American history. He caught pneumonia while delivering his two-hour inaugural address in a cold rain and his condition deteriorated until his untimely death.

Harrison had eloped many years before with Anna Symmes, the daughter of the former Chief Justice of the New Jersey Supreme Court. Beginning their marriage in a log cabin on the Indiana frontier, the Harrisons had ten children and enjoyed a solid partnership. There are no records of any extra-marital romances during his long military career, and, since he spent his entire month as President in a sick bed, he was not a possible subject for gossip or scandal.

Vice President John Tyler assumed the Presidency upon Harrison's sudden death. A Virginia aristocrat, Tyler had married Letitia Christian when he was twenty-three. It was a very happy marriage and produced seven children. However, circumstances were to conspire to eventually catapult John Tyler into one of the most talked-about romantic scandals in White House history.

Before Tyler became President, his wife had developed a partial paralysis and she became an invalid as her health declined rapidly. Two years after entering the White House, Letitia Tyler died. The president genuinely mourned for his wife for several months, but customs of the times would have liked a much lengthier period of grief. Tyler was a man almost helplessly dependent upon feminine support and companionship. The void in his life, now, was nearly intolerable. Within a year of his wife's death, he was going out with the ladies. Washington society looked on with severe disapproval. Although Tyler's behavior was most gentlemanly and circumspect, gossip flourished and the unpopularity of his Presidency hit a new low.

Matters did not improve when Tyler focused his interest on one target, Julia Gardiner, the daughter of a New York millionaire. When a gun exploded accidentally during a pleasure cruise on the Potomac, Julia's father was killed and Tyler tenderly escorted the stunned and grief-stricken daughter back to the White House. The President's great kindness and sympathy totally conquered Julia's heart, and four months later, on June 28, 1844, the fifty-four-year-old President and his twenty-four-year-old sweetheart were married in New York City.

The wedding shocked the nation and kept people talking for the remainder of Tyler's term of office. Julia, with her raven-haired beauty and spectacular hourglass figure, proudly took her place as First Lady while Washington society smiled to her face and whispered viciously behind her back. Tyler left office a half year later and retired to an exceptionally happy life with his new wife. Julia, not to be surpassed by her predecessor, also presented Tyler with seven children, the last one born in the ex-President's seventieth year!

The next President was James K. Polk, a grim, uninspiring little man who was a work-obsessed bureaucrat. He married Sarah Childress, a strict Presbyterian like himself, when he was twenty-nine. Their quarter-century of marriage never produced any offspring, but James and Sarah were an inseparable couple who found fulfillment in the advancement of his political career.

Sarah worked closely with her husband as his personal secretary, putting in twelve-hour days. Dancing and drinking were banned at the White House, and there was so little social diversion during Polk's administration that the question of extramarital dalliance was a preposterous one. Polk's dying words were addressed to his devoted wife: "I love you, Sarah, for all eternity, I love you."

The twelfth President of the United States, Zachary Taylor, was the second one to die in office. A military career man rather than a politician, he resided in the White House for little more than a year before his sudden death from over-eating. A rough-living Army officer, Taylor married Margaret Smith of Maryland and spent almost their entire marriage dragging her and their six children from one remote frontier post to another. The extreme hardship of their existence combined with the danger and the long periods of separation while Taylor was on campaign made Margaret a bitter, somber woman. Almost an invalid by the time her husband became President, she became something of a recluse in the White House and refused to appear in public or attend special ceremonies. A crude and masculine man, Zachary Taylor may have sought brief romantic liaisons elsewhere, but no proof of this has ever come to light.

———————

Taylor's Vice President, Millard Fillmore, who succeeded him, was an average man of great respectability. As a high school student he had fallen in love with his teacher, Abigail Powers, a girl only two years his senior. Abigail was a kindly young woman, the daughter of a Baptist minister, and she waited seven years for Fillmore to mature and set himself up in a successful law practice before she married him. They enjoyed a happy comfortable marriage without ever a suggestion of scandal until Abigail died suddenly, just after Fillmore left the White House. Devastated by his wife's death and by that of his only daughter shortly after, Fillmore withdrew from an active social life until he married a wealthy fifty-four-year-old widow five years later.

———————

The fourteenth President, Franklin Pierce, was an unhappily married alcoholic. At college he had fallen in love with Jane Appleton, the daughter of the college's former president. A very beautiful and refined woman, Jane was also extremely sensitive and high-strung. The wedding was postponed for more than ten years while the mercilessly self-disciplined Pierce struggled to gain wealth and legal success. Married at age thirty, Pierce began experiencing tragic sorrows from the very start. Their first son died right after birth, then a second son died in early childhood, and the surviving third was killed in an accident when he was a teenager. Jane Pierce's sanity gradually collapsed and she became an unbalanced religious fanatic, withdrawing from life, always dressing in black, and spending most of her days writing letters to her dead sons.

The marriage was a sad and severely strained relationship. Pierce escaped as best he could into his work and the bottle. There was never any hint of romantic impropriety on his part, and after he served his term of office, he quietly retired to his New England home and his drinking. During his presidential campaign, a favorite slogan of the opposition had been: "Pierce—the hero of many a well fought *bottle*."

Yet each man kills the thing he loves,
By each let this be heard,
Some do it with a bitter look,
Some with a flattering word,
The coward does it with a kiss,
The brave man with a sword!
     —Oscar Wilde

16

THE RELUCTANT
BIGAMIST

A midst the relative calm in the White House during the first half of the nineteenth century came a monumental storm. It was discovered after two years of marriage that Andrew Jackson's wife, Rachel, had another husband, alive and in excellent health. The great scandal that ensued followed Jackson to his grave.

From humble origins, Jackson grew up a wild and untamed personality on the American frontier. He lost his entire family by the time he was fourteen and he had to fight his way through life to get anything he wanted. This extreme adversity helped to create one of the most paranoid and emotionally unbalanced men who ever sat in the Oval Office.

While living in Nashville, Tennessee, Jackson made the acquaintance of the Donelson family and rented a room in their modest home. Also in the household was Rachel Robards, a married daughter of the family who temporarily had fled from her husband and returned home. Rachel was the wife of Captain

Lewis Robards, an insanely jealous and possessive man with an incredibly mean temperament. After raging violently when any man so much as looked in Rachel's direction, he sought to punish and humiliate his innocent wife by sending her home to her mother in Nashville. Plain-looking, gentle, and unassuming, Rachel quickly became friends with the young Jackson. It was probably the woman's maternal qualities that most attracted the acutely insecure Jackson. He was most desperately in need of a solid mother substitute in his life, having lost his own mother when only a child.

When Captain Robards angrily reappeared on the scene to drag Rachel back to his home in Kentucky, the two men quarreled violently. Jackson suddenly realized that he was in love with Rachel and, to avoid trouble, he moved to another boarding house. Robards sullenly returned to Kentucky without his estranged wife, and Rachel quietly let it be known to Jackson that she had also fallen in love with him. In a seemingly hopeless dilemma and constantly threatened by the immediate return of her embittered spouse, Rachel decided to abandon Nashville and spend time visiting friends down the Mississippi River in Natchez.

Offering to escort the docile woman safely on the dangerous journey, Jackson went with her in the early part of 1791 to Natchez. He left Rachel there and sadly returned to Nashville to spend several lonely months trying to reconcile himself to the total hopelessness of his great love. Just as he was reaching the depths of his despair, a rumor arrived that summer that Lewis Robards had been successful in securing a divorce from Rachel from the Virginia legislature.

Jackson, wanting to make sure of the rumor's validity, sent a good friend to Kentucky to confirm it. The friend, John Overton, returned to Nashville convinced that it was true. Not wishing to argue further with his amazing good fortune, Andrew Jackson instantly took off for Natchez and joyfully told Rachel the good news. He proposed on the spot and swept her into an immediate marriage. Returning to live in Nashville, the couple was idyllically happy and extremely popular within the community. Their perfect happiness was to last only a short time: After two years of marriage, the incredible news arrived that Lewis Robards had, in fact, never been granted a legal divorce.

Because of the complex laws of Virginia regarding divorce, Robards had merely begun the proceedings in 1791 and his petition had yet to go to trial when Jackson so impulsively rushed into his marriage with Rachel in Natchez. Thus, he had exquisitely played into the ruthless hands of Robards, who then swiftly moved, after his wife's new marriage, to seek a more simple and damning solution from the Kentucky Supreme Court. They immediately granted Robards a divorce on the grounds of Rachel's obvious adultery.

The embarrassed Jacksons were married in a second ceremony on January 17, 1794. Their friends and neighbors in Nashville stoically accepted the accident of their first ill-timed marriage, but the population at large listened with shock to Lewis Robards' claim that his wife had lived in open adultery with another man. Jackson's reputation was severely injured and his method of putting all and any gossip to rest only made the scandal blaze hotter. Anyone who Jackson felt had questioned his wife's honor, he would madly challenge to a duel. Jackson fought dozens of these avenging duels. Twice he was seriously wounded, and once he killed a man in cold blood.

The talk only increased. It plagued Andrew Jackson every time he ran for public office. Rachel hated his political ambitions for the very reason that she was made the target of savagely vicious personal attacks. During the Presidential campaign of 1828, Jackson kept his wife as secluded as he could at their home in Tennessee,thus hoping to protect her from the vulgar and brutal slurs which were the bulk of the opposition's strategy. Rachel was popularly referred to throughout the country as "the harlot" and "the immoral adulteress." Many went so far as to call her a common prostitute.

A portrait by an unknown artist of Rachel Donelson Jackson. Young Andrew met her in Nashville when she had fled her cruel husband, Captain Lewis Robards, in Kentucky. Jackson married her in 1791 when Robards appeared to have divorced her, but the divorce was not yet complete, and the two were remarried, embarrassingly, three years later.

Sooner or later she became aware of these attacks and the gentle and timid woman collapsed in complete humiliation. She suffered a nervous breakdown and her health rapidly deteriorated until a final heart attack killed her just before her husband was to set off for his inauguration as the seventh President of the United States.

———————————

Andrew Jackson blamed his political enemies directly for his beloved Rachel's death, and he went into the White House filled with hate and bitterness. When the wife of one of his friends was ostracized from society because there too had been gossip about an unproven impropriety in her past, Jackson demanded that all his cabinet members force their wives to receive the unfortunate young woman. When every cabinet member refused, Jackson fired all of them.

It was a futile gesture, but one which served well the sorrowful memory of his adored wife.

Power is pleasure; and pleasure sweetens pain.
—William Hazlitt

17

THE AMBIGUOUS BACHELOR

nly one President of the United States has never married. This was James Buchanan, a rather obscure and mysterious man who assumed leadership of the country just before the Civil War. In examining Buchanan from a romantic and sexual perspective, there is almost a total absence of information concerning this important aspect of his life. However, piecing together the scant data and vague impressions which can be gathered, there is one inescapable question that must be asked: was the fifteenth U.S. President a homosexual?

Buchanan grew up in a small town and was the eldest child of a stern storekeeper and his deeply religious wife. While James was growing up, five younger sisters were born. Thus, he enjoyed a highly prized position in a very feminine environment. His early world was a woman's world, and unfortunately the presence of his father was primarily of a negative nature. The senior Buchanan was a harsh, critical, and domineering parent, and his only son at the time was a rival and a target for his frustrated ambitions. So

205

demanding and forbidding was the father, in fact, that the son greatly feared him.

Early in his youth, James Buchanan displayed the need to fasten his affection on mature males whom he could admire and hero-worship. The first and most profound teenage "crush" was a local Presbyterian pastor named John King. King was a dazzling young man who possessed a prodigious number of attractive qualities, which made him the most popular person in town. Buchanan hung around the minister as much as he could. King, in turn, was a very patient and kindly mentor and eventually made it possible for Buchanan to go off and receive a college education. As President, Buchanan would write: "Never have I known any human being for whom I felt greater reverence than for Dr. King."

At college, Buchanan transferred his affections and admiration to one of his professors, James McCormick. When he was a student, Buchanan began drinking and smoking and behaving in such a vain and conceited manner that his professors could barely stand him. Indeed, they managed to expel him after his first year, but let him return when he promised to tone down his extravagant behavior.

There was no limit to Buchanan's ambition to succeed in the material world. His whole emotional life seemed centered upon achievement and success. He became a lawyer and quickly won an impressive reputation. The bulk of his social energy, though, was still consumed by firm masculine friendships. Then, he met Ann Coleman, the emotionally unbalanced daughter of one of the wealthiest men in America. With the full determination of all his efforts, Buchanan started paying court to Ann. After a year, they became engaged in 1819.

However, there was soon trouble. Most people, and Ann's parents in particular, did not believe that Buchanan really loved the nervous young girl. They believed that the rising lawyer was interested primarily in the Coleman fortune and all that went with it. Within time, Ann also came to this conclusion. And she knew something else that all of the others didn't—the cold, unaffectionate way in which Buchanan treated her. She sensed that the "spark" wasn't truly there in him, nor was the deep and sincere feeling of true love. Ann wrote him a letter in which she complained of his lack of affection towards her and charged him with being interested only in her money.

Buchanan replied in a note with sentiments of polite injury and hurt, but he made no effort to either apologize for or explain his behavior. Ann, confused and upset by his lack of feeling, broke off the engagement shortly after. Abruptly leaving town, she went to visit her sister and became hysterical and died quite suddenly, a probable suicide. Buchanan proceeded more swiftly than ever with his career and began acquiring great wealth.

As James Buchanan matured, he became a handsome man with wavy blond hair, fine features, and bright blue eyes. He was tall, had broad shoulders, and a personable, attentive manner that made a good impression and easily won friends. He was very attractive to women and was considered to be an exceptionally eligible bachelor. Yet Buchanan developed other traits which were not quite so alluring. He was extremely vain and proud. He was also excessively formal, rigid, and precise. But although picky and fussy about everything in his life, he was also uncommonly kind and gentle. Always pleasant and friendly, Buchanan hated conflict or argument and would avoid a fight at almost any cost. In fact, the mere approach of a serious confrontation in his life would make Buchanan acutely ill and cause him to run a fever and vomit for hours.

With his establishment of great wealth and fame, Buchanan devoted himself entirely to politics and won a variety of glittering prizes. As senator, as ambassador to Russia and Great Britain, as Secretary of State, Buchanan climbed higher and higher towards his final goal: the Presidency. To have had a wife would most certainly have been a vital asset for his political career, but Buchanan still remained unmarried.

As a man nears the White House, having a wife, any wife, is an absolute necessity. It was even a greater necessity in the rigidly structured society of Buchanan's era. The fact that Buchanan possessed a gigantic ambition which motivated him to make any number of great sacrifices and compromises for the sake of his career makes it seem incredible that he could not force himself to acquire a wife, even if it was a marriage of convenience, which were far from rare at that time. What makes it even more utterly fantastic is Buchanan's continued and over-stated cries against the loneliness of bachelorhood throughout his life and his constantly voiced enthusiasm for entering into an intended marriage with one seemingly desirable candidate after another.

Thus, either consciously and with deliberate guile, or innocently and unconsciously, Buchanan always made the effort to make it appear as if he were seriously involved with a woman he deeply loved and wished to make his future wife. Although he knew these women and enjoyed their friendship, no romances ever transpired. There were no lingering kisses, no tender caresses. And when things progressed to the stage where he would have to physically demonstrate some affection and commitment, Buchanan would skillfully withdraw from the relationship with anguished cries of regret and a ready and convincing alibi.

With pretty Mary Snyder of Philadelphia it was that he couldn't devote enough time to her, the time she truly deserved, because of his career and the obligation towards his numerous nephews and nieces. When Buchanan later professed to be seriously in love with Anna Payne, the beautiful young niece of Dolley Madison, he finally said that he could not go ahead and marry her because of the great difference in their ages, although it was a commonly accepted social practice at this time for some girls to marry men old enough to be their grandfathers. This broken engagement Buchanan proudly advertised as a shining example of his ability to put his head before his heart and make the sacrifice of his own happiness for the good of another and the best interests of his country. The fact that almost everyone continually fell for his routine is a testament to the total ignorance of even basic psychology during those days. As if to press his luck to see what he could get away with, Buchanan pulled out all of the stops on his extravagant nature and wrote poor Anna Payne the following verses:

In thee my chilled & blighted heart has found
A green spot in the dreary waste around.
Oh! that my fate in youthful days had been
T'have lived with such an one, unknown, unseen,
Loving and lov'd, t'have passed away our days
Sequestered from the world's malignant gaze!
A match of age with youth can only bring
The farce of "winter dancing with the spring."
Blooming nineteen can never well agree
With the dull age of half a century.
Thus reason speaks what rebel passion hates,
Passion,—which would control the very fates.
Meantime, where'ere you go, what e're your lot
By me you'll never, never be forgot.
May heaven's rich blessings crown your future life!
And may you be a happy, loving wife!

Thus, Buchanan artfully disposed of another "love" and firmly protected his own reputation. By the time he became President, the aging Buchanan ceased these charades altogether and no longer felt the need to be actively involved in serious friendships with women. More and more, he entered into very private associations with younger men. In particular, there was a young senator with whom Buchanan was especially close, and when the inseparableness of the relationship eventually drew attention, there was much comment on it, though no public speculation mentioned a sexual tie. In fact, due to his cleverness or luck and the lack of knowledge and understanding at that time, Buchanan was never involved involved in a public scandal involving his masculine friendships and sexual preferences.

There is absolutely no proof that James Buchanan ever led an actively homosexual life. Chances are that he never did. In nineteenth century America homosexuality was an almost unknown phenomenon. In Europe it occurred with regularity in the elite aristocratic class and the lowest criminal segment of the population, but in the United States with its inflexible moral and social codes, it remained a luxurious and exotic personal expression that was totally alien to the nature of the new land and one that the rough challenge of manifest destiny could not afford. From the New England Puritans to the Quakers of Pennsylvania and the Catholics of the South, the United States was an intensely religious nation, and all religions of that time held homosexuality as an absolute taboo.

A latent homosexual, as Buchanan most likely was, could never actively explore his sexuality and successfully rise in the world of politics. The dangers were far too great. It was an era of personal attacks so vicious and unprincipled that the slightest lapse of morals was an open invitation for public shame and ruin. Unless a man were willing to risk all or was so caught up in his passion that he was a helpless victim, to privately engage in a homosexual relationship was an absolute impossibility, especially for someone who had his sights set on the White House.

James Buchanan was not only a cautious man, he was a man who disciplined his passions to the same merciless degree as John Adams had. Buchanan was always in control of himself. He never believed the popular saying that in human conduct the mind may influence, but the heart controls. On the contrary, Buchanan never allowed his heart to control his choices and decisions in life. Passions created chaos and conflict and loss of control. Buchanan was severely threatened by these things and even physically suffered when confronted with them. Not to control himself and his environment precisely would, he must have feared, unleash his true nature—his true sexual self. The great panic he felt when confronted with any loss of control, causing acute illness, must

210

surely have been related to his coming to terms with his hidden desires, something he could never force himself to do.

Although tolerant of homosexuality and even sympathetic when it exists at moderate levels of society, the majority of the public do not wish to think that their heroes and leaders are gay. This reluctance to recognize it in someone they perceive as being above them has protected not only James Buchanan in historical memory, but also several homosexual actors and artists of later generations, and, even some later United States Presidents who certainly had more than their share of homosexual leanings.

Between love and power,
I would choose power.
—Niccolò Machiavelli

18

LOVE FOR SALE

erhaps the most revered President in American history is Abraham Lincoln. If his accomplishments in public life have earned him unlimited admiration, then any knowledge of the particulars of his private existence must surely produce profound sympathy. Lincoln was the most unhappy and melancholy man ever to have lived in the White House. The progress of his personal life was one tragedy after another. The victim of acute psychological problems, Lincoln adjusted and coped by pulling the plug on his deepest emotions and sacrificing his heart and soul to the dark specter of mad ambition. Obsessed by succeeding as far as he could at any price, he ignored trying to deal with the difficult prospect of finding a true and satisfying love relationship and, instead, literally sold himself to the easiest entryway to success.

Death was the theme of Lincoln's early life. He lost almost everyone close to him by the time he was a teenager. This combined with an extremely impoverished environment and a

213

dubious family tree to produce a sensitive, gentle, and dolefully morbid young man who saw his only salvation in life was his ability to excel beyond all others. Poetic and bookish, Lincoln found himself bitterly at odds with his father. The estrangement between father and son was so severe that it approached hatred. When the elder Lincoln was on his deathbed in 1851, the forty-two-year-old Abraham refused his request to come to him and later even refused to attend his funeral.

Lincoln was forever to be the victim of his own acute feelings of inferiority and personal loss. He retreated into an emotional isolation so complete that he was fully protected from ever having to deal with the unbearable trauma of losing a loved one again. The price he paid was a brooding loneliness and intermittent periods of gloom and depression so extreme as to plunge him into dark silences of considerable duration.

Those closest to Lincoln throughout his entire life would each comment that he was the most solitary, secretive, and emotionally withdrawn human being that they had ever known. The one who would make this complaint most furiously was his wife, Mary Todd. Lincoln was also a very strong and earthy man with a wide streak of vulgarity and coarseness in his character. Sex was something that seemed to interest him especially and much of his private humor consisted of off-color jokes of explicit sexual situations. He was the product of the raw frontier and, though extremely soft and sentimental, he felt most at home in the lower circles of society where manners and morals were not strictly enforced.

Lincoln found it impossible to engage in feminine friendships, let alone serious relationships with women. The tall, awkward introvert postponed dealing with the problem of relating to women until he was twenty-seven years old. He, then, out of a sense of aching loneliness, sought out the most unattractive and undesirable maid he could find and proposed marriage. He casually treated her like one of his fellow buddies and definitely had no love whatsoever for her. However, to his horror and humiliation,

Mary Owens, the woman he believed no one else would want, turned him down flat. Feeling himself to be a complete fool, Lincoln wrote at the time: "I have now come to the conclusion never again to think of marrying; and for this reason; I can never be satisfied with any one who would be block-head enough to have me."

His self-pity was overwhelming. He kept his promise, and for two years he convinced himself that he would never have anything else to do with women. Moving to Springfield, Illinois, he made the acquaintance of a fellow Kentuckian named Joshua Speed who ran a general store. He took a great liking to Lincoln and seemed strangely attracted to his acute sadness. "I never saw so gloomy and melancholy a face in my entire life," he later observed.

Speed invited Lincoln to come live with him and share the double bed in his upstairs room. The two bachelors soon became each other's "most intimate friend." They continued to sleep together for some time and expressed their feelings more freely and intensely than they ever would again with anyone else. Lincoln poured out his heart to Speed and told him of his hopes and fears and his problems with women. He also shared dirty jokes and confided in him about his feelings of isolation and loneliness from other people. This was probably the happiest time of Abraham Lincoln's entire life.

Whether or not there was a sexual relationship between the two men can never be definitely known. But even without the intimate evidence, it is very apparent that Lincoln was surely an emotional homosexual at the very least. His awkwardness and almost total lack of interest in women, whatever its cause may have been, made him always much, much closer to men. His masculine relationships were the ones which always meant the most to him. They were the only truly gratifying human interactions that he experienced, save for tender feelings in later years for his sons. With iron will and insatiable ambition, Lincoln evaded trying to either understand or fulfill his complex emotional nature and proceeded to direct all of his passion and energy into his soaring career.

About the same time, Lincoln acquired a new law partner named Billy Herndon. Very successful in his practice, Lincoln could have chosen anyone in town and they would have gladly accepted. But he chose Billy, a young and inexperienced lawyer who seemed to have little to offer professionally. Lincoln had first taken notice of Billy a couple of years before when he worked as a clerk in Speed's general store. He had taken an instant liking to the young man and the friendship he developed with him would be second in importance only to the one with Speed.

After Lincoln's death, Herndon would write and lecture tirelessly in an effort to canonize his dearest friend, the love of his life. It was Herndon who was responsible for humanizing Lincoln and making him a heterosexually romantic figure by fabricating an early romance with Anne Rutledge. The Anne Rutledge story was quickly picked up by Lincoln biographers and became a vital part of the Lincoln legend to demonstrate his intense heterosexuality and help pardon his calculated marriage of convenience to Mary Todd. Anne Rutledge did exist—she was the daughter of one of Lincoln's early friends—but, while Lincoln liked her and considered her a friend, she was always treated like one of the boys, and there certainly were never any romantic feelings of love.

Lincoln was thirty-one when he met Mary Todd. Rich and with the social position that Lincoln single-mindedly aspired to, Mary was an intense and domineering woman of almost masculine firmness and resolve. She also had a burning ambition as all-consuming as Lincoln's. Mary took one look at the tall, homely lawyer and instinctively knew she had found the pliable raw material she had been searching for. She aggressively pursued him, did almost all the talking, and steered him into courtship. Tactfully and obliquely, she mentioned marriage and saw to it that they became officially engaged.

Lincoln hadn't fallen in love with her. He was flattered by her attention and he found her easy to be with and interesting to talk to, but he lacked the warm and deep feelings for her that he did possess for Joshua Speed and Billy Herndon.

But Lincoln wanted marriage. He especially wanted a marriage that would serve as a solution to several of his seemingly insurmountable problems. Still feeling an extreme sense of inferiority and alienation from the proper social classes, he realized that the easiest and possibly the only way to achieve acceptance and respectability was through a marriage with a socially prominent and wealthy woman. Mary Todd fit the bill ideally. And, to her advantage, she was comfortable for him to be around, a quality he found rare in women.

As the date of the wedding approached, Lincoln soon had second thoughts. His doubts became so severe that he couldn't go through with it. He suddenly broke off the engagement. But the agony he now experienced was so intolerable, a physical collapse and paralyzing depression, that he finally was able to push himself back into facing the ceremony. Mary Todd, as determined as ever to capture Lincoln, accepted him back and they were married in November of 1842. Before the date of the wedding, Lincoln still wasn't convinced he was doing the right thing, but he confided to a friend that he believed he would be "less miserable" living with Mary than alone. On his honeymoon he wrote to another friend reporting that there was no news to talk about "except my marrying, which to me, is a matter of profound wonder."

The marriage did provide some mutual benefits, but Mary Todd Lincoln was precariously balanced when it came to her sensitive emotions,and her husband's constant lack of warmth and affection and his periodic brooding silences transformed her into a nervous and bitter shrew. Lincoln centered most of his affection on his sons, and, although he was an unfailingly patient and sympathetic husband, he and Mary were of too drastically different temperaments and characters to have a successful or satisfying marriage.

By the time Lincoln entered the White House, he and his wife were each quietly going their own separate ways. While President, Lincoln had no inclination or available time for any extra relationships. There was never any romantic scandal involving his name.

Whether or not Lincoln was ever actively homosexual will always be a subject for speculation and debate. The fact of his emotional homosexuality is an inescapable conclusion from the information available on his life. In the extraordinarily unnatural motivating drive which relentlessly pushes a man against all odds towards the White House, frustrated passion is one of the most potent forces. The inability to establish a fulfilling love relationship has often proved to be the most effective ingredient in driving a man to the highest level he can attain. In an era when homosexual feelings could only be repressed, what stronger force could feed a man's material ambition and his lust for power?

Love is the wisdom of the fool and the folly of the wise.
                                              —Samuel Johnson

19

SEX AND THE
SEVEN SAINTS

*A*fter the American Civil War, the weight of the Victorian era fully descended upon the United States. With one major exception, the Presidency would be of the highest sexual moral tone and completely free of romantic scandals for the next half century. The men who occupied the Executive Office during this dignified and placid period were exceptionally decent, devoted family men of deep religious beliefs and firmly conservative personal values. They were as good and sound as they were mediocre and unremarkable.

When Lincoln was assassinated in 1865, his Vice President, Andrew Johnson, took over the Presidency. Johnson was a modest man of exceptionally austere origins. A poor man, he had been a tailor for many years and gradually rose in the world of politics. When he was eighteen he married a girl of sixteen who was almost as poor as himself. However, the girl, Eliza McCardle, had a good education, and it was she who taught the illiterate Johnson to read and write. Sharing this bond and a very deep religious faith, the husband and wife forged a solid and tender relationship that enabled them to progress through a life of struggle and hardship and eventually rise all the way to the White House.

When he unexpectedly became President, Johnson brought his unpretentious family to the most exalted residence in the country. His wife, an invalid, remained close to her husband and provided him with great comfort and support during the trauma of his impeachment proceedings. Somber, unimaginative, and devout, Andrew Johnson was never the subject of romantic gossip. He and Eliza remained devoted to one another until their deaths in 1875.

President Ulysses S. Grant was a bumbling ne'er-do-well who failed at everything he touched until he found his true calling in the military and became the Union's number-one hero during the Civil War. As President, Grant's two administrations were rocked by more scandals than any of the previous ones. However, these ignoble disgraces only involved the dishonest actions and misuse of power by Grant's political appointees, not any dishonesty of his own or any illicit personal affairs involving sexual relationships.

Grant was a happily married man. He was a doting husband who adored his wife and was totally dependent on her emotionally and professionally. The object of this great affection was the former Julia Dent, a fat and physically unattractive Southerner of high spirits and a warm, loving heart. Julia had a cast in one of her eyes and was so self-conscious about it that she never looked directly at a camera, only allowing herself to be photographed in protected profile.

With no interests beyond his family and his political career, Grant was a staid and somewhat dour personality in the White House. In spite of the constant storm of scandals that thundered throughout his terms of office, no charge of political or sexual misconduct could ever be leveled truthfully against him. It was symbolic that his wife Julia redecorated the interior of the White House in the cozy, cluttered trappings of the iron-clad Victorian style.

Love and sex were a bit more of a problem for the nineteenth President of the United States, Rutherford B. Hayes. Beginning life in a tragic and problematic family constellation, Hayes was born a few months after his father's death. His youth was dominated by his devoutly Methodist mother and his beautiful older sister. His rigidly strict mother, indeed, wanted Rutherford to become a minister in the church and she relentlessly pushed him towards the pulpit.

The most disturbing element in Hayes' adolescence was the nature of his relationship with his older sister. She was as nervous and high-strung as she was beautiful, and Hayes became more and more passionately attached to her as he approached manhood. Whether his feelings for her were incestuous or not it is not known, but his love and emotions were so centered on his sister that he failed to form any other female relationships throughout his entire young adulthood. He remained a bachelor until he was thirty and met Lucy Webb, a woman of even stronger character and commanding personality than his beloved sister.

Hayes found it difficult to choose Lucy over his sister, and it took him some time to commit himself to a decision. Finally, he went ahead with this practical and sensible union and formed an exceptionally solid Victorian marriage. His disappointed sister later spent many years in an insane asylum.

Lucy Hayes made a superb First Lady. Dignified and absolutely correct in her every action, she was also very energetic and possessed a fine intellect, being the first President's wife to have graduated from college. True to her firm beliefs, she enforced a ban on all alcohol in the White House and became popularly known as "Lemonade Lucy." The marriage produced several children and was held up as a model of virtue and respectability for the whole nation. Hard-working and disciplined, Rutherford and Lucy were paragons of sexual morality.

James Garfield and his wife, Lucretia, were worthy successors to the the Hayes White House. Garfield, probably the handsomest and most charming man to have ever lived in the White House, learned early in life both the advantages and hazards of his great natural gifts. He was avidly pursued by young women and found himself in a series of awkward and strained situations which made him wary of being caught in an unwanted marriage. Turning to religion, he vented his passion in a near fanatical devotion to the Disciples of Christ. It was his involvement in the church that brought him in contact with his wife. Despite Garfield had a considerable dilemma in deciding whether or not to marry Lucretia Rudolph. She was a serious woman of considerable learning and unbending character. Garfield was attracted to these qualities and felt a kinship with her, but he was not physically attracted to her plain face and her total lack of sensuality.

But, for whatever reasons, he finally gave himself, he compromised, and entered into a practical partnership based on common interests and mutual respect, a basis for many a presidential marriage during this extraordinarily sedate era. Despite Garfield's lengthy absences from home and the ubiquitous presence of his mother, even in the White House, the marriage was serene and rewarding for both husband and wife. The family was an extremely devoted one and no whisper of scandal ever directed itself toward their personal lives.

Unfortunately, Garfield became the second President to be assassinated in office, only six months after beginning to serve his term. Chester Alan Arthur became the next President. Arthur had never run for public office before being elected Vice President. His elevation to the Presidency shocked everyone who knew him. Tragically, the person who would have been most pleased and surprised by his success had died suddenly only a few months before. This was his wife, Nell, who had been the center of his life.

Thus, when Chester Arthur entered the White House he was a devastated and broken man. Feeling no need whatsoever to replace Nell with other feminine companions, Arthur remained a mourning widower until his death four years later. He indulged his senses only at the dinner table, and was celebrated as a great and dedicated eater, as his ample frame soon attested. When towards the end of his Presidency gossips began talking about a beautiful woman with whom Arthur was involved, they gave as proof the fact that he was known to keep a picture of her by his bed and devotedly place fresh flowers in front of it each and every morning.

But the gossip did not last long. When hearing of it, President Arthur smiled sadly and gently explained that the picture was of his dead wife.

The twenty-third President was the next saint in the White House. Benjamin Harrison was the scion of one of America's oldest and most illustrious dynasties, the grandson of a former President, William Henry Harrison. He was a remarkably religious man, and married early, at age twenty. His wife was Caroline Scott, the daughter of one of his college professors; together they raised a family and became stolid pillars of their local Presbyterian church, faithfully teaching Bible classes and Sunday school for many years.

The Harrisons provided the nation with an unusually staid and unexciting First Family. They were admired and respected for their dedication to their high-minded principles. At the very end of Benjamin's term of office, his wife suddenly contracted typhoid fever and died. Three years after leaving the White House, he married his late wife's niece, Mary Dimmick. She had been a member of his household while he was President and worked for his wife as her companion and secretary. The marriage may have seemed natural and reasonable to Harrison, but it provoked a minor scandal and his children refused to accept the match. So shocked and alienated were they that they became estranged from their father permanently and never saw him again during the remaining five years of his lifetime.

William McKinley was another saintly President. He occupied the White House during the last years of the nineteenth century. Kind and gentle, beloved by even his political opponents, McKinley was a tragic figure in every sense of the word. He had married a local celebrated beauty named Ida Saxon. After only a couple of years of marriage, their world began to collapse. First, Ida's mother died, then shortly after, her two small daughters died. Ida suffered a complete nervous and physical breakdown from which she never recovered. Afflicted with a special form of epilepsy, she lived the existence of an invalid, her mind precariously balanced on the edge of madness.

McKinley's tender devotion to his suffering wife was a marvel to everyone who witnessed it. As President, his entire routine and schedule was centered upon the health and moods of his Ida. He rushed to her side after he finished his work and spent every free moment with her. On the rare occasions when she needed to appear at state dinners, he always sat next to her and took care of her, gracefully dealing with her sudden loss of control and seizures.

In fact, so extreme was McKinley's concern and attention to his wife that the cynical minds of Washington were convinced that it surely must be the result of a guilty conscience—a clever cover for his own torrid extramarital affairs. However widespread this ignoble suspicion, it was the opposite of the truth. The saintly McKinley was so selflessly devoted to his wife that even as he lay dying from an assassin's bullet, he whispered to those next to him, "My wife—be careful how you tell her—oh, be careful!"

Reaching a little ahead, into the twentieth century, perhaps an eighth saint should be added to this privileged list of Victorian Presidents. Certainly William Howard Taft was a contemporary of this group in both mind and years. A genial and good-natured man of immense girth and vitality, Taft possessed many talents and

224

abilities which enabled him to succeed in almost every aspect of government. Loyal and honest, he was exceptionally patient and understanding with his colleagues and especially with his difficult wife.

Taft had married the imperious Helen Herron. Although she deeply loved her husband, she tended to dominate him and the advancement of his career was her entire life's interest. Highspirited and with a sharp temper, it was her personality which usually had its way. Taft's dream was the Chief Justiceship of the Supreme Court, but Helen insisted he pass it by when he was offered the prestigious chance of becoming President in 1908. Ironically, Helen Taft suffered a serious stroke the first year her husband was in office and her much-looked-forward-to reign as First Lady was not spent regally at her husband's side, but instead in a sick bed convalescing from her severe paralysis.

With his typical display of loving-kindness, Taft devoted all of his free time to nursing his irritable wife to a full recovery, even meticulously teaching her how to speak again. An object of grat personal admiration, William Howard Taft remained a faithful and exemplary husband for the rest of his life.

*There is no greater nor keener pleasure than that of
bodily love—and none which is more irrational.*
                                                    —Plato

20

A MAN'S MAN AND THE
MARTYRED MESSIAH

"I felt a great admiration for men who were fearless
and could hold their own in the world, and I had a
great desire to be like them," President Theodore
Roosevelt once confessed. "But owing to my asthma I was not
able to go to school, and I was nervous and self-conscious."

This straightforward statement is the key to understanding one
of the most individual and complex personalities to have ever
become President of the United States. Theodore Roosevelt
unfailingly made every effort to present himself in the most basic
and simple manner possible, yet his eternally flawless posing hid
a character intricately woven with ambiguities and opposites. His
love life was perhaps the greatest victim of his life-long addiction
to obsessive overcompensation.

Roosevelt started off in an enviable position. He was the only
son of an old, ultra-rich New York family. Home was a warmly
protective mansion in the best part of town, and puny little
Theodore was a pampered and spoiled child. His health was

atrocious and, as he grew, he remained frail and sickly. Concerned, his intelligent father impressed upon his son the absolute need to build up his body if he were to have a life worth living. Theodore worshipped his father and took his words to heart. He commenced a manic routine of exhausting exercise from which he would not deviate for the rest of his life. Putting all of his energy into struggling against his weak and passive nature, young Roosevelt developed his famous aggressive personality and mercilessly drove himself in constant motion, charging off in every direction with a bold, confident smile. Incredibly insecure beneath the loud, bombastic surface, Roosevelt discovered early that this was the best technique for pushing forward in life while maximally protecting his sensitive and delicate core.

By the time he got to Harvard, he had succeeded admirably in building his body and perfecting his health. His precariously balanced ego was also gaining confidence and strength, especially after he courted and married the sweetest and most beautiful girl in Boston, Alice Lee. For three years Theodore Roosevelt and his adored wife lived a storybook romance of prefect love and luxurious wealth.

Then, his entire world shattered to pieces. On Valentine's Day, 1884, his beautiful young wife and his beloved mother died within hours of each other. They were the two people whom Theodore loved most in the world. He had built his life around them. The shock of the double loss was so profound that Roosevelt totally abandoned his solid existence and fled as far away as he could get. Beyond the reaches of civilization, he lived on a secluded ranch in South Dakota. It would be more than two years before the crushed psyche of the exiled aristocrat would be healed enough to return home to New York.

His body returned to the East Coast and his mind to politics, but his heart and soul had closed down forever. Roosevelt never said a single word about his late wife or mother for the rest of his life. It was as if they never existed. Emotionally, he not only stopped growing, but he retreated to a happier and more problem-free age in his past, an early adolescent age unthreatened by the adult cruelty of death and painful loss. Much of Theodore Roosevelt's remarkably zestful and boyish personality had its roots in his extreme adjustment to this dark chapter of his life. Without fully appreciating the truth of his witty comment, the British ambassador, Cecil Spring-Rice, once said of Roosevelt: "You must always remember that the President is about six."

Forging ahead in life with greater energy and shriller bravado than ever, Roosevelt could only deal with people on the most superficial level. Even his most intimate relationships were armored with the protective shield of manically grinning teeth and brusque back slapping. Feelings were kept at bay by endless activity, emotions were made light of by a relentless flow of high-spirited energy. The tender and the romantic were thoroughly sliced from his heart. There was no crack of vulnerability for affection to touch and communicate with.

The death of Roosevelt's softer emotions was a bonanza for his political career. It enabled him to charge forward and rapidly climb to the top. He would be the youngest man in history to become President. However, his personal life could not have been satisfying. Women never again held a mesmerizing charm for Roosevelt. He viewed the feminine sex without any of his former romantic ardor. Love was something that he could not allow himself to get involved with and, thus, possibly destroyed by again. The women in his life existed only as "buddies" and good-natured "chums." The feminine aspects of the world were negative ingredients in his desperate plan for survival. Women won your heart and touched your most sensitive elements—they made you dependent on their love and understanding—then they left, they died, and you were hurt and destroyed and worse than dead.

Roosevelt's delicate ego necessitated such a total withdrawal from women that his hyper-aggressive, almost insane glorification of masculinity—the manly man's man—gave him the typical persona of the modern-day masculine-type homosexual. It is extremely doubtful that Theodore Roosevelt had any homosexual feelings on a conscious level, and his character and lifestyle could certainly never have tolerated any form of such then-illicit expression, but the sensibility was much the same. His deepest emotional relationships were with men. The majority of his time was spent in manly pursuits in masculine society.

When Roosevelt shrewdly surveyed his life and saw that its structure would best be supported by a conventional marriage, he proposed to an old childhood friend, Edith Carow. She was a quiet but strong-willed woman who had an efficient approach to living that organized and controlled everything that entered her environment. Plain-looking and extremely practical-minded, she seemed to possess a high degree of the masculine in her personality and character. It was a non-romantic marriage based on the sound tenets of a well-disciplined partnership. Theodore and Edith liked each other and had a jovial, casual way of relating that is most often seen in the fellow members of a college fraternity. Several children were born, and there was never the slightest breath of gossip concerning any extramarital love life of the President. In fact, in every area of his life, Theodore Roosevelt was one of the most respected and scandal-free Presidents the nation has ever enjoyed.

The exact opposite of Roosevelt was Woodrow Wilson. Wilson was an equally complex man, but a gentle introvert who felt comfortable only in the company of women—preferably admiring, doting, docile women like his mother and sisters and cousins who surrounded him when he was young. Refined and thoroughly domesticated, Wilson was also acutely insecure and suffered from an inferiority complex so severe that it drove him to the same extreme limits of over-achievement as Roosevelt. The son of a strait-laced Calvinistic minister, he could not tolerate criticism in any form and felt weak and unimportant in the competitive company of other men.

The founding father of psychiatry, Sigmund Freud, wrote a book in which he intricately dissected Woodrow Wilson's full psychological character. Freud's chief thesis was that the twenty-eighth President unconsciously identified himself with Jesus Christ. Because Wilson viewed his own father in such an exalted, saintly light, it is understandable how he could have unknowingly assumed the role of the son of God. The need to save his fellow man through his hard work and moral perfection and the need to suffer were certainly the strongest motivating forces in Wilson's life. First, he attempted to reform and save the people of the United States and almost invited unnecessary suffering to accomplish it, then with the coming of World War I he expanded his goal—now he was going to "Save the World for Democracy." The failure of his famous League of Nations ideal was guaranteed by his inescapable need to be a martyr. To be the messiah, he knew that he had to accept his doom.

What is most astounding about this Christ-figure is that he was the subject of one of the most vicious and sensational romantic scandals in the history of the Presidency. No other President while in office was ever the target of such scathing personal attacks for outrageous sexual misconduct. Perhaps because Wilson was so extreme in his moralizing and his self-righteous rigidity, he was suspected by a majority of the public of being just the opposite. The presidential public facade seemed far too perfect to be true; therefore, it had to be merely the clever cover for something highly immoral, and it became a national hobby speculating just what it was exactly.

The dignified and Puritanically proper Wilson had enjoyed a thirty-year marriage to Ellen Axson that was as deeply felt and as passionate as few marriages have the good fortune to be. They had three charming daughters and were an exceptionally happy and devoted family. Wilson relied so completely on his wife that she

The only recently widowed President Woodrow Wilson and his future second wife, Edith Bolling Galt, herself a widow, enjoy a day at the ballpark as the 1915 World Series opens. They seem oblivious to the impending avalanche of public condemnation and scandal that will follow the revelation of their assignations.

functioned as his alter ego. After many years of joyous home life, he wrote her: "I would a thousand times rather repay you a tithe of the happiness you have brought me than make my name immortal without serving you as the chief mission of my life. Ah, my little wife, do you know that my whole self has passed over into my allegiance for you?" In a tragic stroke of fate, Ellen Wilson died from the complications of Bright's disease only two years after her husband moved into the Oval Office.

Wilson was so grief-stricken by her death that he refused to leave his vigil by her body for days. In the months that followed, his confusion and despair only increased, and, finally, his doctors and friends feared for his health and sanity. To lift this crushing depression, those closest to him arranged a meeting with a beautiful Washington widow named Edith Bolling Galt. Six months after his wife's death, Wilson met the refined widow and began escorting her to social events about the city. The friendship quickly became a romance. Two months later they were engaged to be married. The public heard rumors of the romance and reacted violently.

For a sad, lonely widower, the nation had a deep and genuine sympathy. However, for this same man to be dating and romancing an attractive woman so short a time after the tragic death of his wife, they now had only anger and contempt. The most conservative opinion centered on the extreme haste of the President's departure from mourning. Women across the country, most especially, felt insulted and degraded by Wilson's apparently faithless behavior. But this was only the beginning. The criticism of the President's lack of respect for his dead wife's memory was only a springboard for imaginative gossips and vicious character assassins.

Soon, the vast anti-Wilson forces were spreading the "news" that the President had been in love with Mrs. Galt before his wife's demise—and that the shock of his infidelity was responsible for carrying her off to an early grave. Many others insisted that Wilson and his paramour had conspired with Ellen's doctor to have her quietly poisoned and disposed of. Others contradicted this story only because they knew for certain that Wilson had pushed his ailing wife down a flight of stairs so he would be free to remarry. The rumors were so widespread and persistent that even the most logical and level-headed citizens believed there must be some validity to them.

With Wilson's decision to run for a second term and the approach of the 1916 election, the gossip concerning his "immoral" behavior and sexual improprieties automatically became the chief campaign issue. With little effort, the Republican Party totally misrepresented Wilson's personality and character. They took his emotional need for feminine companionship and support and translated it into purely sexual terms. Whereas he associated so harmlessly with women that he related to them as almost one of their kind (his sensibilities being so kindred with those of refined matrons), his enemies insisted that these friendships were entirely base and illicitly sexual.

Reaching back in time, the Republican press used the affair of a Mrs. Peck to prove their point. It seems that Wilson had first met this rich divorcee in 1907 when he spent the winter in Bermuda for his health. They had become very good friends and had written to each other and visited many times since then. Mrs. Peck was an amusing, accomplished hostess who fully appreciated the brilliant intellectual talents of the reserved Wilson. He, in turn, was always in desperate need of female adulation and attention. Theirs was never anything more than a very proper friendship of shared cultural interests and mutual respect.

Said with a thoroughly obscene snicker, the nickname of "Peck's Bad Boy" became a popular way of referring to Woodrow Wilson from coast to coast. Every detail of their friendship was given a vulgar interpretation. The President was supposed to be paying Mrs. Peck hush money to keep quiet about their affair. Love letters written by him were said to be appearing very soon in the newspapers. Rumors of Wilson's immoral and insatiable sexual lust gradually became common knowledge.

Meanwhile, Wilson and Edith Galt were making immediate plans to be married. This greatly shocked the nation and fed the fires of malicious personal attacks. Even those few friends of the President who fully understood the complete situation were begging him to, at the very least, postpone the wedding until after the November election. Public reaction became so extreme that Wilson offered to release his fiancee from her promise to marry him, but Edith, a courageous woman of firmly resolute character, smiled tenderly and insisted they carry on with their plans.

As the barrage of slander continued to sweep over the White House, the President showed his true instinct for martyrdom by suffering silently and taking no active steps whatsoever to refute or even defend himself against the evil lies. When he was first confronted with a detailed account of the gossip, he cried. After that, he placed the burden of clearing his reputation on his friends. Fortunately for him, they rallied to his defense like vengeful warriors and bombarded public opinion with their glowing testaments of praise.

The marriage went ahead as scheduled. Public sentiment, as fickle and unpredictable as ever, suddenly jumped its tracks and abruptly soared off in the opposite direction. America was now captivated by the new great joy of their President and the officially sanctioned romance was greeted with enthusiasm and sympathy. As quickly and ferociously as the ugly stories had spread and been enjoyed by the people in the streets, they just as rapidly evaporated into thin air. War threatened from the European continent, and popular feeling wanted America to remain at peace. This greatly helped Woodrow Wilson escape his personal scandal and become re-elected to a second term in 1916.

Edith Galt proved to be even a better helpmate than Wilson's first wife. When the President suffered a severe stroke in 1919 and was partially paralyzed, his devoted spouse kept the world at bay and virtually performed the entire task of the Executive Office from behind the closed doors of her husband's sickroom. Indeed, when the full extent of her sacrifice for her marriage and her country finally came to the public's notice, there undoubtedly were many who hung their heads in shame when they remembered the riddle they had gleefully repeated after the announcement of her wedding: "What did Mrs. Galt do when the President proposed to her?" "She fell out of bed."

Try to reason about love, and you will lose your reason.
—Old French proverb

21

THREE SQUARES IN THE OVAL OFFICE

ollowing the Harding scandals, it was inordinately fortunate for the country that Calvin Coolidge and Herbert Hoover were in command of the Presidency. These two men who occupied the Oval Office for almost a decade were the most dignified, reserved, and circumspect Chief Executives in American history. Both were solidly old-fashioned traditionalists, as conservative as it was humanly possible to be, and morally correct in every aspect of their lives. Enjoying happy, devoted marriages, they were completely invulnerable to character attacks. However, there were brief incidents which did promote gossip of illicit sexual activity, although much imagination was needed to sustain any interest.

Calvin Coolidge was from the lonely hills of Vermont and was an unusually stoic and cold personality whom one famous Washington wit claimed "was weaned on a pickle." He married his opposite: warm, amiable Grace Goodhue. Their life together was so quiet and placid that when even a ripple appeared on the

Though Calvin Coolidge and Mrs. Coolidge—seen here on the lawn of the old Coolidge homestead in the Vermont village of Plymouth—were anything but a wild and exciting pair, their placid surfaces masked passionate natures that, at one point, became public, and kept the nation entertained for weeks.

surface, it made headlines and sent rumors flying for months.

The incident, undoubtedly innocent enough, occurred during a vacation trip to the Black Hills of South Dakota in June 1927. The austere husband and wife were having a leisurely stay at a mountain lodge. One morning the First Lady said she was taking a short hike with James Haley, a very handsome Secret Service agent. They disappeared into the woods while the President patiently waited. Hours went by and they failed to return for lunch. Coolidge became very worried. By afternoon a search party was sent out to find them. Finally, Grace and her good-looking escort staggered back to the lodge. Exhausted, Haley sheepishly explained to the President that he and the First Lady had ventured into an unfamiliar part of the forest and had become lost. It had taken them the better part of the day to find their way back.

Coolidge became enraged and shouted at Haley, firing him and ordering his immediate departure. He refused to speak to his wife and remained silent for days. Reporters at the lodge happily picked up the story and wrote about it for weeks. Anyone who knew Grace Coolidge was certain that nothing improper had occurred on the "hike," but a gossip-starved country made the most of it.

No less a pillar of respectability was Coolidge's successor, Herbert Hoover. A devoutly religious Quaker and a compulsive worker, Hoover married Lou Henry when he was twenty-four and they traveled the world together. A modest, loving couple, they bestowed an immaculate moral image on the Presidency while living in the White House.

The nearest Hoover ever came to being linked to an illicit affair was in 1929, when an obviously unbalanced woman tried to force her way through the White House gates, loudly claiming that the President was the father of her unborn child. She was quickly taken care of by the guards, but news of the incident was humorously whispered around Washington for some time.

Another completely "square" President would hold office in the late 1940s.

Harry S. Truman was a plain, no-nonsense personality who had a unquestioned reputation as a faithful husband. Towards the end of his life he observed: "Three things can ruin a man—money, power, and women. I never had any money, I never wanted power, and the only woman in my life is up at the house right now."

Truman had been a physically weak, bookish "mama's boy,"

239

a frightened and timid child. When he was six years old, he met a beautiful little blond girl at Sunday school named Bess Wallace. Bess came from the most prominent family in town and was an extroverted, popular, athletic girl. She would win local shot-put and basketball championships and appeared during their youth to be the far more masculine of the two. Harry later confessed: "I was smitten at once and still am." His infatuation turned into an intense and enduring love. It seemed a perfect blending of opposites. The future President waited patiently for nearly thirty years before he was finally able to marry her.

Bess Wallace Truman was definitely the senior partner of the married couple and her doting husband the junior. He openly and unashamedly referred to his wife in public as "the Boss" and always gave evidence that he considered her his superior in almost every way. As President, Truman was greatly influenced by the First Lady's ideas and opinions, both personal and political, and she ruled at the absolute center of his world.

The Trumans were an extremely tight-knit family, and both Bess' and Harry's mothers lived at the White House during the nearly eight-year Presidency. By temperament, character, and psychological nature, Harry S. Truman was a one-woman man who, fortunate in having found that very special woman, was incapable of carrying on an illicit love life.

*One must be firm, have a firm heart—otherwise one
has no business mixing in war and government.*
                              —Napoléon Bonaparte

22

THE REAL FIRST LADY

On a warm, quiet evening in the spring of 1798, ex-President George Washington paced restlessly down the hillside of his property to the Potomac River. He stared somberly at the wide stretch of dark water. His thoughts were not of his cheerful, placid wife, Martha, waiting for him inside the distant house—they were of a woman named Sally who was living alone and impoverished far beyond the sea. Washington returned to his study that night and wrote Sally a letter in which he said: "None of the important events since I have last seen you nor all of them together have been able to eradicate from my mind the recollection of those happy moments, the happiest of my life, which I have enjoyed in your company."

Since the national hero had not seen his one true love in almost thirty years, the "important events" he was referring to were the magnificent victories of the American Revolution and the glory of his Presidency. At the end of his illustrious career, these glories meant nothing to Washington in comparison to the great love he had sacrificed to get them. In his almost pathetic letter to Sally, the greatest man in America humbly begged the widow to leave her modest home in England and come to live at Mount Vernon and keep him company in his old age. Sally never answered his pleas.

Contrary to one of the most popular and firmly believed legends of all time, George and Martha Washington were not a romantic love match. Their marriage was a calm and serene partnership, a union of two friends who joined together in a convenient arrangement of mutual material benefit. Each respected the other and possessed a very real affection, but there was no passion ever present and the myth of their great romance is as apocryphal as the sacred cherry tree.

Throughout history, there has been a full range of theories and legends regarding our first President's true sexuality. Because he was most likely sterile, many have claimed that he was a eunuch, and a few have even gone so far as to claim that he was actually a woman in disguise. Some early stories sought to win for him the title of "The Stallion of the Potomac." Other more reliable witnesses testify to Washington's complete abstinence from sexual activity in his later life. To resolve the conflicting claims of such extremes, it is necessary to examine the personality of the man and evaluate all of the evidence available.

To begin with, George Washington inherited an extraordinarily passionate temperament. His mother, again in direct contrast to the time-honored myth of soft and gentle maternal perfection, was a wild-tempered woman of great emotional energy who made life miserable for everyone around her. Widowed early in life and left with meager financial resources, Mary Washington had channeled all of her passionate nature in a negative direction. Her great frustration had created a narrow-minded, grudging, shrewish personality which seldom showed any degree of warmth or affection. George never got along at all with his mother and left home as soon as he could go to live with his older half-brother.

Without ever admitting it or even consciously realizing it,

George Washington was very much like his mother. However, instead of being destroyed by the same passionate nature, he learned very early in life that his success and survival in the world would depend upon his ability to master and control his over-powering impulses and desires.

Thus, due to the threatening example of his mother's painful failure to cope with life, Washington began his relentless, almost superhuman struggle to control his passions, and, when unable to do so, to eliminate and destroy them.

George Washington's progress through life had only one theme: self-control.

The celebrated American painter Gilbert Stuart made several life portraits of our first President, and he put as much effort as anyone into observing the appearance and true essence of the great hero. Stuart later would state: "All of his features were indicative of the most ungovernable passions, and had he been born in the forests, it is my opinion that he would have been the fiercest man among the savage tribes."

Washington's unfortunate relationship, or lack of it, with his mother would affect all of his love relationships during his lifetime. His ambivalent feelings for his mother would create not only complex and contradictory attitudes towards women in general, but also intense needs for certain attachments in particular. There would be both the compelling desire to replace the cold, disapproving mother with a warm, affectionate and appreciative woman and the unsettling impulse to distrust the feminine and resist any deep involvement at all cost.

This great need for female acceptance and support, combined with a suspicion and aversion to the feminine, produced in Washington unique psychological needs.

As a youth, the future President masked and protected his vulnerable feelings and passionate nature behind the facade of an almost foolishly theatrical and histrionic disposition. The chal-

243

lenging circumstances and early hardships of his existence had prompted him to adapt and flourish by experiencing life as a great drama. By the time he was a teenager, it was second nature to Washington to respond intuitively to the elements of drama in any important moment, and especially in the expression of his deeper feelings. This trait would serve him well in later life when he would perform like a great actor in seizing center stage with the perfect word, tone, or gesture and making the most of it in a flawlessly natural way.

But before having reached this polished and mature level of development, Washington suffered through a youth in which his heart grew stronger by means of an excess of theatricality and playacting that sometimes approached the absurd. He loved going to the theater and liked dancing and all of the other pleasant amusements of proper society. He especially showed a strong attraction for beautiful young women. Unfortunately, the teenage boy was socially awkward, being larger and taller than almost all of the other young men and intensely manly and masculine which somewhat intimidated and frightened the girls and kept them away. Nearing his mature stature of 6'3" and 190 pounds, the muscular Washington was a commanding figure.

The adolescent young man was further hampered by a distinct lack of wealth and worldly position. It had been difficult for the Washington family to make ends meet, and it certainly did not escape George's impressionable young eyes when his favorite brother, Lawrence, advanced himself considerably by marrying into a wealthy Virginia dynasty.

Socially unskilled, physically awkward, and of a humble family background, it is no wonder that the affection-starved Washington retreated into the role of a dreamy romantic and fell in love with love. To an obscure girl named Frances Alexander the sixteen-year-old boy wrote a poem which began: "From your bright sparkling I was undone,/Rays you have more transparent than the sun."

There was no romance with Frances, however, and she remained just a distant object to kindle Washington's dreamy imagination and dramatic flamboyance. Another of the boy's poetic efforts during this same time showed even more his romantic nature and passionate yearnings:

> Oh, ye Gods, why should my poor resistless heart
> Stand to oppose thy might and power
> At last surrender to Cupid's feather'd dart
> And now lays bleeding every hour
> For her that's pitiless of my grief and woes
> And will not on me pity take
> I'll sleep amongst my most inveterate foes
> And with gladness wish to wake.
> In deluding sleepings let my eyelids close
> That in an enraptured dream I may
> In a soft lulling sleep and gentle repose
> Possess those joys denied by day.

It was at this tender time that Washington became friendly with the Fairfax family and met the incomparable Sally. The Fairfax dynasty was one of the richest and most illustrious families in Virginia. They were also the in-laws of George's favorite older brother, Lawrence. George was a shy, impressionable sixteen-year-old and the talented, sophisticated Fairfax family showed kindness and understanding in taking him into their socially brilliant circle of elegant dinner parties, card games, dances, and amateur dramatics.

Sally Fairfax was the eighteen-year-old wife of George Fairfax, Washington's good friend and the son of his former employer. She had been a member of the prominent Cary family before her recent marriage and was very popular because of her lively personality, vivacious wit, and sparkling good humor. She was also a very attractive young woman possessed of a prodigious amount of flirtatious charm. The awkward young Washington fell under

Sally's spell and found himself deeply in love.

For her part, Sally was, at first, amused and flattered by her adolescent admirer's exaggerated infatuation. She was an uncomplicated woman of purely feminine charm and superficial qualities. With no intellectual interests or any serious spiritual depth to temper her carefree, frivolous character, Sally Fairfax was exactly the type of woman that so often captures the hearts and imaginations of hyper-masculine men. Playfully alluring, she made every effort to attract and, then, gracefully pull back, always keeping one step ahead and out of reach, and, thus, confusing and frustrating her prey.

Washington would forever be a man who was a helpless victim to the Machiavellian machinations of the feminine mystique. Women were always a total mystery to the rugged, manly first President. He was never to understand anything about them. Although he idealized women, he was never obsessed by them. Finding them to be rather strange creatures of a far superior quality, Washington ensured himself with maximum protection against the early hurt in life which his mother inflicted on him. He also could safely tie up his heart and vent his dramatic feelings of romance on a hopeless situation, the love of a married woman— a woman married to one of his closest friends, and also be free and unhampered to pursue his most important goals in life—wealth, fame, social prominence, and admiring recognition. By placing his women on pedestals, he gained the advantage of never having to take his opinions from them and most certainly never having to fashion his life to fit any woman's ideas or conceptions.

The platonic romance with Sally grew in intensity until her relatives couldn't help but take notice and become uncomfortable and concerned. Young Washington was finally sent off on a military campaign against the Indians and one observer of his indiscreet affections advised him in a letter that it was far better to spend his passions fighting the Indians instead of in the pursuit of "an impossible love."

As time passed, the young man's ardor would surge and wane like the Atlantic tides. Sally never failed to do exactly the right thing to keep Washington on tenterhooks. In the beginning the true extent of her feelings for him was questionable. Certainly she didn't take the awkward lad seriously in the least and was flattered by his devotion. The tone of her responses was clearly that of a tease. Next to her sophisticated, successful husband, the clumsy youth of modest background was never even a serious rival. Sally was amused by Washington and had fun with him. She was enough of a coquette to ignore the depth of his feeling and the consequences of her actions. When the young man reached his breaking point, he would vow he'd had enough and storm off never to return. But, of course, he would.

The memory of Sally would be ignited by a place or face and Washington would once more become enraptured with her. He would write her letters and she would respond begging him not to communicate with her again. But when he finally would stop writing and retreat in utter frustration, Sally would always send him an appealing little note which never failed to revive his flame of love.

When her feelings changed and became more serious and committed is not known definitely. However, as the two young people matured and progressed through life, their love also matured and developed from the uncertain playfulness of teenagers into the grand passion of worldly experience. Of most importance was the growing success and stature of Washington and the gradual reversal of contrast with Sally's rich, but tranquil and unambitious husband.

Unfortunately for Washington's dilemma, the passing of time only seemed to enhance Sally's physical beauty. Her classic features became even more perfect as she progressed through her twenties. With her very long neck, clear white skin, large dark eyes, lustrous chestnut-colored hair, and willow-thin figure, Sally was always the center of masculine attention. Bubbling with charm and laughter, she was also full of a variety of feminine vanities, and she would become annoyed when other women received more attention from men than she did. Sally took great care to always attract and charm, no matter who she was around.

Washington described Sally to a friend as "an amiable beauty, filled with mirth, good humor, and ease of mind." Yet, she still confounded him. Her unerring technique of always following her advances with skillful little retreats never failed to leave the future military master-strategist disturbed and thoroughly confused.

Because divorce was almost unknown in Colonial Virginia and, even if possible, a union with a divorced woman would bring instant death to all of his ambitions, Washington began looking elsewhere for a wife. Perhaps reconciling himself to his hopeless eternal love for Sally Fairfax, he seems to have stopped looking for romantic or sexual love in the women he would pursue. Whether he was reluctant to give his deepest love a rival or unable to be aroused again to an equal passion, he somewhat single-mindedly ventured forth on a determined quest to marry a woman of both impressive wealth and social position. Between his periodic romantic visits to Sally in her husband's home, Washington began channeling his great feelings of frustration into courting eligible women who could fulfill his glittering material desires.

When he was twenty, Washington started seriously courting Betsy Fauntleroy, the sixteen-year-old daughter of a rich Virginia planter. Although Betsy was attractive with her petite figure, her turned-up nose, and her smiling high spirits, it is difficult to believe that Washington had any sincere or deep affection for her. But it really didn't matter. Betsy's father considered young George to be from a second-rate family and not nearly good enough for his daughter. His suit was promptly rejected.

This rejection, emphasizing more than ever his distance from the prestige and worldly position that he sought, only strengthened Washington's resolve to capture these elusive prizes through a brilliant marriage. Moving on to his next candidates, he never mentioned Betsy's name again and never even wrote of her in his memoirs.

Without specific documentation, legend has it that during his early twenties Washington proposed to and was rejected by many young, rich and aristocratic beauties. Indeed, almost every self-respecting Tidewater mansion in Virginia which dates back to that period boasts a prized room in which the eager young Washington was supposed to have proposed marriage to the daughter of the house and been duly rejected. If even a fraction of these legendary stories were true, it would tax credibility. At the most, Washington might have had two or three of his marriage offers turned down, but he was much too calculating and shy to have exposed himself more than a few times to such humiliation and embarrassment.*

At age twenty-four, he met Eliza "Polly" Philipse during a trip to New York City. Polly was two years older than Washington, single, beautiful, and rich. Very rich! She was the heiress of one of New York's great Dutch baronial families. Advancing rapidly toward spinsterhood, Polly Philipse was very available for marriage and appears to have been captivated by the huge young man from Virginia. She most definitely showed the first interest and she encouraged him to pay her court. However, being of a strong-willed and almost dominating temperament, Polly had both the advantages and disadvantages of reminding Washington of his disagreeable mother. Therefore, he was both attracted and put off by her at the same time.

Washington might have hoped to have fallen in love with Polly, but he never did. He was enamored of her vast material assets, though, and he began a half-hearted courtship that lasted almost a year. He had to borrow money from his friends to finance

---

*In fact, the discouragement of these early rejections made Washington reluctant, if not unwilling, to make the first courting moves in the future. It would be older, more mature women who would aggressively pursue the cautious young Washington.

his trips to New York, as few as they were, to see Polly. He vaguely hoped to marry her and felt guilty he couldn't summon up enough enthusiasm to visit her more often.

But then he came into contact with Sally Fairfax again—met her at a party, shared a dance and laughter on a moonlit lawn—and he realized once again that it was she whom he loved and no other. He did not return to New York to call on Polly and the potential relationship finally collapsed under the unbearable weight of Washington's total lack of interest.

The platonic affair with Sally continued. Washington devoted more and more of his time to visiting her and her good-natured husband. The flirtations became stronger, the affectionate looks lingered longer, the laughter louder and more constant, and the tension reached a fever pitch between the two frustrated lovers. When Washington could stand no more, he applied his unfailing self-control, packed up his passion, and moved on to a self-imposed exile. He again sought a solution to this seemingly unsolvable romantic problem by trying to contract an advantageous marriage. He began socializing more freely and made the acquaintance of several new friends. One of these was Martha Custis.

Martha was several months older than George, but she always seemed much more his senior. Plump and attractive, her short stature was further exaggerated by the contrast with Washington's unusual tallness. Martha Custis was a widow with two small children. Her charming, placid, good-natured personality was permeated with a strong sense of the maternal. It may well have been this outstanding trait of the secure, gentle mother that Washington found so attractive. Martha was certainly an ideal mother type, one that was far different from Washington's own parent and one that he undoubtedly had been searching for his entire life.

What most definitely did attract the rising young military leader was the fact that the death of Martha's husband had left her the wealthiest woman in Virginia. Washington needed her money and her social prestige, while Martha Custis needed a just and firm administrator for her numerous estates and a kindly and devoted father for her two young children. They each fulfilled the other's needs. They each liked and respected the other, finding a pleasant matching of personalities and harmonious temperaments.

A sensible and honest woman, Martha played no games of pretended romance. She gently led Washington to the logical conclusion that their wedded union would provide them both with excellent benefits, and she even helped him in his awkward and anxious proposal.

Plans for the marriage were made. It was 1759. Washington was twenty-seven years old. Now, his thoughts suddenly drifted back to Sally Fairfax. He couldn't risk seeing her as he had done before when courting Polly Philipse. So, he wrote her a long letter. In it he said: "Misconstrue not my meaning; doubt it not, or expose it. The world has no business to know the object of my love declared in this manner to you, when I want to conceal it." Shortly after he sent Sally the letter, he married Martha.

The marriage is well documented and has taken its place in history as one of the most successful of wedded unions. There is absolutely no evidence that George was ever unfaithful to Martha. However, there is also nothing to indicate that there was even any small degree of romantic love or passion in the marriage. They were best friends to each other and the harmony and tranquility of their relationship was, to a great extent, based on the fact that it rested on a solid, calm foundation of practicality and logical reason rather than upon one with the slightest trace of exciting sexual passion.

George Washington's love letters to Martha were filled only with affectionate expressions of friendship. They would have been appropriate between friends of the same gender or members of the same family. George more than once commented on the superiority of "domestic felicity" to that of "the giddy rounds of promiscuous pleasure." However, throughout his entire marriage

THE BETTMAN ARCHIVE

In this little-known painting by H.A. Ogden, George Washington's marriage to Martha Custis is romantically depicted. Although the President-to-be here appears moonstruck, and Martha looks equally smitten, history would conspire to conceal the fact that theirs was a marriage of convenience, a union of friends, and not a love match.

he continued to be romantically devoted to Sally Fairfax. He still penned numerous letters to her declaring his feelings and assuming the tone of a complaining lover trying to revive and win back the exalted prize he has once known.

Sally, for her part, also continued writing Washington ultra-romantic letters during his marriage. She was careful to write them without her husband's knowledge, and Washington always cautiously destroyed them as soon as he read them. It was during these years after George and Martha's marriage that Sally finally abandoned her role of coquette and fell more deeply in love with Washington.

Thus, the emotional passion of the relationship grew stronger with the passing of years. At the time of the American Revolution, Washington wrote to a close friend about Sally: "I feel the force of her amiable beauties in the recollection of a thousand tender passages that I wish to obliterate till I am bid revive them."

The exact nature and full extent of the Sally Fairfax affair can never be known for certain. It seems doubtful if their physical passion was ever gratified. No scandal ever occurred publicly and Washington and Sally's husband remained very close friends. The absence of sexual communion between Washington and Sally Fairfax would also explain the prolonged and heightened state of romantic limerance between the two frustrated lovers.

Thus, the founding father of the United States was truly successful throughout his entire life in mastering his passion and re-directing it to achieve material gain and stable personal relationships. At the end of his life, Washington could well speak from experience when he wrote warningly to his step-granddaughter:

> . . . beware, lest love become an involuntary passion. In the composition of the human frame there is a great deal of inflammable matter, however dormant it may lie for a time, and when the torch is put to it, *that* which is *within you* must burst into a blaze.

George Washington valiantly avoided that "blaze" until the very last year of his life. But, then, it finally consumed him while idling away his lonely days of retirement on the banks of the Potomac. His begging letter to Sally clearly shows his feelings of aching regret at the choices he had earlier made—the compromises and sacrifices of his heart in exchange for wealth and glory. As Washington looked back upon his life, he finally realized that all of the material rewards he had won, far greater than he could have ever dreamed of, meant nothing to him because of the price he had to pay for them.

Staring towards the hollow prospect of illustrious immortality, George Washington only wished to see the face of the woman he had loved his whole life but had always denied himself. He would give up anything, now, to be at last united with his beloved Sally. When his letter arrived in London his beloved might have experienced a variety of emotions. But whatever her response, her greatest gift to Washington was that she remained silent and never answered it.

George Washington died suddenly a year later. His first and final breach of iron self-control passed unnoticed and produced no disaster upon his godly reputation. He and his wife entered history as the ideal American couple, and Sally Fairfax, the real First Lady in Washington's life, vanished into obscurity.

One word frees us of all the weight and pain
of life: that word is love.
                            —Sophocles

23

A PURITAN IN PARIS

George Washington's successor to the Presidency was John Adams, a short, plump man from Boston who was an even more severe self-disciplinarian. Adams enjoyed, perhaps, one of the happiest and most successful marriages of any President in history. For fifty-four years he and his superb wife, Abigail, were as well matched intellectually and emotionally and as devoted to each other as two people could possibly be. They very simply existed as the entire world to each other. As President, John openly sought out and took seriously his brilliant wife's direction and advice, a practice that his political enemies attacked with outraged vigor.

A deeply religious New Englander who vented his great natural passion in embracing the rigid Puritanical maxims of working harder and longer than anyone else and almost completely denying all of life's sensual pleasures, Adams was able to maintain these impossibly high standards for all of his days, with the exception of a brief sojourn in Paris when he faced the greatest

255

personal conflict of his life. In Paris the staunch young Puritan from Boston confronted head-on all that he had avoided and denied himself. The temptations were overwhelming, and John Adams' response to them is as interesting as it was curious.

In his autobiography, Adams candidly wrote:

> I was of an amorous disposition and very early from ten or eleven Years of Age, was very fond of the Society of females. I had my favorites among young women and spent many of my evenings in their company and this disposition although controlled for seven years after my entrance into college returned and engaged me too much until I was married.

Regardless of this self-confessed romantic disposition, the pudgy, serious-minded young Adams was not very successful with women. To compensate, he channeled most of his overflowing passion into a single-minded ambition to progress as far as he could in the material world.

John's first romantic involvement was with Hannah Quincy, the playfully flirtatious daughter of the wealthy Colonel Josiah Quincy. Adams was twenty-four and was so carried away by his passionate feelings that he couldn't work because he was constantly thinking of her. The courtship came to its conclusion one afternoon in Hannah's house when John found himself alone in the room with her. He began mildly making love to her and, swiftly being swept away by his great natural ardor, was on the verge of proposing marriage. Suddenly, the young couple were interrupted by another member of the household. John was instantly brought back to his senses. He promptly got up and left, resolving once and for all to end the potentially dangerous relationship with Hannah.

Later, with large, bold strokes of self-satisfaction, Adams wrote in his diary: "The thing is ended. A tender scene! A great sacrifice to reason!"

John Adams' passionate nature was so overwhelming to him that he honestly believed that he only had two rigid choices in life: a complete and dissipated indolence, or a ruthless and unrelenting self-control and harsh discipline. Like Washington, Adams committed himself to the security of the latter choice and directed his passion into politics and his career. When he finally met his intellectual match in the talented Abigail, Adams realized that the firm cerebral basis of the marriage would not only accommodate his physical desires, but also serve as the strongest support for his exalted career ambitions.

After breaking up with Hannah Quincy, John Adams had also declared to his sacred diary: "Let love and vanity be extinguished, and the great passions of Ambition and Patriotism break out and burn." Abigail offered him a superb focus and control of all that was best in him.

In 1778, when Adams was forty-three, he was selected as a representative of the fledgling United States government on an important mission to France to secure that country's continued support for the Revolutionary War in America. Because it was necessary for his wife, Abigail, to remain at home in Massachusetts with their children, Adams sailed alone. The separation from his wife some became an agony for Adams and resulted in the most crushing personal crisis of his life.

On first arriving in France, the dour Bostonian was instantly the victim of his senses. He was overwhelmed by his first French meal. He found the cooking so superb and the dishes so elaborate that they were hardly to be believed. Soon, everything in France was actively seducing Adams from his rigid abstinence from pleasure. The graceful and sumptuous design of the architecture, the glamourous style of the fashions, the splendor of society gatherings, the polished learning and manners of the culture, even the perfect textures and colors of the natural French landscapes— all of these things almost seemed to conspire to conquer the

257

Puritan's self-discipline and sacred vow to sensual denial.

At the first elegant dinner party Adams attended in Bordeaux, the young and beautiful Madame de Texel smilingly asked the shy, middle-aged diplomat:

> Mr. Adams, by your name I conclude you are descended from the first Man and Woman, and probably in your family may be preserved the tradition which may resolve a difficulty which I could never explain. I never could understand how the first couple found out about the Art of lying together?

Adams had never heard a woman speak in such a manner as this before and he found it "shocking" and "surprising." He later wrote:

> I believe at first I blushed; then, I replied: "There was a physical quality in us resembling the power of electricity or of the magnet, by which when a pair approach within a striking distance they flew together like the needle to the pole or like two objects in electrical experiments."

Madame de Texel smiled and replied: "Well, I know not how it was, but this I know—it is a very happy shock." Adams, undoubtedly, blushed again.

Without time to resist, Adams' extremely sensuous nature was deeply and immediately touched by French society. In his first, delayed letter to his wife he confessed: "The Delights of France are innumerable. The Politeness, the Elegance, the Softness, the Delicacy is extreme. In short, stern and haughty Republican as I am, I cannot help loving these people."

Adams spent the first few weeks of his long stay freely rejoicing in the delights of his senses. However, it was not long before he became fully aware of the basic immortality of French society. The commonly accepted practice of lovers and mistresses and totally loose morals in Paris was increasingly difficult for Adams to accept. The fact that he did so at all was motivated by his sense of duty to do so for the sake of his job. Within time, Adams began working harder and harder, practicing a high degree of self-sacrifice, and only going out socially when he absolutely had to.

The crisis had begun for John Adams. Assaulted by the irresistible temptations of Parisian life, Adams had struggled to hold his own, but suddenly he was engaged in a conflict that critically threatened his beliefs more than any other he would ever encounter. The conflict very simply stepped forward in the genial presence of Benjamin Franklin.

Franklin had preceded Adams to France on the same important mission of American support. As the senior representative of the United States, Franklin had conquered French society completely and was respected and revered as almost a god. Everything about him had won the hearts and minds of the French people and his fame spread throughout Europe and exceeded that of any other person from the New World.

But there was a private side to this elderly, kindly sage that Adams discovered during his sojourn. It was a side that shook Adams to his core and almost produced a serious breakdown. The wise and witty Franklin, it seemed, was every bit as immoral as the French, if not more so. Living in Paris in the company of his illegitimate son and his illegitimate son's illegitimate son, Franklin was chiefly interested in the pursuit of pleasure, and sexual pleasure most especially.

The ordinarily jealous and paranoid Adams found his comparison with Franklin to be unbearable. Under Franklin's leadership, very little in the way of diplomacy had been accomplished in Paris and papers and reports were in a total mess. It was up to Adams to work double-time to put things in a workable state. He slaved night and day while his esteemed associate was not only glitteringly honored and given all of the credit but was unfairly being hailed for all of the qualities that he did not really possess but that Adams did.

Abigail and John Adams, in old age. The two corresponded, in great volume, when he was away from Boston and, if not passionate lovers, were always great friends and sources of mutual support. Mrs. Adams' portrait is by Gilbert Stuart.

The portrait of President John Adams is an engraving after an earlier portrait (artist unknown).

261

Adams grew to despise Franklin. He bitterly contrasted the reputation of the "great man" with the true immortality of his character. While Adams cultivated the greatest virtues and performed most of the work, the proper reward for such efforts was being showered upon Franklin for his cunning and immoral behavior.

Never popular in France and certainly never acclaimed, Adams enviously directed his entire frustration towards the portly target from Philadelphia. A logical implication may have been, to Adams, that his own strict code of behavior was, after all, not the ticket to success that he had always thought it was. All of his goals and ambitions in life were being obtained by a man who was engaging in the hedonistic pursuits of total abandon. Maybe Adams had been wrong all this time. Maybe the example of Franklin was one that should be emulated if Adams hoped to gain an equal position and fame in society.

These were the doubts that haunted John Adams during the lonely hours of the night in his Paris home. Franklin's persona was the deepest personal challenge of Adams' life. Parisian life in general and Franklin in particular served as a neat little drama in which Adams was forced to do mortal combat with the strongest elements of his nature. It was a contest almost ideally designed to bring out his full capacities for self-control and the renunciation of all and any pleasures. After many months of enduring such a contest, Adams wrote to his wife back home: "I believe I am grown more austere, severe, rigid, and miserable that I ever was."

Never at a loss for the intellectual, Adams sought to bury his emotional responses in thoughtful conclusions and theories. He later wrote: "From all that I had read of history and government, I had drawn this conclusion, that the manners of the women were the most infallible barometer to ascertain the degree of virtue and morality in a nation."

Adams firmly believed that it was, indeed, women who determined the moral standards of a society, especially the sexual standards. He viewed the immorality of France's culture as being the direct result of the French woman's loose morals and casual approach to sex. Adams greatly feared that if this influence spread to America it would be certain to destroy the fiber of the nation.

His concerns may have been so great because of his own situation being so threatened by the shadow of sexual license. The severe anxiety caused by his forced separation from his beloved wife and the prolonged state of celibacy which it created was made even harder to endure because of the overpoweringly sensuous sophistication of his environment and the challenging example of his illustrious fellow countryman.

It can never be known if Adams ever did give in to Franklin's joyous example. If he did have any affairs in Paris, they surely must have been secret, brief flings that caused much guilt to his Puritanical New England conscience. Within time, Adams seems to have traveled full cycle and gradually returned to an active social life during the later part of his stay. To his close friend, Richard Henry Lee, he wrote from France: "He must be of a strange disposition who cannot be happy at Paris where he may have the choices of all the pleasures, amusements and studies which human life affords."

What *is* known is the telling fact that for the rest of his life, whenever Adams would write about Franklin, his pen would slip and make many unnecessary mistakes.

AFTERWORD

Love and pride stock Bedlam.
—Thomas Fuller

*F*or those who constantly contend that a man's private life has nothing to do with his public performance, the study of our forty-one Presidents and the secret love affairs of many of them proves just the opposite. There may not be a precise parallel between an individual's personal morality and his public conduct, but there is, indeed, a solid consistency of behavior that it impossible to ignore. The way in which a man controls or indulges his passions indeed has a vital effect on how he performs in the other areas of his life. To fully understand the actions and characters of a political leader, it is necessary to examine the nature of his love relationships. How such a man deals with his sexuality can tell us more about him than any other single fact.

Had John F. Kennedy not indulged his sexual compulsions, the history of the United States might have taken a quite different path. His lack of sexual control certainly undermined the success of his Presidency. Lyndon Johnson's descent into paranoia and his inability, ultimately, to come to terms with the problems of his administration were obviously related to the fear of the discovery of his illicit affairs and his frustration in obtaining the love he so desperately wanted.

The moral and psychological dilemmas of Richard Nixon can be attributed to his repressed sexuality and unsatisfactory emotional relationships. His self-destructive debacle, Watergate, probably would never have occurred had he enjoyed a better sexual adjustment to life. And would Carter or Reagan have been elected had they been men of entirely different moral characters? Was the serenity of the Eisenhower White House the direct result of Ike's listless acceptance of his frustrated passion?

Franklin Delano Roosevelt very nearly gave up his early political career to marry his true love, and Abraham Lincoln might never have pursued the Presidency had he freely followed out the feelings and inclinations of poet Walt Whitman.

The entire history of our nation has been shaped by the characters of its leaders, and their characters have largely been formed and molded by their sexual natures and their love relationships. Whatever we might think of them and however we may judge them, the passions of our Presidents have ruled *our* lives as much as they have *theirs*.

266

SELECTED
BIBLIOGRAPHY

Of the approximately 930 sources used in researching *Presidential Passions*, those following are the primary sources consulted.

General

Bannett, Carole. *Partners to the Presidents*. New York: Citadel Press, 1966.

Barber, James. *The Presidential Character*. Englewood Cliffs, NJ: Prentice-Hall, 1977.

Boller, Paul F. *Presidential Character*. New York: Oxford University Press, 1984.

Brown, Roger. *Social Psychology*. New York: Fred Press, 1965.

Burns, James MacGregor. *Leadership*. New York: Harper & Row, 1977.

Califano, Joseph. *A Presidential Nation*. New York: W. W. Norton, 1975.

Davidson, James West. *After the Fact: The Art of Historical Detection*. New York: Alfred A. Knopf, 1986.

Donovan, Hedley. *Roosevelt to Reagan*. New York: Harper & Row, 1985.

Edwards, George. *The Public Presidency*. New York: St. Martin's Press, 1983.

Goldberg, Herb. *The Hazards of Being Male: Surviving the Myth of Masculine Privilege*. New York: New American Library, 1976.

Hatch, Louis. *A History of the Vice Presidency*. Westport, CT: Greenwood Press, 1970.

Hollander, E. P. *Current Perspectives in Social Psychology*. New York: Oxford University Press, 1963.

Graff, Henry. *The Presidents: A Reference History*. New York: Charles Scribner's Sons, 1984.

Greenstein, Fred. *A Sourcebook for the Study of Personality and Poli-*

tics. Chicago: Markham, 1971.

Hughes, Emmett. *The Ordeal of Power*. New York: Atheneum, 1963.

Kane, Joseph. *Facts About the Presidents*. New York: W. W. Norton, 1974.

Kellerman, Barbara. *All the President's Kin*. New York: Free Press, 1981.

Koenig, Louis. *The Chief Executive*. New York: Harcourt Brace Jovanovich, 1975.

Levinson, Daniel. *The Seasons of a Man's Life*. New York: Alfred A. Knopf, 1978.

Monaco, James. *Celebrity*. New York: Delta, 1978.

Neustadt, Richard. *Presidential Power*. New York: John Wiley, 1960.

Novak, Michael. *Choosing Our King*. New York: MacMillan, 1974.

Parks, Lillian Rogers. *Backstairs at the White House*. New York: Doubleday, 1972.

Parsons, Talcott. *Social Structure and Personality*. New York: Free Press, 1964.

Pessen, Edward. *The Log Cabin Myth: The Social Backgrounds of the Presidents*. New Haven: Yale University Press, 1984.

Polsby, Nelson. *Presidential Elections*. New York: Charles Scribner's Sons, 1976.

Reedy, George. *The Twilight of the Presidency*. New York: New American Library, 1970.

Rossiter, Clinton. *The American Presidency*. New York: Harcourt Brace, 1956.

Schlesinger, Arthur. *The Imperial Presidency*. New York: Popular Library, 1973.

Spragens, William. *Popular Images of the American Presidents*. Westport, CT: Greenwood Press, 1986.

Sochen, June. *Herstory: A Woman's View of American History*. New York: Alfred A. Knopf, 1974.

Southwick, Leslie. *Presidential Also-Rans and Running Mates*. London: MacFarland & Company, 1984.

Stone, Irving. *They Also Ran*. Garden City, NY: Doubleday, 1944.

Taylor, Tim. *The Book of Presidents*. New York: E. P. Dutton, 1972.

West, J. B. *Upstairs at the White House*. New York: Warner, 1974.

Wildavsky, Aaron. *The Presidency*. Boston: Little, Brown, 1974.

Chapters 1–4

Adler, Bill. *The Kennedy Children*. New York: Franklin Watts, 1980.

Baldridge, Letitia. *Of Diamonds and Diplomats*. Boston: Houghton Mifflin, 1968.

Barrow, Andrew. *Gossip: A History of High Society from 1920 to 1970*. New York: Coward, McCann, and Geohegan, 1978.

Bishop, Jim. *A Day in the Life of President Kennedy*. New York: Random House, 1964.

Blair, Joan and Clay. *The Search for JFK*. New York: Berkeley, 1976.

Bradlee, Benjamin. *Conversations with Kennedy*. New York: W. W. Norton, 1975.

———. *That Special Grace*. Philadelphia: Lippincott, 1964.

Bryant, Traphes, and Frances Spatz Leighton. *Dog Days at the White House: The Outrageous Memoirs of the Presidential Kennel Keeper*. New York: Macmillan, 1975.

Burns, James McGregor. *Edward Kennedy and the Camelot Legacy*. New York: W. W. Norton, 1976.

———. *John Kennedy*. New York: Harcourt Brace, 1961.

Cameron, Gail. *Rose: A Biography of Rose Fitzgerald Kennedy*. New York: Putnam, 1971.

Clinch, Nancy. *The Kennedy Neurosis*. New York: Grosset and Dunlap, 1973.

Collier, Peter, and David Horowitz. *The Kennedys: An American Drama*. New York: Summit, 1984.

Curtis, Charlotte. *First Lady*. New York: Pyramid Books, 1962.

Damore, Leo. *Senatorial Privilege*. Washington, DC: Regnery-Gateway, 1988.

David, Lester and Irene. *Bobby Kennedy: The Making of a Folk Hero*. New York: Dodd, Mead, 1986.

Davis, John H. *The Kennedys: Dynasty and Disaster*. New York: McGraw-Hill, 1984.

De Toledano, Ralph. *R.F.K.: The Man Who Would Be President*. New York: Putnam, 1967.

Exner, Judith. *My Story*. New York: Grove Press, 1977.

Gallagher, Mary Barelli. *My Life with Jacqueline Kennedy*. New York: John McKay, 1969.

Goodwin, Doris. *The Fitzgeralds and the Kennedys: An American Saga.* New York: Simon and Schuster, 1987.

Guiles, Fred. *Legend: The Life and Death of Marilyn Monroe.* New York: Stein and Day, 1984.

Hall, Gordon Langley. *Jacqueline Kennedy.* New York: Frederick Fell, 1964.

Heymann, C. David. *A Woman Named Jackie.* New York: Lyle Stuart, 1989.

Kelly, Kitty. *Jackie Oh!* Secaucus, NJ: Lyle Stuart, 1978.

Kennedy, Robert. *Thirteen Days.* New York: W. W. Norton, 1969.

Kennedy, Rose Fitzgerald. *Times to Remember.* New York: Doubleday, 1974.

Koskoff, David. *Joseph P. Kennedy: A Life and Times.* Englewood Cliffs, NJ: Prentice-Hall, 1974.

Kramer, Frieda. *Jackie: A Truly Intimate Biography.* New York: Grosset and Dunlap, 1979.

Lasky, Victor. *J.F.K.: The Man and the Myth.* New York: Macmillan, 1963; Trident Press, 1968.

Lincoln, Evelyn. *Kennedy and Johnson.* New York: Holt, Rinehart and Winston, 1968.

————. *My Twelve Years with John F. Kennedy.* New York: David McKay, 1965.

Logan, Joshua. *Movie Stars, Real People, and Me.* New York: Delacorte Press, 1978.

Mailer, Norman. *Marilyn.* New York: Grosset and Dunlap, 1973.

Manchester, William. *The Death of a President.* New York: Harper and Row, 1967.

Meyers, Joan Simpson. *John Fitzgerald Kennedy: As We Remember Him.* New York: Atheneum, 1965.

Morrow, Robert. *The Senator Must Die: The Murder of Robert Kennedy.* Santa Monica, CA: Roundtable Press, 1988.

Navasky, Victor. *Kennedy Justice.* New York: Atheneum, 1970.

Newfield, Jack. *Robert Kennedy: A Memoir.* New York: Dutton, 1969.

Paper, Lewis. *John F. Kennedy: The Promise and the Performance.* New York: Da Capo, 1980.

Parmet, Herbert. *The Struggles of John F. Kennedy.* New York: Dial Press, 1983.

Plimpton, George. *An American Journey: The Times of Robert Kennedy.* New York: Harcourt Brace, 1970.

Powers, David, and Kenneth O'Donnell. *Johnny, We Hardly Knew Ye.* Boston: Little, Brown, 1972.

Rachlin, Harvey. *The Kennedys.* New York: World Almanac Company, 1986.

Riese, Randall, and Neil Hitchens. *The Unabridged Marilyn.* New York: Congdon and Weed, 1987.

Romero, Gerry. *Sinatra's Women.* New York: Manor, 1976.

Salinger, Pierre. *With Kennedy.* Garden City, NY: Doubleday, 1966.

Scheim, David E. *Contract on America: The Mafia Murder of John F. Kennedy.* New York: Shapolsky, 1988.

Schlesinger, Arthur M. *A Thousand Days.* Boston: Houghton Mifflin, 1965.

————. *Robert Kennedy and His Times.* Boston: Houghton Mifflin, 1978.

Sciacca, Tony. *Kennedy and His Women.* New York, Manor, 1976.

Shannon, William. *The Heir Apparent.* New York: Macmillan, 1967.

Sidey, Hugh. *John F. Kennedy: President.* New York: Atheneum, 1964.

Slatzer, Robert. *The Life and Curious Death of Marilyn Monroe.* New York: Pinnacle, 1974.

Smith, Gene. *When the Cheering Stopped.* New York: Morrow, 1964.

Sorensen, Theodore. *Kennedy.* New York: Harper and Row, 1965.

————. *The Kennedy Legacy.* New York: Macmillan, 1969.

Speriglio, Milo. *The Marilyn Conspiracy.* New York: Pocket Books, 1986.

Strait, Raymond. *The Tragic Secret Life of Jayne Mansfield.* Chicago: Henry Regnery, 1974.

Summers, Anthony. *Goddess: The Secret Lives of Marilyn Monroe.* New York: Macmillan, 1985.

Swanson, Gloria. *Swanson on Swanson.* New York: Random House, 1980.

Tanzer, Lester. *The Kennedy Circle.* Washington, DC: Luce Inc., 1961.

Taylor, Robert. *Marilyn Monroe in Her Own Words.* New York: Delilah Press, 1983.

Thompson, Nelson. *The Dark Side of Camelot.* Chicago: Playboy Press, 1976.

Weatherby, W. *Conversations with Marilyn.* New York: Ballantine, 1977.

Whalen, Richard. *The Founding Father.* New York: New American Library, 1964.

White, Theodore. *In Search of History: A Personal Adventure.* New York: Harper and Row, 1978.

————. *The Making of the President — 1960.* New York: Atheneum, 1961.

Wicker, Thomas. *JFK and LBJ: The Influence of Personality upon Politics.* Baltimore: Penguin Books, 1972.

Wills, Gary. *The Kennedy Imprisonment: A Meditation on Power.* Boston: Little, Brown, 1981.

Chapters 5 and 6

Bornet, Vaughn. *The Presidency of Lyndon B. Johnson.* Lawrence, KS: University of Kansas Press, 1983.

Caro, Robert. *The Years of Lyndon Johnson: The Path to Power.* New York: Alfred A. Knopf, 1982.

Carpenter, Liz. *Ruffles and Flourishes.* New York: Doubleday, 1970.

Dugger, Ronnie. *The Politician: The Life and Times of Lyndon Johnson.* New York: W. W. Norton, 1982.

Evans, Richard. *Lyndon B. Johnson: The Exercise of Power.* New York: New American Library, 1966.

Goldman, Eric. *The Tragedy of Lyndon Johnson.* New York: Alfred A. Knopf, 1969.

Hall, Gordon Langley. *Lady Bird and Her Daughters.* Philadelphia: Macrae Smith, 1967.

Johnson, Lady Bird. *A White House Diary.* New York: Holt, Rinehart and Winston, 1970.

Johnson, Sam Houston. *My Brother Lyndon.* New York: Cowles, 1969.

Kearns, Doris. *Lyndon Johnson and the American Dream.* New York: Harper and Row, 1976.

Miller, Merle. *Lyndon: An Oral Biography.* New York: G.P. Putnam, 1980.

Montgomery, Ruth. *Mrs. L.B.J.* New York: Holt, Rinehart and Winston, 1964.

Schandler, Herbert. *The Unmaking of the President.* Princeton, NJ: Princeton University Press, 1977.

Valenti, Jack. *A Very Human President.* New York: W. W. Norton, 1976.

White, Theodore. *The Making of the President.* New York: Atheneum, 1965.

Chapter 7

Ambrose, Stephen. *Eisenhower.* New York: Simon and Schuster, 1983.

Brendon, Peirse. *Ike: His Life and Times.* New York: Harper and Row, 1986.

Chandler, Alfred. *The Papers of Dwight David Eisenhower.* Baltimore: Johns Hopkins University Press, 1980.

Eisenhower, Dwight. *Mandate for Change.* New York: Doubleday, 1963.

Eisenhower, John. *Strictly Personal.* New York: Doubleday, 1975.

Eisenhower, Milton. *The President Is Calling.* New York: Doubleday, 1974.

Ferrell, Robert. *The Eisenhower Diaries.* New York: W. W. Norton, 1981.

Lee, R. Alton. *Dwight D. Eisenhower.* New York: Nelson-Hall, 1981.

Melanson, Richard. *Reevaluating Eisenhower.* Champaign, IL: University of Illinois Press, 1986.

Morgan, Kay Summersby. *Past Forgetting: My Love Affair with Dwight D. Eisenhower.* New York: Simon and Schuster, 1976.

Chapter 8

Abrahamsen, David. *Nixon vs. Nixon: A Psychological Study.* New York: Farrar, Straus, and Giroux, 1976.

Barber, James D. *The Presidential Character: Predicting Performance in the White House.* Englewood Cliffs, NJ: Prentice-Hall, 1972.

Brodie, Fawn. *Richard Nixon: The Shaping of His Character.* New York: W. W. Norton, 1981.

David, Lester. *The Lonely Lady at San Clemente: The Story of Pat Nixon.* New York: Thomas Crowell, 1978.

De Toledano, Ralph. *One Man Alone: Richard Nixon.* New York: Funk and Wagnalls, 1969.

Hiss, Tony. *Laughing Last*. Boston: Houghton Mifflin, 1978

Hoyt, Edwin P. *The Nixons: An American Family*. New York: Random House, 1972.

Hughes, Arthur J. *Richard M. Nixon*. New York: Dodd, Mead, 1972.

Hutschnecker, Arnold. *The Drive for Power*. New York: M. Evans, 1974.

Korff, Baruch. *The Personal Nixon: Staying on the Summit*. Washington, DC: Luce Inc., 1974.

Kornitzer, Bela. *The Real Nixon: An Intimate Biography*. New York:Rand McNally, 1960.

Lurie, Leonard. *The Running of Richard Nixon*. New York: Coward, McCann, and Geoghegan, 1972.

Mankiewicz, Frank. *Perfectly Clear: Nixon from Whittier to Watergate*. New York: Popular Library, 1974.

Mazlish, Bruce. *In Search of Nixon: A Psychohistorical Inquiry*. New York: Basic Books, 1972.

McGinniss, Joe. *The Selling of the President—1968*. New York: Trident Press, 1969.

Nixon, Richard. *Six Crises*. Garden City, NY: Doubleday, 1968.

Price, Raymond. *With Nixon*. New York: Viking Press, 1977.

Reedy, George. *The Twilight of the Presidency*. New York: New American Library, 1970.

Safire, William. *Before the Fall: An Inside View of the Pre-Watergate White House*. New York: Doubleday, 1975.

Spalding, Henry D. *The Nixon Nobody Knows*. Middle Village, NY: Jonathan David, 1972.

Willis, Garry. *Nixon Agonistes*. Boston: Houghton Mifflin, 1970.

White, Theodore. *Breach of Faith: The Fall of Richard Nixon*. New York: Atheneum, 1975.

Woodward, Bob, and Carl Bernstein. *All the President's Men*. New York: Simon and Schuster, 1974.

———. *The Final Days*. New York: Simon and Schuster, 1976.

Chapter 9

Boyarsky, Bill. *Ronald Reagan*. New York: Random House, 1981.

Carter, Jimmy. *Keeping Faith: Memoirs of a President*. New York: Bantam Books, 1982.

Carter, Jimmy and Rosalynn. *Everything to Gain*. New York: Random House, 1987.

Carter, Rosalynn, *First Lady from Plains*. Boston: Houghton Mifflin, 1984.

De Gregorio, William A. *The Complete Book of the United States Presidents*. New York: Dember Books, 1984.

Dugger, Ronnie. *On Reagan: The Man and His Presidency*. New York: McGraw-Hill, 1983.

Edwards, Anne. *Early Reagan*. New York: William Morrow, 1987.

Ford, Betty. *The Times of My Life*. New York: Harper and Row, 1978.

Ford, Gerald. *A Time to Heal*. New York: Harper and Row, 1979.

Glad, Betty. *In Search of the Great White House*. New York: W. W. Norton, 1980.

Kucharsky, David. *The Man from Plains: The Mind and Spirit of Jimmy Carter*. New York: Harper and Row, 1983.

Leamer, Lawrence. *Make Believe: The Story of Nancy and Ronald Reagan*. New York: Harper and Row, 1983.

Leighton, Frances Spaty. *The Search for the Real Nancy Reagan*. New York: Macmillan, 1987.

Mazlish, Bruce, and Edwin Diamond. *Jimmy Carter: An Interpretive Biography*. New York: Simon and Schuster, 1979.

Reagan, Nancy. *My Turn*. New York: Random House, 1989.

————. *Nancy*. New York: Berkley, 1981.

Reagan, Ronald. *Where's the Rest of Me?* New York: Duell, Sloan, Pearce, 1965.

Ross, Shelley. *Fall from Grace*. New York: Ballantine Books, 1988.

Sidey, Hugh. *Portrait of a President*. New York: Harper and Row, 1975.

ter Horst, Jerald. *Gerald Ford and the Future of the Presidency*. New York: Third Press, 1974.

Vestel, Bud. *Jerry Ford, Up Close*. New York: Coward, McCann, and Geoghegan, 1974.

Wooten, James. *Dasher: The Roots and Rising of Jimmy Carter*. New York: Simon and Schuster, 1978.

Chapters 10 and 11

Adamic, Louis. *Dinner at the White House*. New York: Harper and Row, 1946.

Burns, James. *Roosevelt*. New York: Harcourt Brace, 1973.

Farr, Finis. *FDR*. New York: Arlington House, 1972.

Flynn, John. *Country Squire in the White House*. New York: Doubleday, 1940.

————. *The Roosevelt Myth*. New York: Devlin-Adair, 1957.

Freidel, Frank. *Franklin D. Roosevelt*. Boston: Little, Brown, 1973.

Goldberg, Richard. *The Making of Franklin D. Roosevelt*. New York: New York University Press, 1984.

Gunther, John. *Roosevelt in Retrospect*. New York: Harper and Row, 1950.

Hansen, William. *Eleanor Roosevelt*. New York: Chelsea House. 1987.

Hassett, William. *Off the Record with FDR*. New Brunswick, NJ: Rutgers University Press, 1958.

Israel, Fred. *Franklin D. Roosevelt*. New York: Chelsea House, 1985.

Lash, Joseph. *Eleanor: The Years Alone*. New York: W. W. Norton, 1972.

————. *Eleanor and Franklin*. New York: W. W. Norton, 1971.

Lash, Joseph. *Eleanor Roosevelt: A Friend's Memoir*. Garden City, NY: Doubleday, 1964.

McIntire, Ross. *White House Physician*. New York: Putnam, 1946.

Morgan, Ted. *FDR*. New York: Simon and Schuster, 1986.

Nash, Gerald. *Franklin Delano Roosevelt*. Englewood Cliffs, NJ: Prentice-Hall, 1967.

Parks, Lillian Rogers. *My Thirty Years Backstairs at the White House*. New York: Fleet Publishing, 1961.

Perkins, Francis. *The Roosevelt I Knew*. New York: Viking Press, 1947.

Roosevelt, Eleanor. *Autobiography*. New York: Harper and Row, 1961.

————. *This I Remember*. New York: Greenwood Press, 1975.

Roosevelt, Elliot. *As He Saw It*. New York: Duell, Sloan, and Pearce, 1946.

————. *The Roosevelt Letters*. London: Harrap and Company, 1949.

Roosevelt, James. *My Parents: A Differing View*. Chicago: Playboy Press, 1976.

Tugwell, Rexford. *The Democratic Roosevelt.* Baltimore: Penguin Books, 1969.

Ward, Geoffrey. *Before the Trumpet.* New York: Harper and Row, 1986.

White, William. *Majesty and Mischief.* New York: McGraw-Hill, 1961.

Chapter 12

Bates, James. *The Origins of Teapot Dome.* New York: Greenwood Press, 1977.

Daugherty, Harry. *The Inside Story of the Harding Tragedy.* New York: Western Islands, 1975.

Downe, Randolph. *The Rise of Warren Gamaliel Harding.* Columbus: Ohio State University Press, 1970.

Means, Gaston. *The Strange Death of President Harding.* New York: Doubleday, 1930.

Mee, Charles. *The Ohio Gang.* Lawrence, KS: University of Kansas Press, 1977.

Russell, Francis. *The Shadow of Blooming Grove.* New York: Bobbs-Merrill, 1968.

Trani, Eugene. *The Presidency of Warren G. Harding.* Lawrence, KS: University of Kansas Press, 1977.

Chapter 13

Cleveland, Grover. *The Letters of Grover Cleveland.* Boston: Houghton Mifflin, 1933.

McElroy, Robert. *Grover Cleveland: The Man and the Statesman.* New York: Harpers, 1923.

Nevins, Allan. *Grover Cleveland: A Study in Courage.* New York: Dodd, Mead, 1932.

Parker, George. *Recollections of Grover Cleveland.* New York: Ayer, 1970.

Tugwell, Rexford. *Grover Cleveland.* New York: Macmillan, 1968.

Vexler, Robert. *Grover Cleveland.* New York: Oceana Publishers, 1968.

Chapter 14

Adams, William Howard. *The Eye of Thomas Jefferson*. Charlottesville: University of Virginia Press, 1981.

Binger, Carl. *Thomas Jefferson*. New York: W. W. Norton, 1970.

Boorstin, Daniel. *The Lost World of Thomas Jefferson*. Chicago: University of Chicago Press, 1981.

Brodie, Fawn. *Thomas Jefferson: An Intimate History*. New York: W. W. Norton, 1974.

Butterfield, L. H. *The Papers of Thomas Jefferson*. Princeton, NJ: Princeton University Press, 1950.

Dabney, Virginius. *The Jefferson Scandals: A Rebuttal*. New York: Dodd, Mead, 1981.

Dewey, Frank. *Thomas Jefferson, Lawyer*. Charlottesville: University of Virginia Press, 1986.

Dos Passos, John. *The Shackles of Power*. Garden City, NY: Doubleday, 1966.

Lehman, Karl. *Thomas Jefferson: American Humanist*. Chicago: University of Chicago Press, 1965.

Malone, Dumas. *Thomas Jefferson and His Times*. Boston: Little, Brown, 1986.

Martin, Edwin. *Thomas Jefferson: Scientist*. New York: Macmillan, 1952.

Peterson, Merrill. *The Jefferson Image in the American Mind*. New York: Oxford University Press, 1960.

———. *Thomas Jefferson and the New Nation*. New York: Oxford University Press, 1970.

Randall, Henery. *The Life of Thomas Jefferson*. New York: Da Capo Press, 1970.

Sanford, Charles. *The Religious Life of Thomas Jefferson*. Charlottesville: University of Virginia Press, 1984.

Weymouth, Lally. *Thomas Jefferson: The Man, His World, and His Influence*. New York: G. P. Putnam, 1973.

Chapter 15

Allen, David. *The Diary of John Quincy Adams*. Cambridge, MA: Belknap Press, 1981.

Ammon, Harry. *James Monroe*. New York: Shoe String Press, 1971.

Barre, W. L. *The Life of Millard Fillmore*. New York: Benjamin Franklin Press, 1971.

Bauer, K. *Zachary Taylor*. Baton Rouge: Louisiana State University Press, 1985.

Bell, Carl. *They Knew Franklin Pierce*. New York: April Hill Publishing, 1980.

Bemis, Samuel Flagg. *John Quincy Adams and the Union*. New York: Alfred A. Knopf, 1956.

Brant, Irving. *The Fourth President*. Indianapolis: Bobbs-Merrill, 1970.

Brugger, Robert. *The Papers of James Madison*. Charlottesville: University of Virginia Press, 1986.

Burns, Edward. *James Madison*. New Brunswick, NJ: Rutgers University Press, 1938.

Cresson, William. *James Monroe*. New York: Shoe String Press, 1971.

Curtis, James. *The Fox at Bay*. Lexington: University of Kentucky Press, 1970.

Ellert, K. T. *Young John Tyler*. New York: Diety Press, 1976.

Esaray, Logan. *The Letters of William Henry Harrison*. New York: Ayer, 1975.

Farrell, J. J. *Zachary Taylor and Millard Fillmore*. New York: Oceana Publishing, 1971.

Fitzpatrick, John. *Autobiography of Martin Van Buren*. New York: Augustus Kelley, 1969.

Gunderson, Robert. *The Log Cabin Campaign*. Westport, CT: Greenwood Press, 1977.

Hamilton, Holman. *The Three Kentucky Presidents*. Lexington: University of Kentucky Press, 1978.

Hargreaves, Mary. *The Presidency of John Quincy Adams*. Lawrence: University of Kansas Press, 1985.

Hawthorne, Nathaniel. *The Life of Franklin Pierce*. New York: Somerset Publishing, 1872.

Hecht, Marie. *John Quincy Adams: A Personal History of an Indepen-*

dent Man. New York: Macmillan, 1972.

Ketcham, Ralph. *James Madison.* New York: Macmillan, 1971.

McCoy, Charles. *Polk and the Presidency.* New York: Haskell Publishers, 1973.

Moore, Virginia. *The Madisons: A Biography.* New York: McGraw-Hill, 1979.

Morgan, Robert. *A Whig Embattled: The Presidency Under John Tyler.* New York: Shoe String Press, 1974.

Nagel, Paul. *Descent from Glory: Four Generations of the John Adams Family.* New York: Oxford University Press, 1983.

Nichols, Roy. *Franklin Pierce.* Philadelphia: University of Pennsylvania Press, 1958.

Niven, John. *Martin Van Buren.* New York: Oxford University Press, 1983.

Richards, Leonard. *The Life and Times of Congressman John Quincy Adams.* New York: Oxford University Press, 1986.

Rutland, Robert Allen. *James Madison: The Founding Father.* New York: Macmillan, 1987.

Schultz, Harold. *James Madison.* New York: Twayne Publishing, 1970.

Sellers, Charles. *James K. Polk.* Princeton, NJ: Princeton University Press, 1966.

Sloan, Irving. *Franklin Pierce.* New York: Oceana Publishing, 1968.

Tyler, Leon. *The Letters and Times of John Tyler.* New York: Da Capo, 1970.

Weaver, Herbert. *The Correspondence of James K. Polk.* Nashville: Vanderbilt University Press, 1969.

Chapter 16

Bassett, John. *The Life of Andrew Jackson.* Hamden, CT: Archon Books, 1967.

Bowers, Claude. *The Party Battles of the Jackson Period.* New York: Chatauqua Press, 1923.

Curtis, James. *Andrew Jackson and the Search for Vindication.* Boston: Little, Brown, 1976.

Davis, Burke. *Old Hickory: A Life of Andrew Jackson.* New York: Dial Press, 1977.

Goodwin, Philo. *The Biography of Andrew Jackson.* New York: R. H. Towner, 1833.

James, Marquis. *Andrew Jackson: The Border Captain.* New York: Bobbs-Merrill, 1933.

———. *Andrew Jackson: Portrait of a President.* New York: Bobbs-Merrill, 1937.

Ogg, Frederic. *The Reign of Andrew Jackson.* New Haven, CT: Yale University Press, 1919.

Remini, Robert. *Andrew Jackson and the Course of American Freedom.* New York: Harper and Row, 1981.

———. *The Election of Andrew Jackson.* Philadelphia: Lippincott, 1963.

Sellers, Charles. *Andrew Jackson: A Profile.* New York: Hill and Wang, 1971.

Smyth, Clifford. *Andrew Jackson.* New York: Funk and Wagnalls, 1931.

Stone, Irving. *The President's Lady.* New York: Doubleday, 1944.

Sumner, William Graham. *Andrew Jackson.* Boston: Houghton Mifflin, 1924.

Walker, Alexander. *The Life of Andrew Jackson.* Philadelphia: G. G. Evans, 1867.

Ward, John. *Andrew Jackson: Symbol for an Age.* New York: Oxford University Press, 1974.

Chapter 17

Auchampaugh, Philip. *James Buchanan and His Cabinet.* New York: Conner Books, 1965.

Curtis, G. T. *The Life of James Buchanan.* New York: Macmillan, 1883.

Klein, Philip. *President James Buchanan: A Biography.* Philadelphia: Pennsylvania State University Press, 1962.

McFarland, I. D. *Buchanan.* New York: Biblio Distributors, 1981.

Moore, John. *The Works of James Buchanan.* New York: Ayer Publishing, 1911.

Smith, Elbert. *The Presidency of James Buchanan.* Lawrence: University of Kansas Press, 1978.

Chapter 18

Anderson, Dwight. *Abraham Lincoln: The Quest for Immortality.* New York: Alfred A. Knopf, 1982.

Angle, Paul. *The Lincoln Reader.* New Brunswick, NJ: Rutgers University Press, 1947.

Baringer, William. *Lincoln's Rise to Power.* Boston: Little, Brown, 1937.

Barton, William. *The Life of Abraham Lincoln:* Indianapolis: Bobbs-Merrill, 1925.

Basler, Roy. *Abraham Lincoln.* New York: Grosset and Dunlap, 1962.

———. *Lincoln.* New York: Octagon Press, 1976.

Bell, J. E. *The Story of Lincoln.* New York: Beekman Publishing Company, 1971.

Charnwood, Godrey. *Abraham Lincoln.* Garden City, NY: Garden City Publishing, 1929.

Conwell, Russell. *Why Lincoln Laughed.* New York: Harpers, 1922.

Current, Richard. *The Lincoln Nobody Knows.* New York: Hill and Wang, 1963.

Daugherty, James. *Abraham Lincoln.* New York: Viking Press, 1943.

Donald, David. *Lincoln's Herndon.* New York: Alfred A. Knopf, 1948.

Fehrebacher, Don. *Prelude to Greatness: Lincoln in the 1850's.* Stanford, CA: Stanford University Press, 1962.

Herndon, William. *The Hidden Lincoln.* New York: Viking Press, 1938.

Hill, John. *Abraham Lincoln: Man of God.* New York: G. P. Putnam, 1926.

Holzer, H. *The Lincoln Image.* New York: Charles Scribner's Sons, 1984.

Horgan, Paul. *Citizens of New Salem.* New York: Farrar, Strauss, 1961.

Horner, Harlan. *Lincoln and Greeley.* Urbana: University of Illinois Press, 1953.

Keckley, Elizabeth. *Behind the Scenes.* New York: Arno Press, 1968.

Kolpas, Norman. *Abraham Lincoln.* New York: McGraw-Hill, 1981.

Ludwig, Emile. *Lincoln.* Boston: Little, Brown, 1930.

Mearns, David. *The Lincoln Papers.* Garden City, NY: Doubleday, 1948.

Morse, John. *Abraham Lincoln.* Boston: Houghton Mifflin, 1895.

Nevins, Allan. *The Emergence of Lincoln.* New York: Charles Scribner's Sons, 1950.

Randall, James. *Lincoln.* New York: Dodd, Mead, 1945.

Randall, Ruth Painter. *Mary Lincoln: Biography of a Marriage.* Boston: Little, Brown, 1953.

Ross, Ishbel. *The President's Wife: Mary Todd Lincoln.* New York: G. P. Putnam, 1973.

Rothschild, Alonzo. *Lincoln: Master of Men.* Boston: Houghton Mifflin, 1905.

Sandburg, Carl. *Abraham Lincoln.* New York: Harcourt, Brace, 1946.

———. *Abraham Lincoln: The Prairie Years.* New York: Harcourt, Brace, 1929.

Shaw, Archer. *The Lincoln Encyclopedia.* New York: Macmillan, 1950.

Stern, Philip Van Doren. *The Life and Writings of Abraham Lincoln.* New York: Modern Library, 1950.

Tarbell, Ida. *The Life of Lincoln.* New York: Doubleday, 1900.

Thomas, Benjamin. *Abraham Lincoln: A Biography.* New York: Alfred A. Knopf, 1952.

Thomasp, B. P. *Abraham Lincoln.* New York: Modern Library, 1968.

Weik, Jesse. *The Real Lincoln.* Boston: Houghton Mifflin, 1926.

Williams, Thomas. *Lincoln and His Generals.* New York: Alfred A. Knopf, 1952.

Wolf, William. *Lincoln's Religion.* Philadelphia: Pilgrim's Press, 1970.

Chapter 19

Anderson, J. *William Howard Taft: An Intimate History.* New York: W. W. Norton, 1981.

Barber, James. *U.S. Grant: The Man and the Image.* Springfield: Southern Illinois University Press, 1986.

Barnard, Harry. *Rutherford B. Hayes and His America.* New York: Russell and Russell, 1967.

Benedict, Michael. *The Impeachment and Trial of Andrew Johnson.* New York: W. W. Norton, 1973.

Bishop, A. *Rutherford B. Hayes.* New York: Oceana Publishing, 1969.

Brown, Harry James. *The Diary of James Garfield.* Lansing: Michigan State University Press, 1967.

Burton, David. *William Howard Taft*. New York: Krieger, 1986.

Clancy, Herbert. *The Presidential Election of 1880*. Chicago: Loyola University Press, 1958.

Conger, Arthur. *The Rise of U. S. Grant*. New York: Ayer Publishing, 1974.

Coolidge, Louis. *Ulysses S. Grant*. New York: AMS Press, 1975.

Duffy, Herbert. *William Howard Taft*. New York: Minton Balch, 1930.

Gould, Lewis. *The Presidency of William McKinley*. Lawrence: University of Kansas Press, 1980.

Greer, Emily. *First Lady: The Life of Lucy Webb Hayes*. Kent, OH: Kent State University Press, 1984.

Hayes, Ruth. *The Diary of a President*. New York: David McKay, 1964.

Howe, George. *Chester A. Arthur*. New York: Ungar Publishing, 1957.

Howells, William Dean. *The Life and Character of Rutherford B. Hayes*. New York: R. West, 1980.

Josephson, Matthew. *The Politicos*. New York: Harcourt, Brace, 1963.

McFreely, William. *Grant: A Biography*. New York: W. W. Norton, 1982.

McKitrick, Eric. *Andrew Johnson and Reconstruction*. Chicago: University of Chicago Press, 1964.

Morgan, H. Wayne. *William McKinley and His America*. Syracuse, NY: Syracuse University Press, 1963.

Olcott, Charles. *The Life of William McKinley*. New York: AMS Press, 1972.

Pringle, Henry. *The Life and Times of William Howard Taft*. New York: Farrar and Rinehart, 1939.

Sievers, H. J. *Benjamin Harrison*. New York: Oceana Publishing, 1969.

Simon, John. *The Papers of Ulysses S. Grant*. London: Feffer and Simons, 1969.

Smith, Gene. *High Crimes and Misdemeanors*. New York: McGraw-Hill, 1985.

———. *Lee and Grant*. New York: McGraw-Hill, 1984.

Taft, Helen. *Recollections of Full Years*. New York: Dodd, Mead, 1919.

Winston, Robert. *Andrew Johnson: Plebeian and Patriot*. New York: AMS Press, 1970.

Chapter 20

Beale, Howard K. *Theodore Roosevelt and the Rise of America to World Power*. Baltimore: Johns Hopkins University Press, 1956.

Blum, John. *The Republican Roosevelt*. Cambridge, MA: Harvard University Press, 1977.

————. *Woodrow Wilson and the Politics of Morality*. Boston: Little, Brown, 1956.

Burton, David. *Theodore Roosevelt*. New York: G. K. Hall, 1973.

Cooper, John Milton. *The Warrior and the Priest*. Cambridge, MA: Harvard University Press, 1983.

Cutright, P. *Theodore Roosevelt the Naturalist*. New York: Harper and Row, 1956.

Einstein, Lewis. *Roosevelt: His Mind in Action*. Boston: Houghton Mifflin, 1956.

Elletson, D. H. *Roosevelt and Wilson: A Comparative Study*. London: J. Murray, 1985.

Freud, Sigmund. *Thomas Woodrow Wilson: A Psychological Study*. New York: Houghton Mifflin, 1967.

George, Alexander. *Woodrow Wilson and Colonel House*. New York: John Day, 1956.

Grantham, Dewey. *Theodore Roosevelt*. Englewood Cliffs, NJ: Prentice-Hall, 1971.

Grayson, Cary. *Woodrow Wilson: An Intimate Memoir*. New York: Holt, Rinehart and Winston, 1960.

Hagedorn, Hermann. *The Roosevelt Family of Sagamore Hill*. New York: Macmillan, 1954.

Harbaugh, William. *The Life and Times of Theodore Roosevelt*. New York: Collier, 1963.

Link, Arthur. *Woodrow Wilson*. Princeton, NJ: Princeton University Press, 1947.

————. *Woodrow Wilson: Confusion and Crisis*. Princeton, NJ: Princeton University Press, 1964.

————. *Woodrow Wilson: A Critical Study*. New York: Harlan Davidson, 1979.

Lorant, Stefan. *The Life and Times of Theodore Roosevelt*. New York: Doubleday, 1959.

Markham, Lois. *Theodore Roosevelt.* New York: Chelsea House, 1985.

Morris, Edmund. *The Rise of Theodore Roosevelt.* New York: Coward, McCann, 1979.

Mulder, John. *Woodrow Wilson.* Princeton, NJ: Princeton University Press, 1978.

Pringle, Henry. *Theodore Roosevelt: A Biography.* New York: Harcourt, Brace, 1931.

Putnam, Carleton. *Theodore Roosevelt: The Formative Years.* New York: Charles Scribner's Sons, 1958.

Roosevelt, Theodore. *An Autobiography.* New York: Charles Scribner's Sons, 1925.

————. *The Strenuous Life.* New York: Review Company, 1904.

Tumulty, Joseph Patrick. *Woodrow Wilson As I Know Him.* New York: Doubleday, 1921.

Wagenknecht, Edwin. *The Seven Worlds of Theodore Roosevelt.* New York: Longmans Green, 1958.

Weinstein, Edwin. *Woodrow Wilson: A Medical and Psychological Biography.* Princeton, NJ: Princeton University Press, 1981.

Wilson, Edith Bowling. *My Memoirs.* Indianapolis: Bobbs-Merrill, 1938.

Chapter 21

Burner, David. *Herbert Hoover.* New York: Alfred A. Knopf, 1979.

————. *Herbert Hoover: A Public Life.* New York: Atheneum, 1984.

Burns, Richard. *Harry S. Truman.* New York: Scholarly Resources, 1984.

Coolidge, Calvin. *The Autobiography of Calvin Coolidge.* New York: Tuttle Publishing, 1972.

Eckley, Wilton. *Herbert Hoover.* Boston: Twayne Publishing, 1980.

Ferrell, Robert. *Dear Bess: The Letters of Harry S. Truman to His Wife.* New York: W. W. Norton, 1983.

Jenkins, Roy. *Truman.* New York: Harper and Row, 1986.

Lyons, Eugene. *Herbert Hoover.* Garden City, NY: Doubleday, 1964.

McCoy, Donald. *Calvin Coolidge: The Silent President.* New York: Macmillan, 1967.

Miller, Merle. *Plain Speaking: The Life of Harry S. Truman.* New York: Berkley, 1986.

Nash, George N. *The Life of Herbert Hoover.* New York: W. W. Norton,1983.

Robinson, Eugene. *Herbert Hoover: President of the United States.* Stanford, CA: Hoover Institute Press, 1975.

Ross, Ishbel. *Grace Coolidge and Her Era.* New York: Dodd, Mead, 1962.

Truman, Harry. *Memoirs.* Garden City, NY: Doubleday, 1955.

Truman, Margaret. *Harry S. Truman.* New York: William Morrow, 1973.

Wilson, Joan. *Herbert Hoover.* Boston: Little, Brown, 1975.

Chapter 22

Abbot, W. W. *The Papers of George Washington.* Charlottesville: University of Virginia, 1985.

Alden, John. *George Washington: A Biography.* Baton Rouge: Louisiana State University Press, 1984.

Ambler, Charles. *George Washington and the West.* Chapel Hill: University of North Carolina Press, 1936.

Andrist, Ralph. *George Washington: A Biography in His Own Words.* New York: Harper and Row, 1972.

Borden, Morton. *George Washington.* Englewood Cliffs, NJ: Prentice-Hall, 1969.

Callahan, North. *George Washington.* New York: William Morrow, 1972.

Cleland, Hugh. *George Washington in the Ohio Valley.* Pittsburgh: University of Pittsburgh Press, 1955.

Conkling, Margaret. *Memoirs of the Lives of the Mother and Wife of Washington.* Auburn, MA: New Publishers, 1851.

Cunliffe, Marcus. *George Washington: Man and Monument.* Boston: Little, Brown, 1958.

Fitzpatrick, John. *The Diaries of George Washington.* Boston: Houghton Mifflin, 1925.

Flexner, James. *George Washington: Anguish and Farewell.* Boston: Little, Brown, 1972.

———. *George Washington: The Forge of Experience.* Boston: Little, Brown, 1965.

————. *George Washington and the New Nation.* Boston: Little, Brown, 1970. *George Washington in the American Revolution.* Boston: Little, Brown, 1967.

Ford, Henry Jones. *George Washington and His Colleagues.* New Haven, CT: Yale University Press, 1920.

Ford, Paul. *The True George Washington.* Philadelphia: Lippincott, 1896.

Freeman, Douglas Southall. *George Washington.* New York: Charles Scribner's Sons, 1948.

Haworth, Paul. *George Washington: Country Gentleman.* Indianapolis: Bobbs-Merrill, 1925.

Hughes, Rupert. *George Washington.* New York: William Morrow, 1926.

Knollenberg, Richard. *George Washington: The Virginia Period.* Durham, NC: Duke University Press, 1964.

Lodge, Henry Cabot. *George Washington.* Boston: Little, Brown, 1899.

Moore, Charles. *The Family Life of George Washington.* New York: Macmillan, 1926.

Nettels, Curtis. *George Washington and American Independence.* Westport, CT: Greenwood Press, 1951.

Smyth, Clifford. *George Washington: The Story of the First American.* New York: Funk and Wagnalls, 1931.

Sparks, Jared. *The Life of George Washington.* Boston: Charles Tappan, 1839.

Stephenson, Nathaniel. *George Washington.* New York: Oxford University Press, 1940.

Van Dyke, Paul. *George Washington: The Son of His Country.* New York: Charles Scribner's Sons, 1931.

Wilson, Woodrow. *George Washington.* New York: Harper Brothers, 1897.

Woodward, W. E. *George Washington: The Image and the Man.* New York: Liveright Publishing, 1946.

Chapter 23

Adams, Abigail. *The Letters of Mrs. Adams.* Boston: Wilkens, 1848.

Adams, Charles Francis. *The Letters of John Adams Addressed to His Wife.* Boston: Little, Brown, 1841.

Adams, James. *The Adams Family.* New York: Literary Guild, 1930.

Bowen, Catharine. *John Adams and the American Revolution.* Boston: Little, Brown, 1950.

Butterfield, L. H. *The Book of Abigail and John: Selected Letters of the Adams Family.* Cambridge, MA: Harvard University Press, 1975.

————. *The Diary and Autobiography of John Adams.* Cambridge, MA: Belknap Press, 1961.

Chinard, Gilbert. *Honest John Adams.* Boston: Little, Brown, 1964.

Hutson, James. *John Adams and the Diplomacy of the American Revolution.* Lexington: University of Kentucky Press, 1980.

Mitchell, Stewart. *New Letters of Abigail Adams.* Boston: Houghton Mifflin, 1947.

Morse, John. *John Adams.* Boston: Houghton Mifflin, 1894.

Oliver, Andrew. *Portraits of John and Abigail Adams.* Cambridge, MA: Belknap Press, 1967.

Peabody, James. *John Adams: A Biography in His Own Words.* New York: Harper and Row, 1973.

Russell, Francis. *Adams: An American Dynasty.* New York: McGraw-Hill, 1976.

Shaw, Peter. *The Character of John Adams.* Chapel Hill: University of North Carolina Press, 1976.

Smith, Page. *John Adams.* Garden City, NY: Doubleday, 1962.

Smyth, Clifford. *John Adams: Father of American Independence.* New York: Funk and Wagnalls, 1931.

Taylor, Robert. *The Papers of John Adams.* Cambridge, MA: Belknap Press, 1977.

Whitney, Janet. *Abigail Adams.* Boston: Little, Brown, 1947.